Revolutionary War
Journals of
HENRY DEARBORN
1775-1783

A Da Capo Press Reprint Series

THE ERA OF THE AMERICAN REVOLUTION

GENERAL EDITOR: LEONARD W. LEVY
Claremont Graduate School

Revolutionary War
Journals of
HENRY DEARBORN
1775-1783

Edited from the Original Manuscripts by
LLOYD A. BROWN *and* HOWARD H. PECKHAM

With a Biographical Essay by
HERMON DUNLAP SMITH

DA CAPO PRESS · NEW YORK · 1971

A Da Capo Press Reprint Edition

This Da Capo Press edition of the
*Revolutionary War Journals of Henry Dearborn,
1775-1783,* is an unabridged republication of
the 1939 edition published in Chicago.

Library of Congress Catalog Card Number 74-146143

SBN 306-70107-3

Published by Da Capo Press
A Division of Plenum Publishing Corporation
227 West 17th Street, New York, N.Y. 10011

Manufactured in the United States of America

77450

Revolutionary War Journals
of Henry Dearborn

Revolutionary War
Journals of
HENRY DEARBORN
1775-1783

Edited from the Original Manuscripts by
LLOYD A. BROWN *and* HOWARD H. PECKHAM

With a Biographical Essay by
HERMON DUNLAP SMITH

THE CAXTON CLUB, CHICAGO
1939

⁓ CC ⁓

Foreword

S HORTLY *after attending the meeting of The Caxton Club at which Mr. Hermon D. Smith read his paper on General Dearborn, Mr. John T. McCutcheon published a cartoon in the Chicago* Tribune, *which, to a considerable extent, was illustrative of his own experience. It depicted several Chicago businessmen as pupils in a school room replying to a question put to them by the teacher:" Gentlemen, you have all heard of Father Dearborn. What is your conception of him?" One pupil replies: " An old cartoon character with chin whiskers and a cigar, standing for Chicago." Another says: " He was one of our early settlers. He was named after Fort Dearborn, or the other way around." And another: " He ran a big department store near Fort Dearborn in the first ward."*

These replies express with little exaggeration the opinions held by many substantial and even history conscious Chicagoans in regard to their" patron saint." A few, like Mr. McCutcheon, discovered the real General Dearborn through hearing Mr. Smith's paper, which includes quotations from Dearborn's journals of the Revolutionary War, as well as his important and apparently hitherto unpublished letter giving orders for the erection of the Fort.

Because of its long association with Chicago, The Caxton Club feels that it is especially appropriate that it should present General Dearborn and his writings to the city with which his name is so closely identified. It is accordingly publishing this

v

book which contains, in addition to Mr. Smith's paper, the complete Revolutionary War journals, including the journal of the Yorktown campaign, which has never been published. In order to provide the historical setting necessary for the fullest understanding and appreciation of the journals, The Caxton Club secured as editors of the journals two distinguished Revolutionary scholars, Lloyd A. Brown and Howard H. Peckham of the William L. Clements Library. The Club believes the book to be an important contribution to American historical scholarship.

Publication of the present volume is in keeping with the traditions of the Club, for its earliest publications were in the field of American history—translations of three accounts of LaSalle's voyages and discoveries. These were followed by Mrs. John H. Kinzie's Wau-Bun; *Wakefield's* History of the Black Hawk War; The Development of Chicago, 1674–1914, Shown in a Series of Contemporary Original Narratives; *Charlevoix's* Journal of a Voyage to North America; *John Steele's* Across the Plains in 1850; *Jesse Applegate's* A Day with the Cow Column; *Jesse A. Applegate's* Recollections of My Boyhood; *and* The Journal of Paul Du Ru, [February 1 to May 8, 1700], Missionary Priest of Louisiana.

THEODORE W. KOCH
President, The Caxton Club

⇜ H D ⇝

Contents

List of Plates

Introduction

HENRY DEARBORN *served as an officer in the American Revolution from April, 1775, until the reduction of the New Hampshire line on March 1, 1783. He fought at Bunker Hill and marched on the expedition to Quebec. He was active in the Burgoyne campaign, and following the surrender joined Washington at Valley Forge. He attacked with the advance division at Monmouth and afterward did garrison duty in Connecticut. In 1779 he marched on the expedition under Sullivan against the Indians, then rejoined Washington and later took part in the Yorktown campaign. Dearborn kept a journal during the entire war, with the exception of a six months' period in 1782 when he was engaged in a special mission that took him away from the army. The six parts published in this volume constitute one of the very few complete, eye-witness accounts now extant of the American side of the Revolution.*

Their value to historians is enhanced by the advantages for observation enjoyed by an officer of Dearborn's rank. First as a captain, then as a major, and finally as a lieutenant-colonel in the Continental forces, he was in a position to learn the movements and objectives of the army, of which a private or noncommissioned officer would not be informed. He was able therefore to view the tactics of his own company or regiment in their relation to the general strategy. Moreover, Dearborn did not attain a rank which would have kept him off the field and out of direct contact with his men. Even after he was appointed deputy quartermaster general in July, 1781, he continued to move with the main army.

The entries in Dearborn's journal vary widely in length and importance, but in nearly every instance they are impersonal and objective. He rarely philosophizes, and he wastes little space in damning the enemy. Never does he even imply any wavering of loyalty to the cause of the patriots, nor does he show any slackening of faith in the principles for which he was fighting. Commenting on the death of several popular officers after the first battle of Freeman's Farm, Dearborn observed: "the Loss of those Brave men are very greatly Lamented in the Army, But as it was a Debt that they & Every one owe their Country I Beleave they Paid it with Cherefullness." His respect for his commander-in-chief is apparent to the most casual reader, and it seems to have been reciprocated by Washington. Likewise, he never criticizes his immediate superiors. The only hint of his dissatisfaction with a campaign is revealed in an entry made in August, 1777: "Gates takes Command of the Northern army this Day which I think will Put a New Face upon our affairs." This opinion would pass unnoticed among the loud complaints raised against Schuyler at that time.

Personally brave, Dearborn was evidently an able leader of men. Frequent assignments to command special corps of picked riflemen attest his ability, although he apparently remained oblivious to the honor implied by these special duties. More than once he was sent out to reconnoiter the enemy, to assault a position or turn the opposing flank during battle. In the attack on Quebec, while his company was caught between the barriers in the driving snow and semi-darkness, he coolly exchanged abusive remarks with the defenders, and while facing a brisk fire urged his men to reprime their wet muskets and attempt a volley. Again, at Monmouth, Colonel Cilley and Dearborn were ordered to attack the British right wing, which was then passing through an orchard. Casually Dearborn relates the advance of his men, their taking down two rail fences under heavy fire, and their approaching within four rods of the British before "we then gave them a very heavy fire." In consequence of this temperament and style of writing, one feels that his comments on what he experienced may be relied upon as sincere and usually accurate.

Five of Dearborn's journals have been published before, though not annotated nor within one cover. The remaining journal, covering the important period from October, 1779, to December, 1781, has never before been printed. In this volume the complete series of journals is published for the first time, with annotations and a biographical sketch of the author. The division into parts, although based on the six notebooks used by Dearborn, is to some extent topical.

The first journal covers forty folio pages in manuscript, and dates from September 10, 1775 to July 16, 1776. It is the only one not in Dearborn's handwriting, although corrected in a score of places by the author. Dearborn's original manuscript has not been located. This copy was made in a fine flowing hand, sprinkled with excess punctuation. It was purchased by the Boston Public Library at the sale in 1878 of the library of John W. Thornton, executor of the will of Henry A. S. Dearborn, the son of Henry Dearborn. It was first published in the Proceedings *of the Massachusetts Historical Society, second series, volume II (1885-86). The editor, Judge Mellen Chamberlain, added no historical footnotes, but did indicate the corrections made in Dearborn's hand. The journal was reprinted from the above* Proceedings *in the* Magazine of History, *volume XXXIV (1928), number 3, extra number 135. Kenneth Roberts published it again in his* March to Quebec *(New York, 1938), with a few notes.*

The second journal dates from July 25, 1776, to December 4, 1777, and fills fifteen folio pages, numbered in continuation of the first journal, with which it is bound. It, too, is owned by the Boston Public Library and was purchased with the first. Judge Chamberlain published it, without notes, in the Proceedings *of the Massachusetts Historical Society, second series, volume III (1886–87).*

Journal number three is contained in a notebook of 144 octavo pages. The first five pages, comprising copies of Congressional resolves relating to the army, and the last seventy pages, containing accounts, receipts, and songs, are not printed here. The actual diary is 69 pages long, covering the period from December 5, 1777, to June 16, 1779. It was printed in the above Proceedings, *with an error in the final date of the heading. The manuscript belongs to the Boston Public Library.*

The fourth journal is in the possession of the Massachusetts Historical Society through the gift of Charles P. Greenough, who had owned it for many years. He may have obtained it from John S. Fogg, who is reported to have had it in 1879. Mr. Fogg probably acquired it at the Thornton sale in 1878. The journal covers eighty octavo pages and dates from June 17 to October 25, 1779. While it was in the hands of Mr. Greenough, it was published in the Journals of the Military Expedition of Major General John Sullivan against the Six Nations of Indians . . . *edited by Frederick Cook in 1887. There the journal was annotated with seven footnotes credited to General John S. Clark.*

The unpublished fifth journal, covers the war from October 28, 1779, to December 10, 1781. The original manuscript, in the possession of the New York Public Library, fills 99 octavo pages. It was acquired as part of the Dr. Thomas Addis Emmet Collection in 1896. Dr. Emmet purchased the diary at the Thornton sale in 1878. Henry A. S. Dearborn made a copy of journals three, four and five, the manuscript of which is also in the New York Public Library.

The last journal is eighteen octavo pages long, with a few additional pages of oaths, accounts, and memoranda of little

*importance. The manuscript is in the Boston Public Library
with the first three Dearborn journals, and was printed without notes in the* Proceedings *of the Massachusetts Historical
Society with journals two and three. Its entries date from June
20, 1782, to June 18, 1783, bringing to a close Dearborn's
military service of eight years.*

*The journals were transcribed and are here printed exactly as
Dearborn wrote them, insofar as is possible with type. His
punctuation, spelling, and abbreviations have been scrupu-
lously observed; but to help the reader, sentences that run together have been separated by extra space in the absence of
periods. Omitted words and letters, the lack of which was con-
fusing, have been supplied in brackets. Liberty was taken to
indent the date of each new entry, whereas Dearborn usually
set the date in the margin.*

*In annotating the journals, the persons and places men-
tioned by the author were identified, his accounts of battles as he
saw them were clarified by summaries of the engagements as a
whole, and the rumors he set down were corrected or amplified.
In general Mr. Brown identified place names, and Mr. Peckham the persons referred to by Dearborn. Since place names
often were located only after consulting several maps, both
printed and manuscript, in the map collection of the William
L. Clements Library, sources have not been cited for these notes.
Biographical sketches were inserted the first time a person was
mentioned. The introductions to each journal were designed to
supply briefly the background of the campaign or operation in
which Dearborn was engaged.*

*The biographical essay is not intended to be a complete ac-
count of Dearborn's life, and purposely passes rapidly over
certain episodes, such as the War of 1812 campaigns, which,
it was felt, would not be of interest to the general reader. For
a more inclusive biographical sketch of Dearborn, the reader is referred to volume V of the* Dictionary of American Biography,

and for a full account of Fort Dearborn, to M. M. Quaife's, Chicago and the Old Northwest.

No work of this kind could be published without the interest and coöperation of many persons. We are glad to acknowledge our gratitude to the several institutions and individuals that have extended courtesies to us. First of all, we wish to thank the Boston Public Library, the Massachusetts Historical Society, and the New York Public Library for their permission to publish the journals in their possession; The National Archives for permission to print an unpublished Dearborn letter; and the Maine Historical Society for permission to reproduce the portrait of Dearborn. We are grateful also for information obtained from the American Antiquarian Society, the Chicago Historical Society, Harvard University Library, the University of Chicago Library, Yale University Library, and the Newberry Library.

Several persons have freely given us the benefit of their expert knowledge: Randolph G. Adams, director of the William L. Clements Library; R. W. G. Vail, librarian of the American Antiquarian Society; Allyn Forbes, librarian of the Massachusetts Historical Society; Victor H. Paltsits of the New York Public Library; Alexander C. Flick of the New York State Library; Hugh P. Graham of the Cohoes Department of History; Henry V. Greenough of Boston; Carroll A. Wilson of New York; Marjory Gane Harkness of Wonalancet, New Hampshire; and Kathleen Scott of Waldoboro, Maine.

LLOYD A. BROWN
HOWARD H. PECKHAM
HERMON DUNLAP SMITH

Ann Arbor, October 1, 1939

Revolutionary War Journals
of Henry Dearborn

General Henry Dearborn

A BIOGRAPHICAL ESSAY BY HERMON DUNLAP SMITH

TO CHICAGOANS, the name of Dearborn signifies a fort, a street, or the cartoonists' "Father Dearborn", but to very few would it suggest a real person. A letter signed "H. Dearborn" would seem to most of them as improbable as one signed "J. Bull" or "Uncle Sam." It is therefore not surprising that the curiosity of a Chicagoan should be aroused by finding the following letter.

> "Portsm^th, Monday
> ½ after 11: o'clock P. M—
> "My dear Sarah
> This is the first minuit that I have been able to write a line today. We set off at 6 o'clock tomorrow morning for Portland, where the President intends to arrive before night. Mrs W. & Julia are at Portland & will come back with me. I hope to see you on Saturday.
> Your affectionate,
> H. Dearborn"

The letter is addressed to Mrs. Sarah B. Dearborn, Boston, and is postmarked Portsmouth, New Hampshire, July 15,—no year shown.

This is indeed a sketchy document from which to create a portrait of its writer, but its gaps, such as the omission of the year, and the mention of the "President," "Julia," and "Mrs. W.," are a challenge to further investigation. The search for the information

3

needed to explain these references produced a vivid picture of a colorful personality.

*   *   *

The first Dearborn to settle in America was Godfrey Dearborn, who came to the Massachusetts colony about 1639. Henry Dearborn was the twelfth child of the ninth child of Godfrey's grandson,—a prolific family, by modern standards, but exceeded by one of his uncles, who had seventeen children. Born in 1751 at North Hampton, in the extreme southeastern corner of New Hampshire, Henry grew up as a strong, athletic boy—a champion wrestler. After a course of medical instruction under Dr. Hall Jackson of Portsmouth, he took up the practice of medicine in nearby Nottingham. At twenty-four, when in his third year of practice, news of the battle of Lexington reached him, on April 20, 1775. He and sixty of his fellow-townsmen, with squirrel guns on shoulders, at once set off on foot for Cambridge, arriving there the next morning at sunrise, having marched fifty-five miles in less than twenty-four hours. Finding there was no immediate need for their services, they soon returned home, but before long young Dr. Dearborn had become Captain Dearborn of the first New Hampshire regiment, under command of Colonel John Stark, formerly of Rogers' Rangers, and later the hero of the Battle of Bennington. Dearborn's popularity enabled him to enlist his own company, which marched southward in time to take an important part in the Battle of Bunker Hill.

THE BUNKER HILL CONTROVERSY

Dearborn's participation in the Battle of Bunker Hill was responsible for his being involved in a curious controversy with unfortunate political ramifications, more than forty years later. There is a general agreement as to the disposition of the troops at the battle, but there is widespread disagreement in regard to the parts played by the various American officers—a confusion to which Dearborn contributed in no small degree by the publication of an account of the battle in 1818. To give very briefly the accepted facts regarding the battle: on the night of June 16, 1775, the American forces had fortified Breed's Hill, which commanded the northern portion of Boston and is connected with the neighboring Bunker Hill by a ridge extending about 700 yards. On the following afternoon, June 17, 1775, General Howe's veteran British regulars attempted three times to storm the hill, which was held by a motley handful of undisciplined volunteers barricaded behind a hastily constructed redoubt and a post-and-rail fence. Among the defenders of the fence was Captain Dearborn, who was on Colonel Stark's right wing. Of these men, Dearborn later said, "Not an officer or soldier of the continental troops engaged was in uniform, but were in the plain and ordinary dress of citizens; nor was there an officer on horseback."[1] Only when their ammunition was exhausted did the American troops retreat towards Bunker Hill. The significance of the battle lies largely in the stubborn resistance of the provincials, who, by driving the British regulars back in disorder two times, showed the colonies that there was hope of ultimate victory in their struggle for independence.

The effectiveness of the American troops is largely attributable to their coolness in holding their fire until the British were almost upon them. As expressed in General Wilkinson's account of the battle, "Colonel Stark's men were directed to reserve their fire until they could see the enemy's half-gaiters."[2] From this it would seem that the

1. Dearborn, *An Account of The Battle of Bunker Hill*, p. 14.
2. Coffin, comp., *History of the Battle of Breed's Hill*, p. 12.

often quoted order, "Don't fire until you can see the white of their eyes," was more nearly, "Don't fire until you can see the white of their gaiters."

Unfortunately, the last shot of Bunker Hill was not fired on the battle field. In fact, some of General Dearborn's ammunition was set off posthumously. In 1843 there was published an attack on General Israel Putnam's military reputation, under the intriguing title, "The Veil Removed." The author of this remarkable work states, "The controversy respecting the conduct of General Putnam at the Battle of Bunker Hill appears to have originated principally from an article on that battle written by the late General Dearborn and published in 1818."[3] In this article Dearborn describes General Putnam of Connecticut as occupying a safe position on Bunker Hill, "on the declivity towards Charleston neck," while the New Hampshire and Massachusetts troops were holding the post-and-rail fence on Breed's Hill against the fierce British attack. When, with ammunition exhausted, the retreating Continentals arrived at the summit of Bunker Hill, Dearborn writes, "We found General Putnam with nearly as many men as had been engaged in the battle; notwithstanding which no measures had been taken for reinforcing us, nor was there a shot fired to cover our retreat, or any movement made to check the advance of the enemy to this height, but on the contrary, General Putnam rode off, with a number of *spades and pickaxes in his hands* and the troops that had remained with him *inactive*, during the whole of the action, although within a few hundred yards of the battle ground, and no obstacle to impede their movement but *musket balls*."[4]

3. Fellows, *The Veil Removed*, p. 113.
4. Dearborn, *op. cit.*, p. 9.

This reputedly ignoble conduct of General Putnam is confirmed by various eyewitnesses, including one who reports the following conversation with Colonel Prescott, who was at the redoubt. Said Prescott, when, upon retreating to Bunker Hill, he met Putnam armed with a spade, "Why did you not support me General, with your men, as I had reason to expect, according to agreement?" Putnam answered, "I could not drive the dogs up." Prescott pointedly said to him, "If you could not drive them up, you might have led them up."[5]

But contradicting eye witnesses, and the muse of poesy as well, have rallied to Putnam's defence. "An Historic Poem in Four Cantos," entitled, "The Battle of Bunker Hill, or The Temple of Liberty" reports quite a different conversation between Prescott and Putnam.—

> Prescott to Putnam as he clears the steep:
> "Thy swift return makes new pulsations leap.
> "Revered art thou—the chosen of the field—
> "This day is thine to be in history sealed.
> "How glows my breast to see our minds as one,
> "Centred as rays collected from the sun . . ."[6]

The same poet places Putnam, not safely on Bunker Hill, but by the post-and-rail fence on Breed's Hill, with his sword poised aloft, as a signal to the minutemen to withhold their fire as the British draw closer and closer.—

> Still Putnam keeps his sword suspended high—
> They now so close, he looks them in the eye!—
> They caught the rising vengeance of his soul,
> Which shock'd them, as keen lightning from the pole.
> They paused—so terrible the veteran's ire,
> His glance appear'd an arrow tipp'd with fire.
> His sword the instant like a meteor fell!—
> A shriek of agony convulsed the hill![7]

5. Fellows, *op. cit.*, p. 132.
6. Emmons, *The Battle of Bunker Hill*, p. 55.
7. *Ibid.*, p. 82.

And like Satan in "Paradise Lost," he proves even more magnificent in defeat.—

> Putnam yet lingering on the rear the last,
> Back on the foe a stern defiance cast.
> His countenance appear'd like Jupiter's, when he
> Summon'd the gods to reverence his decree.
> The hero leads th' immortals o'er the plain,
> At whom the vessels pour'd their wrath in vain.
> The Eagle, though retreating, waves her plumes
> In radiant light and victory assumes.
> Soon on a neighboring steep the flag is seen,
> Touch'd with a ray of setting sun serene.
> While round the glorious Height a rainbow curl'd—
> A sign—that Liberty would bless the world.[8]

The opposing views of the Putnam controversy were well expressed by Colonel Francis J. Parker, who wrote, "If one party were to be believed, General Putnam was the Alpha and Omega of the battle and always commanding, but if the other side were to be credited, he was never there at all, except that late in the day he was skulking behind the great hill, presiding over the army of terrified bummers, who occupied that important position."[9]

We have no reason to doubt that Dearborn's statement represented his honest recollections, although undoubtedly dimmed by the passage of 43 years. A contemporary compiler said of his account of the battle, "When General Dearborn, who always acted without fear or reproach, adds his opinion, . . . there seems to be no sufficient reason why he should not be fully credited."[10] But Putnam had a strong popular following, and when Dearborn was nominated for Governor of the Commonwealth

8. *Ibid.*, p. 126.
9. Parker, *Could General Putnam Command at Bunker Hill?* p. 1.
10. Coffin, comp., *op. cit.*, p. 35.

of Massachusetts, the popularity of Putnam was brought to bear against his election, and contributed to his defeat.[11] The modern historian, however, has long since dismissed the attack on Putnam as "a strange and not very creditable outgrowth of political animosities."[12]

THE REVOLUTIONARY WAR

To return to the adventures of young Captain Dearborn in the Revolutionary War. Shortly after the Battle of Bunker Hill, on September 10, 1775, he joined the forces which were preparing to march to Quebec under the leadership of Colonel Benedict Arnold. Other participants in the Canadian campaign were two young soldiers who were to cast a shadow across his later life, —Colonel Arnold's personal aide, Aaron Burr, and Burr's subsequent confederate, James Wilkinson, who did not join Arnold till spring, but who, like Dearborn, had given up the practice of medicine to fight for liberty. Dearborn's journal gives a vivid picture of the terrible hardships of the desperate march through the wilderness. For thirty days in the early Canadian winter, he was overcome by fever in a rude cabin with no medicine but a "Tea of Piggen plumb Roots, and Spruce" and no attendants, except for two boys. He rejoined his company, which had supposed him dead, just in time to take part in the disastrous attack on Quebec on December 31, 1775. The attack was commenced before daylight on that morning, and Dearborn's troops, which were detached from the main body, lost their way in the snow and darkness. Dearborn says in his journal, that in coming upon some soldiers in the early dawn, "I was at a Stand to know whether They were our men, or the enemy, as

11. Fellows, *The Veil Removed*, p. 140.
12. French, *The First Year of the American Revolution*, p. 228.

they were dress'd like us, I was Just about to Hail them, when one of them hail'd me, he asked who I was . . I answer'd a friend; he asked me who I was a friend to, I answer'd to liberty, he then reply'd God-damn you, and then rais'd himself partly above the Pickets, I Clapt up my Piece which was Charged with a ball and Ten Buck shott Certainly to give him his due, But to my great mortification my Gun did not go off, I new prim'd her, and flushed and Try'd her again, but neither I, nor one in Ten of my men could get off our Guns they being so exceeding wet . . . we Now found ourselves surrounded by Six to one, I now finding no possibility of getting away, my Company were divided, and our arms being in such bad order, I thought it best to Surrender after being promis'd good quarters and Tender usuage . . . I with my other officiers, ware Carry'd to the main, guard-House . . . where we had a good Dinner, and aplenty of several sorts of wine."

Unfortunately, such good treatment could not last for long. Dearborn was held in close confinement for several months, and was frequently taunted with the threat that in the spring he would be sent to England and hanged as a rebel. On May 16, 1776 he was extremely fortunate in arranging to return home on parole, as most of his companions were confined till the close of the war. After a long sea voyage, during which he was "treated with the usual contumely and hauteur of English officers,"[13] he finally reached Portsmouth on July 16.

In the following spring, he was relieved of his parole through an exchange of prisoners, and, having been appointed a Major of the Third New Hampshire Regiment, set out for Ticonderoga early in May. Throughout the balance of the war he turned up at nearly every important

13. Massachusetts election! . . . p. 4.

engagement. On September 19, 1777, he wrote of the first Battle of Saratoga, "The Enimy Brought almost their whole force against us, together with 8 Peices of Artilery. But we who had something more at Stake than fighting for six Pence Pr Day kept our ground til Night, Closed the scene, & then Both Parties Retired . . . on this Day has Been fought one of the Greatest Battles that Ever was fought in Amarrica, & I Trust we have Convincd the British Butchers that the Cowardly yankees Can & when their is a Call for it, will, fight."

On October 17, 1777, he records the surrender at Saratoga, "this Day the Great Mr Burguoyn with his whole Army Surrendered themselves as Prisoners of war with all their Publick Stores, & after Grounding their armes march.d of[f] for New England, the greatest Conquest Ever known." By a most interesting coincidence, one of the British prisoners taken with Burgoyne was John Whistler (grandfather of James McNeill Whistler), who, after later joining the American army, was the first commandant of Fort Dearborn.

Hastening from Saratoga by a spectacular forced march to Albany, Dearborn's regiment next went on to join Washington. He records in his journal, under date of December 18, 1777, "this is Thanksgiving Day thro the whole Continent of America—but god knows We have very Little to keep it with this being the third Day we have been without flouer or bread—& are Living on a high uncultivated hill, in huts & tents Laying on the Cold Ground, upon the whole I think all we have to be thankful for is that we are alive & not in the Grave with many of our friends—we had for thanksgiving breakfast some Exceeding Poor beef which has been boil.d & Now warm.d in an old short handled frying Pan in which we ware Obliged to Eat it haveing No other Platter . . ."

After a short leave at home, he rejoined General Washington at Valley Forge early in 1778. He distinguished himself and his regiment by a gallant charge at the Battle of Monmouth, for which he received the commendation of General Washington. In 1779, he served in Sullivan's expedition against the Indians in western New York; in 1780 he was with the Army of New Jersey; and in 1781 at the siege of Yorktown and the surrender of Cornwallis. On June 18, 1783, at the age of thirty-two, Henry Dearborn, now a Colonel, was honorably discharged after eight years of war service remarkable for its activity and ubiquity.

As would be expected, a campaign of this duration was replete with contrast. On February 22, 1779, for example, we find the following entry. "We had an Elligant Ball at which was a Learge numbar of very fine Ladies." But by April 14th of the same year the scene had changed. He records, "Arivd at Peeks kill found our brigade Quartered in Huts in the Highlands where we have no neighbors but Owls, Hedghogs, & Rattlesnakes, & them in plenty." The next day, April 15th, he notes, "A Small guard of ours was Surprisd this week in Gersey by a party of Tories from N. York, & every man put to the bayonet on the Spot under the cover of a dark night." This report would seem to confirm an impression of the Loyalists he received about two years earlier, when he referred to the "Indians, and their more savage brothers, the Tories." By April 17, however, more tranquil conditions seemed to have been restored, for he reports, "We ware oblige'd to walk 4 miles to day to find a place leavel enough to play ball."

From perusing the journals, one gets the impression that most of the time not occupied in fighting was spent in observing glorious anniversaries by drinking toasts.

Even during Sullivan's expedition against the Indians, this was not overlooked. The Fourth of July, being Sunday, was observed by an appropriate sermon, and the real festivities were postponed until the 5th, apparently with cumulative force. Dearborn's entry for that day is, "Gen! Poor made an Entertainment to day for all the Officers of his Brigade, to celibrate the Anniversary of the declaration of American Independence. 87 Gentleman ware present at dinner, after which the 13 following Patriotick toasts ware drank. 1ˢᵗ 4th of July 76, the ever Memoriable Eara of American Independence 2ᵈ the United States 3ᵈ the Grand Counsel of America 4ᵗʰ Gen! Washington & the Army 5ᵗʰ The King & Queen of France 6ᵗʰ Gen! Lincoln & the Southern Army 7ᵗʰ Gen! Sullivan & the Western Army 8ᵗʰ May the Counsellors of America be wise, & her Soldiers Invincible 9ᵗʰ A Successful & decisive Campaign 10ᵗʰ Civilization or death to all American Savages 11ᵗʰ the Immortal Memory of those heroes that have fallen in defence of American Liberty 12ᵗʰ May this New World be the last Asylum for freedom and the Arts. 13ᵗʰ May the Husbandman's house be bless'd with peace, & his fields with plenty.

"The whole was conducted with such Joy & festivity, as demonstrated an Independent Elevation of Spirit, on this Important & enteresting Occation."

It is certainly a remarkable tribute to the stamina of our Revolutionary ancestors that they could not only drink thirteen toasts, but remember every one of them!

On the 7th, Dearborn notes a decided change of diet, "I eat part of a fryed Rattle Snake to day, which would have tasted very well had it not been snake."

But the most poignant contrast between the carefree interludes in the life of a soldier and tragedy is found in the following sequence: "October 17, 1778—this being the first Anniversary of the Glorious 17th of Octob^r 1777. the field Officers of this Division Make an Entertainment for all the Officers of the Division, & Gentlemen of the Town.— we Eat Dinner on a small hill between two of the brigades,— after the officers of the three Brigades had assembled, . . . thirteen Cannon ware Discharg^d from Each Brigade at which time Gen.^{rl} Gates arivd with a number of other Gen.^{rl} Officers. there was then three Cheers from the whole Division. at Dinner we had about 350 Officers & other gentlemen. after Dinner there was 13 toasts Drank— & a Cannon Discharged for Each.— at Evining we Retire'd to the Town, & spent the Evining very agreably.

18th—we are geting sober.— . . .

19th—we march at 10 O Clock towards Hartford. I Receiv'd News this Day by Express that my wife Lay Dangerously sick with a Nerveous Fever. In Consequence of which I got Leave of absince & set out for home this Evining.

24th—I ariv'd at my House at 7 O Clock in the Evining. found my wife Senceless & almost Motionless, which was a very shocking sight to behold. at half after Eleven she Expired. much Lamented not only by her Relation but by all her Neighbours.— this was a very Trying Scene to me. I seem'd to be Quite alone in the world. Except my two Little Daughters who are two small to feel their Loss, or offer me any Comfort.

25th—the most Malloncolly Sunday I Ever Experiencd.''

After the war had ended, Colonel Dearborn, having recorded in his journal with remarkably poor foresight, ''Thus ends my millatery life,'' settled down with his family at Pittston on the Kennebec River in southern Maine. In 1780, two years after the death of his first wife, Mary Bartlett, described above, he had married a young widow, Dorcas Marble. Before the close of the war, she presented him with two children—a daughter, Julia, and that son, Henry A. S. Dearborn, who was to be the pride of his later years. In reference to Julia's beauty, a contemporary writer stated, "We are told that Venus rose out of the sea, but I once thought she came out of the waters of the Kennebec."

But peace and semi-retirement did not bring inactivity to this vigorous character. Shortly after the organization of the government, President Washington designated him United States Marshal for the District of Maine; the State of Massachusetts appointed him a Major General of Militia; and in 1792 he was elected to Congress, where he demonstrated his independence of thought by opposing the Jay Treaty of 1794 against the wishes of his beloved chief, President Washington. Even the seclusion of the Maine woods failed to provide protection from callers, for Louis Philippe, and Talleyrand, who was interested in the lumber trade, visited him in Pittston in 1794. It is recorded that Talleyrand fell into the cold waters of the Kennebec while fishing, and was only rescued from drowning by the efforts of a small boy who held his fishing pole to him.[14]

THE FOUNDING OF THE FORT

In 1801, President Thomas Jefferson invited General Dearborn to become Secretary of War—one of the four positions in the Cabinet. In reference to this appointment, General Reid, one of Dearborn's companions of the Revolution, was asked, "How could you get along with such a democrat as General Dearborn is?" In reply, General Reid said, "I always was sorry Harry was a democrat, but that is of no consequence among old

14. Goodwin, *The Dearborns*, p. 22.

officers. He is a noble fellow; there is no man I esteem and love more, and if Jefferson had always made as good appointments as Dearborn to the war-office, I should think much better of him than I do now."[15] It was of course his position as Secretary of War which was responsible for General Dearborn's association with Chicago.

The period following the Revolution had been one of great disorder along the western frontier, until the Treaty of Greenville in 1795, which was made possible by "Mad Anthony" Wayne's victory over the Indians at Fallen Timbers in the year previous. In consideration of the distribution of presents and annuities, and after an adjournment of two or three days "to have a little drink,"[16] as was customary, the Indians signed this Treaty, which recognized the American title to a large tract of land in what is now southern Ohio, and to certain "isolated reservations" including "One piece of Land Six Miles square at the Mouth of Chikago River emptying into the Southwest end of Lake Michigan where a fort formerly stood." With the surrender of the British military posts in the northwest in 1796, in accordance with the terms of the Jay Treaty—the Treaty, incidentally, which Congressman Dearborn had opposed—the way was clear for the United States to take possession of the West. But it was not for another seven years that the pending Louisiana Purchase made further delay perilous and urged immediate fortification.

Realizing the necessity of establishing a base of communication with this vast new territory, Secretary Dearborn, under date of March 9, 1803, wrote Adjutant General Thomas H. Cushing to take up the matter with

15. *Ibid.*, p. 20.
16. Quaife, *Chicago and the Old Northwest*, p. 123.

Colonel John F. Hamtramck of the First Infantry, in command at Detroit, thus linking two names which are still joined in the neighboring Michigan cities of Dearborn and Hamtramck. After giving instructions relative to various frontier posts, this letter states:[17]

"Colonel Hamtramck should be directed to send a suitable Officer with Six men and one or two guides across the Country to the mouth of St. Josephs at the south end of Lake Michigan and from thence to Chikago on the opposite side of the lake to examine the situation with a view to the establishment of a Post, and to look out and mark a track by which a Company may march from Detroit to the St. Josephs and to asurtain what supplies of provisions can be obtained from Mr. Burnit[18] and others, and to decide on a suitable scite for an encampment at St. Josephs as a temporary stand for a Company, until preparations can be made at Chikago for the Company.

"And if it should be found that a Company can march from Detroit to the St. Josephs with pack Horses for transporting the light baggage and such provisions as may be necessary Col. Hamtramck will order a Company under the Command of a discreet judicious Captain to take post as above and he should send by water two field pieces, and a suitable quantity of amunition and other Stores for a Post at Chikago with a suitable number of axes, spades and other tools for erecting Barracks and a Strong stockade work of the kind which is skitched on the enclosed[19]—which should be forwarded to Colonel

17. This letter, which gives the original instructions for the establishment of the Fort, apparently has not been published hitherto. It is in the National Archives, Secretary of War Military Letter Book, Vol. I., 1800-03. pp. 385-387.

18. William Burnett, a French trader on the St. Joseph River, with Montreal connections, who at times extended his trading operations around the Lake as far as Chicago.

19. This sketch has unfortunately been lost or destroyed.

Hamtramck with the directions and explenations accompanying it."

By midsummer, with the arrival of two small detachments of troops, one having come overland from Detroit, the other by the schooner "Tracy," the construction of the Fort was in full progress under the command of the "discreet, judicious captain," John Whistler—the same Whistler who had been captured with Burgoyne at Saratoga. It was of course only natural that this fort should bear the name of the Secretary of War, who had determined its location and ordered its construction.

THE BURR CONSPIRACY

The naming of the Fort, which was to give him immortality, must have seemed at the time a trivial incident to General Dearborn. Even twenty years later, the Fort was not considered worth mentioning in the fulsome seven volume manuscript biography which the "young General" wrote to enhance his father's fame. Certainly the Secretary of War of the young Republic had more important things to think about. In 1805, the ambitious Aaron Burr was concluding his term of office as Vice President under Jefferson. Finding himself an outcast in the East, because of his recent fatal duel with Alexander Hamilton, he was hatching a fantastic scheme for the foundation of a colony in Louisiana, which could serve as a base for a military invasion of Texas, if the expected war with Spain should become an actuality.

On his way to New Orleans in the spring of 1805, Burr made a side trip to Nashville for the purpose of securing the support of Andrew Jackson, who was at that time a General of Militia there. Burr held out to Jackson the idea that from his intimacy with Secretary of War

Dearborn, who had been his companion on the march to Quebec, he would obtain a military appointment upon the outbreak of hostilities with Spain. No doubt influenced by this report of the secret backing of Dearborn, Jackson lent his patronage to Burr's project. After cooperating with Burr for a year and a half, Jackson, in November, 1806, received a visit from a certain Captain Fort, who was on his way from New York to join Burr in the southwest. Fort incautiously characterized the project as a scheme "to divide the union."[20] In spite of Fort's hasty attempts at retraction, the quick mind of Jackson was aroused. He immediately warned the Federal authorities at Washington, and advised Burr in "strong tones" that until "my suspicions . . . were cleared from my mind no further intimacy was to exist between us."[21]

With the likelihood of discovery imminent, Burr's confederate, General Wilkinson,—Dearborn's companion of the Saratoga campaign,—decided to try to save his own skin by betraying Burr in a crafty letter to Jefferson. This prompted a presidential proclamation on November 26, 1806, declaring the existence of a military conspiracy.

In Washington, the former friendly relationship between Jackson and Burr was known, but no word of Jackson's indignation at the suggestion of treason had been received. In fact, there were unfounded rumors that Jackson was leading an army to the support of Burr. Accordingly, Secretary Dearborn, perhaps having difficulty in grasping the depth to which Burr and Wilkinson, his two companions of the campaigns of thirty years before, had sunk, dispatched a cautious communication to his

20. Bassett, *Correspondence of Andrew Jackson*, Vol. I, p. 168.
21. *Ibid.*, Vol. I, p. 169.

subordinate, General Jackson. This letter Jackson characterized as "a milk and cider thing," . . . "the merest old-woman letter . . . you ever saw."[22]

"War Department Dec 19, 1806
"General Jackson,
"Sir:
". . . It appears that you have some reason for suspecting that some unlawful enterprise is in contemplation on the western waters. There can be no doubt, but that many persons are engaged in some such enterprise; and before this reaches you, it is not improbable, that a general movement will have commenced.—
"It is presumed that the Proclamation of the President . . . will have produced every exertion . . . and . . . that you will have been among the most jealous opposers of any such unlawful expedition, as appears to be initiated, by a set of disappointed, unprincipled, ambitious or misguided individuals, and that you will continue to make every exertion in your power, as a General of the Militia, to counteract and render abhortive, any such expedition. About Pittsburgh it is industriously reported among the adventurers, that they are to be joined, at the mouth of the Cumberland, by two Regiments under the Command of General Jackson—such a story might afford you an opportunity of giving an effectual check to the enterprise if not too late, I am etc.
"Henry Dearborn"[23]

Jackson promptly put two brigades under arms, and wrote the Secretary of War a letter, which concludes with the following comment: "The first duty of a soldier or good citizen is to attend to the safety and interest of his country, The next to attend to his own feelings whereever the[y] are rudely or wantonly assailed. The Tenor of your letter is such and the insinuations so grating—The ideas and tenor so unmilitary, stories alluded to, and intimations, of a conduct, to stoop, from the charector of a general to a smiling *assasin* (*These hereafter*) . . . Health and respect."[24]

22. *Ibid.*, Vol. I, pp. 161, 164.
23. James, *The Life of Andrew Jackson*, p. 125.
24. Bassett, *op. cit.*, Vol. I, p. 163.

It soon became apparent that the Burr conspiracy had fallen to pieces, and, with his "first duty" as a soldier attended to, the hot-headed Jackson, who was prepared to defend his honor with dueling pistols on the least provocation, had more time to consider the slight to his patriotism implied in Dearborn's letter, over which he had undoubtedly been brooding. In his reply he proved himself as deadly with the pen as with the pistol. At the conclusion of a long preliminary draft, in which he discussed fully Dearborn's supposed intimacy with General Wilkinson, he wrote, "Colo.B. received at my house all that hospitality that a banished patriot . . . was entitled to . . . But Sir when prooff shews him to be a triator, I would cut his throat, with as much pleasure as I would cut yours on equal testimony."[25]

This still did not satisfy Jackson. It was not until March 17, 1807 that he dispatched the final document, omitting the frequent references to "yanky cunning" which adorned the first draft. "After I have given, the most deliber[ate] consideration to your expressions, then, in a degree, ambiguously made, I cannot draw from them any other conclution than this: that you believed me conserned in the con[s]piricy, that I was an fit subject to act the traitor of traitors, as others have done, and that it was only necessary for the Secretary at war of the United States, to buy me up without honour, money or price . . . It is a well known fact that you have been uniformly the intimate friend and Supporter of Genl. Wilkinson . . . It has been not only *storied* in this part of the western country, but has been reported on the most respectable authority, that Colo. Burr and his adventure[r]s held your order as Secretary at War, purporting a furtherence and governmental support of the

25. *Ibid.*, Vol. I, pp. 177-178.

enterprise . . . The government must indeed be tottering with its own imbecility when the principal supportors of it, shall be thus insulted, thus assailed by an officer of government, devoid of talents, integrity and altogether ignorant of the duties attached to his elevated station. The nominal dignity that the Secretary at war acquires at the first entrance upon the duties of his office, will always give to his assertions a degree of credit. I know what he has done is unworthy the character of a genl. or a man of honor."[26] This, so far as we can determine, was the final word in the correspondence between Jackson and Dearborn in regard to the Burr episode. In spite of abominable spelling and grammar, Jackson had made his opinion of the Secretary of War unmistakably clear!

THE WAR OF 1812

With the vituperative Jackson to contend with, it is not surprising that Dearborn welcomed the relative peace that was offered when Madison appointed him to the lucrative post of Collector of the Port of Boston in 1809. But again his retirement proved all too brief, for it was soon interrupted by the threat of hostilities with England. In January, 1812, Congress took steps to increase our military strength, and President Madison immediately asked Dearborn, who was then more than sixty years old, to accept the post of Senior Major General of the Army. He hastened to Washington, and on February 19, 1812 wrote his son,

"I arrived here on the 17th safe and in good health. I do not discover as much harmony as could be wished, but I presume that all will go on very well ultimately.

"We are engaged in forming lists of nominations of officers for the several states. I hope to complete these soon.

26. *Ibid.*, Vol. I, pp. 172-74.

"There are no indications of any adjustment with England, and although there are many different opinions about the measures for preparation for commencing the war, there seems to be a very general agreement in sentiment as to the necessity, unless a satisfactory adjustment is made between this time and spring. I doubt whether war will be declared before it shall be known what the disposition of the British Government will be after the Prince Regent comes into power, but perhaps it will not be expedient for you to mention the last sentence . . . " This letter likewise concludes with a reference to the same two persons as does the undated one to his wife previously quoted,—"I hope Mrs. Wingate and Julia remain with you and that all of you are as happy as can be wished by your affectionate parent, H. Dearborn."[27]

In spite of the several months' warning provided by the full realization of the imminence of hostilities which is clearly indicated by this letter, the declaration of war on June 18, 1812 found the United States badly prepared. There was almost universal opposition to the war in New England. Governor Caleb Strong of Massachusetts, upon the unanimous advice of the Supreme Court of the Commonwealth, refused to respond to General Dearborn's call for troops as being unconstitutional. It is not surprising that with such opposition, and crippled by lack of competent officers and trained men, General Dearborn's ambitious plan of taking Montreal and Quebec— a plan which is easy to identify with his own march through the wilderness thirty-six years previous—was impossible of execution. The failure of this hoped-for pressure in the East by the troops under his command left the western posts vulnerable to attack. With Mackinac

27. Quoted from letter in the collection of the writer.

Island in the hands of the British, and the fall of Detroit imminent, General Hull, who was in command of the Army of the Northwest, issued his historic order for the evacuation of Fort Dearborn. Meanwhile, the Indians around Chicago, emboldened by news of the British successes, which a runner from Tecumseh had brought them, had become increasingly warlike. On August 15, 1812, as the little band of soldiers and their families left the protective stockade of Fort Dearborn and made their way along the sand dunes of Lake Michigan on the route to Fort Wayne, the Indians swept down on them from ambush. The intensely dramatic qualities of this massacre, the story of which is familiar to every Chicagoan, seem chiefly responsible for the association of Chicago with the name of Dearborn.

THE CONTROVERSY WITH GENERAL HULL

It is interesting to speculate as to the extent to which the man who was responsible for the founding of Fort Dearborn, was also responsible for its destruction. Historians generally agree with Quaife's statement that "on the issue of Hull's campaign hung the fate of Fort Dearborn and the Northwest."[28] However, the extent to which Dearborn was to blame for Hull's failure has been the subject of bitter controversy.

Hull had accepted the command of the Army of the Northwest reluctantly. He had repeatedly expressed the opinion that control of the lakes was essential to the safety of Detroit. Accordingly, with Dearborn doing nothing to engage the British by pushing the attack upon Canada from New York, Hull must have looked upon his position as hopeless, and consequently surrendered Detroit without firing a shot. Early in 1814, Hull

28. Quaife, *Chicago and the Old Northwest*, p. 214.

was tried before a court-martial on grounds of treason, cowardice, and neglect of duty. In his defence before the court, General Hull quoted from a memorial to the Administration dated March 6, 1812, in which he had written, "The British force which can be brought to operate against us in the territory, is more than ten to one, without including the Indians . . . who now hold a constant and friendly intercourse with the British agents, and are liberally fed and clothed by the bounty of the British government . . . If a force is not sent sufficient to oppose the British force which may be collected at Amherstberg and its vicinity, Detroit, Michilimackinac and Chicaga must fall—the inhabitants must once more change their allegiance, and the Indians become the exclusive friends and allies of the King their great Father."[29]

In outlining his case, Hull stated, "I did understand, and such it will appear was the understanding of the executive officers of the government, that in the event of a war the operations of my army would be strengthened and secured by a competent naval force on Lake Erie, and by the direction of other forces against the enemy's territory. Had these expectations been realized, instead of having lingered out so many months as a prosecuted criminal, instead of now standing before you as an accused, I might still have shared my country's confidence — The foul charges to which I am now to answer would not have thus blasted the laurels of my youth— But even in the wilds of Canada and amidst these whitened locks they might have retained their pristine verdure."[30]

Unfortunately, even such eloquence did not prevail against the forceful arguments of the special Judge Advocate, young Martin VanBuren. Hull was found guilty

29. Forbes, *Report of the Trial of Brig. General William Hull*, Appendix I, pp. 30–31.
30. *Ibid.*, Appendix I, p. 28.

upon the counts of cowardice and neglect of duty, and was sentenced to be shot, but President Madison remanded execution of the sentence, because of Hull's Revolutionary services. Curiously enough, the court martial was presided over by General Dearborn, a most improper appointment, since Hull had alleged that Dearborn's ineffectiveness had contributed to bring about his surrender. After his conviction, Hull appealed to his countrymen in "An Address to the Citizens of the United States," in which he objected bitterly to the impropriety of General Dearborn being "president of the court-martial which has condemned me for the misfortune which his own misconduct had been a great cause in producing."[31] Ten years later, upon the release of certain pertinent documents, General Hull resumed the attack on General Dearborn, in a series of articles in the "American Statesman." Due to his father's absence as Minister to Portugal, young General Dearborn took up the cudgels on his behalf in a well documented "Defence of General Henry Dearborn Against the Attack of General William Hull." This brought forth another attack from Hull, and further prolonged the fruitless controversy which was only terminated by the death of Hull within a year.

For Dearborn, the period of the war of 1812 was probably the most trying in his long career. Of the officers appointed by Madison, McMaster says "as a class they were old, vain, respectable, and incapable."[32] Describing the rank and file of the militia, a contemporary wrote, "the soldiers are under no more restraint than a herd of swine, reasoning, remonstrating, threatening, and ridiculing their officers, they show their sense of equality

31. *Defence of Brigadier General W. Hull*, p. XI.
32. McMaster, *A History of the People of the United States*, Vol. III, p. 546.

and their total want of subordination."[33] At critical moments they would refuse to cross the line between their state and Canada.

With these difficulties to contend with, it is not surprising that the operations around Niagara lagged, in spite of the capture of York (now Toronto). This campaign has a special interest for Chicagoans, because Dearborn probably was never so near to the site of Chicago as he was during this unhappy period. Finally, in July, 1813, broken with ill health and disappointment, the failing General was replaced by his companion of the Revolution,—that swaggering, incompetent James Wilkinson, of all people! There may be some poetic justice, of a comic opera sort, in the fact that eighteen months later Dearborn was to preside over the court-martial of this same Wilkinson.

THE TOUR OF PRESIDENT MONROE

With the return of peace to the nation, came peace to the General as well,—and a prosperity he had never previously enjoyed. In 1813, three years after the death of his second wife, he married Sarah Bowdoin, widow of James Bowdoin, patron of Bowdoin College, and daughter of William Bowdoin. The Bowdoin fortune made it possible for General Dearborn to give his old home in Roxbury to his son, while he and his new wife took over the Bowdoin mansion on Milk Street in Boston. Here he lived continuously, except for two years abroad as Minister to Portugal, until his wife's death in 1826, which was followed by his own death three years later. His wide acquaintance, set off by his wife's great wealth, made their home a center for the entertainment of visitors of prominence. Here he received the Marquis de

33. Babcock, *The Rise of American Nationality*, p. 79.

Lafayette, and here on July 3, 1817, he and his wife gave a magnificent ball in honor of the newly elected President of the United States, James Monroe.

The observant reader will have noted that by now considerable light has been thrown on the Portsmouth letter. "My dear Sarah" is obviously the General's third wife, Sarah Bowdoin Dearborn, which brackets the date of the letter between 1813 and 1826, the period of their marriage. Julia is his third daughter, the "Venus of the Kennebec," wife of Joshua Wingate, Jr., Collector of United States Customs at Portland;—she whose beauty so affected the gallant Marquis de Lafayette that he presented her with a set of china which had belonged to Marie Antoinette. "Mrs. W" appears to be the Mrs. Wingate of the Washington letter, Mrs. Joshua Wingate, Sr., Julia's mother-in-law. With our knowledge that a ball was given in honor of President Monroe at Dearborn's home in Boston, the "President" of the letter is revealed as Monroe, and the year as 1817. To authenticate these suppositions fully and to determine the exact circumstances of the letter, required detailed information regarding President Monroe's trip to Boston in 1817. This was located in a book published at Hartford in 1818, entitled, *The Tour of James Monroe, President of the United States, in 1817 through the States of Maryland, Pennsylvania, New Jersey, New York, Connecticut, Rhode Island, Massachusetts, New Hampshire, Vermont and Ohio*, by S. Putnam Waldo, Esquire, Compiler of Robbins' Journal.

It is hard for us who are used to streamlined presidential specials and battle ship fishing expeditions to realize the significance and magnitude of President Monroe's tour, which required three and one half months of hard travel on horseback, and in coaches over bumpy roads. Some of the states had never received an official visit from a President, and their reaction to his setting foot on their sovereign soil so soon after the unpopular War of 1812 was problematical. Lacking the advice of a modern public relations counsel, Monroe started off on the wrong foot, arriving in Baltimore, his first stop, on the Sabbath, and thus "excited the indignation and called forth the censure"[34] of many devout citizens. After this ill-starred beginning, the tour continued smoothly, except for some slight tension at the Massachusetts border, occasioned by the tactlessness of the legislature in passing a resolution *directing* the proper local authorities to escort the President through the State, instead of leaving his reception to "Republican munificence and individual hospitality" as had been done elsewhere. Enroute to Boston, he was joined by General Dearborn, who had just been defeated for the governorship, and others of the friendly minority, who presented him with a memorial expressing "their high regard for his official and personal character." With the arrival in Boston, the tour may be said to have inaugurated what the *Columbian Centinel* of Boston referred to as "The Era of Good Feelings," a fortunate phrase, which Monroe adopted, and which has been used by historians since to denote the happy period of Monroe's two terms in office.

The President remained a number of days in the vicinity of Boston, during which, according to the historian of the tour, "he renewed his acquaintance with many of his revolutionary associates, and, at many private parties, witnessed that elegance and refinement, which is in no way inconsistent with republican simplicity, the most striking characteristic of the President. It would be too much in the style of an English tourist, describing the visits of a prince, to designate every splendid

34. Waldo, *The Tour of James Monroe*, p. 50.

mansion and every brilliant party he honored and adorned by his presence."[35]

As stated before, one of the "brilliant parties" was at the home of General Dearborn. In addition, the President was entertained by the Society of Cincinnati, celebrated Independence Day at the Charleston Navy Yard, reviewed the troops at Bunker Hill, and received an honorary degree from Harvard University.

On July 8th, the President, with his suite, left Boston for Marblehead and Salem, escorted by the Boston Light Dragoons. After a journey through northeastern Massachusetts, which partook of the nature of a triumphal tour, he reached Portsmouth about seven o'clock in the evening of Saturday, July 12th. He was met "by the Committee of Arrangements and a numerous cavalcade of citizens on horseback and in carriages, and a company of cavalry belonging to the Thirty-Fifth Regiment. When he passed the lines of the town, it was announced by a national salute from the artillery company stationed on the Plains; and on the arrival of the President at that place, he viewed the First Regiment, which was ordered out for his inspection. When passing Wilbird's Hill, he was again welcomed by a national salute from the company of Sea Fencibles, and by the ringing of bells; after which, he was escorted into town, through lines formed by the scholars of the several public and private schools in this place, who were arranged on each side of the road. The windows on the streets through which the President passed were crowded with the fair, and the streets lined with spectators, anxious to view the man who had been raised to the highest possible honor,— that of being the chief magistrate of a free people." On the entrance of the President into Market Street, he

35. *Ibid.*, p. 140.

passed through an arch of "evergreen which had been tastily formed by the ladies of the town, near which a band of music received him with national and appropriate airs. After arriving at Frost's Hotel, the President and suite, together with the Committee of Arrangements, appeared in the balcony over the door, which was fancifully decorated, when the Honorable Mr. Mason, in behalf of the citizens, delivered an address of welcome."[36]

Mr. Mason, in addition to welcoming the President, made a brief reference to that perennial condition "the temporary depression under which we are now suffering," and in reply, the President philosophically remarked, "occasional depressions ought not to excite surprise. They are inseparably connected with human affairs." Thereupon, the Portsmouth regiment passed in review, and the President was escorted to his lodgings by the Committee of Arrangements and Marshals.

Not wishing to repeat the mistake made at the beginning of his tour, of traveling on the Sabbath, the President attended divine service twice, at St. John's Church on Sunday morning, and again in the afternoon at the Rev. Mr. Putnam's meeting house. Inasmuch as the ostensible purpose of the tour was the inspection of the national defences, it was appropriate that he should devote Monday to a tour of the Navy Yard and the forts in the harbor. On their return, the President and his party were waited upon by a committee from the Society of Associated Mechanics of the State. In reply to the formal address of the President of the Society, President Monroe gave an extemporaneous answer in which "he made some appropriate reflections on the utility of encouraging our native manufacturers." This was followed that

36. *Ibid.*, p. 167.

evening by a concert given by the Social Harmoniac Society at Jefferson Hall, "which was very elegantly decorated."

Because of General Dearborn's intimate connection with Portsmouth, he was undoubtedly called upon to play an active part in this round of festivities. At Salem or Marblehead he might have begged off the concert given by the Social Harmoniac Society, at least, on the grounds of his nearly seventy years, but at Portsmouth, he had to put in an appearance with his fellow townsmen. And so it was not until 11:30 that night that he was free to drag his weary feet up to his room and dash off a hurried line to his wife. We can now understand why he made note of the late hour, but did not bother about the date, which we have determined to be Monday, July 14, 1817. "This is the first minuit that I have been able to write a line today," he starts. The evidence we have seems to support that statement, as he probably got back from the tour of the fortifications and the reception barely in time to dress for a formal dinner before the concert of the Harmoniac Society. His next sentence is, "We set off at 6 o'clock tomorrow morning for Portland, where the President intends to arrive before night." This emphasis on the early morning start further explains the necessity of a brief note. Portland was nearly fifty miles as the crow flies, a long trip by horse, and, furthermore, after crossing the Piscataqua, the President and the General were to be met by more Committees on Arrangements, speeches of welcome, and escorts of cavalry. It is a relief to know that in spite of these delays, the party reached Portland by six that evening. In his closing sentences, the General refers to his expected return home by Saturday. After a two day stay in Portland, where he could enjoy the company of his daughter,

Portsm.th — Monday
½ after 11 oclock. P.M —

My Dear Sarah

this is the first minute
that I have been able to write a line
to day. we set off at 6 oclock, to morrow morning for Portteus, where
the President intends to us view before
night. Mr W. & Julia and Portteus
& will accompany me. I hope to
see you on Saturday. as

your affectionate

H. Dearborn —

Mrs Sarah B. Dearborn

Julia, he would finally be free to return to Boston, and recuperate, while the President journeyed on to Concord, and thence to the West.

* * *

The General's hasty note is thus fully explained, with every reference made clear,—and in seeking its explanation, we have also brought to life its colorful author whose career is so closely interwoven with the principal events of the critical period of our history. It is easy to see how a less vigorous personality whose name was linked by chance with the founding of a metropolis, might well lose his identity, swallowed by the very legends the greatness of the city would create. But in his strenuous Revolutionary career, Henry Dearborn personified the very qualities of untiring energy and widespread activity which have made Chicago great. Yet, he seems destined to share the fate of Count Nesselrode,— the Russian statesman, whose name has survived only as a pudding. His personality has been well-nigh obliterated by the cartoonists' legend of an old dodo, with plug hat, frock coat, and spade beard, labeled "Father Dearborn." Chicago would do better to remember the brave and resolute Revolutionary fighter to whom the name rightfully belongs,—Henry Dearborn.

The Quebec Expedition

ONE *of the first objectives of the Continental army in 1775 was the capture of St. Johns and Montreal. The invasion of Canada was launched after the battle of Bunker Hill. Montgomery led an expedition north by way of Lake Champlain and the Richelieu River, while the main army under Washington was besieging Howe's troops in Boston. To distract Carleton in Canada, Washington ordered a second expedition to march on Quebec. This daring exploit was entrusted to Arnold. The route selected was the little-used wilderness trail by way of the Kennebec River and the Chaudière. After enduring great suffering and privation for eight weeks, Arnold's expedition emerged from the woods near Point Levis and threatened Quebec. This diversion made possible the capture of Montreal by Montgomery. The wilderness march and the unsuccessful assault on Quebec which followed have evoked commendation from all military historians.*

A JOURNAL kept by Cap:̣ Henry Dearborne,[1] of the Proceedings, and Particular occurrences, which happened within my knowledge, to the Troops, under the Command of Colonel Bennedicte

1. Henry Dearborn was twenty-four years old and a practising physician in Nottingham Square, N. H., when he received news of the battle at Lexington. Being captain of the local militia, he immediately mustered his company and set off for Cambridge. When the 1st New Hampshire regiment was organized under the command of Col. John Stark, Dearborn was appointed a captain. He participated in two skirmishes

Arnold,[2] in the year 1775 Which Troops were detached from the American Army Lying before the Town of Boston, for the purpose of marching to, and taking possession of Quebec:
Said detachment consisted of Eleven hundred Men, Two Battalians of Musket-men, and three Companies of Rifle-men as Light-Infantry—,[3]

around Boston, and on June 17, his regiment checked the British advance at the rail fence barrier running down to the Mystic River from Breed's Hill. After the retreat, Stark's New Hampshire line retired to Winter Hill. In September Dearborn volunteered for Arnold's expedition to Quebec. Charles Coffin, *The Lives and Services of Major General John Thomas . . '. Major General Henry Dearborn* (New York, 1845), 104–8.

2. Benedict Arnold (1741–1801), of a good Connecticut family, began his military career brilliantly. He left a prospering trade to captain a militia company which responded to the Lexington alarm. He obtained a colonel's commission on his offer to seize the cannon and powder at Fort Ticonderoga. The same idea had occurred to Ethan Allen of Vermont, and the two led the victorious assault of May 10, 1775. Arnold went up to Lake Champlain and also captured the fort at St. Johns. Dispute over this command led to his being superseded, and he returned home, where his wife had just died. Next he proposed to Washington an expedition against Quebec by way of the Kennebec River to co-operate with Schuyler's (later Montgomery's) invasion of Canada by way of Lake Champlain. The progress and outcome of this expedition is related in this journal. Arnold was wounded in the leg at Quebec and in the spring gave up the siege of Quebec and fell back to Montreal. Now a brigadier-general, he ordered his force to retreat towards Crown Point, anticipating Gen. Carleton's move to drive the Americans from Canada. At Crown Point Arnold's command built a fleet of green timber and successfully diverted Carleton's fleet carrying 12,000 men after two fierce battles on Lake Champlain. Although Arnold lost his fleet, he nevertheless was responsible for Carleton's retreat to Canada for the purpose of assembling a stronger expedition against the colonies. Arnold spent the winter at home on leave, but routed Tryon's raid on Connecticut, for which service he was made a major-general. In the summer of 1777 he joined Gates who was sent out to stop Burgoyne's army descending from Canada. First he stopped St. Leger at Fort Stanwix, then turned back Burgoyne at Saratoga, where he was again wounded. He rejoined the army in May, 1778, and was placed in command of Philadelphia, recently evacuated by the British. There he married Peggy Shippen, went into debt, and became involved in petty military disputes with the Pennsylvania authorities. In 1779 he began supplying the British with intelligence, and when Washington put him in command at West Point the following year, he negotiated the surrender of that post to the enemy for £20,000 and a commission in the British army. The capture of Maj. André exposed Arnold's plan, and he barely escaped to the British in New York City. He served as an officer in the British army, leading raiding parties into Virginia and along the Connecticut coast. He sailed for England in December, 1781. *Dict. Am. Biog.,* I, 362–6.

3. The British had detached one company from each regiment of foot as "light infantry." These units were equipped less heavily than the regular infantry, and were used primarily for skirmishing, reconnaissance and outpost duties. As the Continental army took shape, the same plan was instituted, (see Dearborn's entry for Aug. 6, 1777)

Officers of the 1ˢᵗ Battalian.	Officers of the 2ᵈ Battalian.
Lieuᵗ Colo: Roger Enos	Lieuᵗ Colo: Cristopher Green
Majʳ Return Jon. Meigs	Maj: Timothy Biggelloe
Capᵗ Thomas Williams	Capᵗ Samˡ Ward
Capᵗ Henry Dearborne	Capᵗ Simeon Thayre
Capᵗ [William] Scott	Capᵗ John Topham
Capᵗ Oliver Hanchett	Capᵗ [Samuel] MᶜCobb
Capᵗ William Goodrich	Capᵗ Jonas Hubbard

The Captains of the Rifle Men.

[Daniel] Morgan
[Matthew] Smith
[William] Hendrick

Septemʳ 10ᵗʰ 1775
I march'd my Company from Winter-Hill[4] to Cambridge 11ᵗʰ 12ᵗʰ and the chief of the 13ᵗʰ We Lay at Cambridge preparing for to March, at 5 O Clock P. M: March'd from Cambridge to Medford, and Encamped,

14ᵗʰ at 12, O Clock march'd from Medford to Salem & Encamp'tᵈ[5]

15 Marched to Ipswich and encamped.[6]

although whole regiments were equipped and employed as light infantry. In this instance the three specially organized companies of riflemen were to serve as light infantry for the expedition.

4. Winter Hill here refers to the works erected on the Charlestown road at the point where the road divides, one branch leading to Concord, the other leading north to Medford. Dearborn marched his men from Winter Hill to Cambridge, a distance of 2¼ miles, where the entire detachment under Arnold was equipped and paraded by Gen. Washington. On the 11th, Dearborn and the other officers attended a council of war, during which Arnold received instructions to proceed to Quebec via the Kennebec. Dearborn started from Cambridge late in the afternoon and camped at Medford, about three miles from Cambridge.

5. A distance of about 9 miles. Salem, situated on a peninsula formed by two inlets of the ocean, was an important maritime city at this time, carrying on a large foreign trade.

6. Ipswich, Essex co., Mass., on the Ipswich River 3 miles from its entrance to the ocean, and about 13 miles from Salem.

16 Marched to Newbury Port and Encamped.[7]

17 Being Sunday, we attended Divine Service there.

18th at 4 Clock, the whole detachment Embarked on Board 10 Vessels.

19 at 10 Clock A: M.. we made Sail, But as Soon as we got outside of the Bar, we hove too,—In order to receive the Several Signals which we were to observe while at Sea, Said Signals were to be given by the Vessel, which Colo: Arnold was on Board of Called the Commodore.

The Signals were as followeth Viz:

1st Signal, for Speaking with the whole Fleet an Ensign was to be Hoisted at the Main-Top: mast head.

2 Signal, for Chasing a Sail, Ensign at fore, top, mast, head.

3 Signal, for heaving too, a Lanthorn at Main, Topmast, head, and two guns if head on Shore, and three Guns, if off shore.

4 Signal, for making sail, in the Night, a Lanthorn at Mast head, and four Guns,—In the day, a Jack at the fore Top: Mast-head.

5 Signal, for dispersing and every Vessel for making the Nearest, Harbour Ensign at the Main-Topmast Peak.

6 Signal, for Boarding any vessel, a Jack at Main Topmast head.

at 12 O Clock we put to Sea, and had a fair wind—at 10 O Clock.. P: M: we hove too, Head, off Shore with a Brisk wind, the Chief of our people were Sea-Sick.

20 In the Morning, we made the mouth of Kennebeck River[8] which we enter'd at 10'Clock an Came

7. Newburyport, Essex co., Mass., on the south bank of the Merrimac River 3 miles from the ocean and about 9 miles from Ipswich.

8. The sail from Newburyport to the mouth of the Kennebec is about 100 miles in a straight line. The sloops and schooners which comprised the fleet encountered favourable weather and a good breeze; the passage was made in about 10 hours. The boats

to an Anchor, at 3.. O: Cl[ock] P: M: we Weighed, Anchor and put up the River a Bout 3 Leagues, and came to an Anchor, I went on Shore at Rousask⁹ where there are a Number of Inhabitants and a Meeting house.

21ˢᵗ Put up the River as far as Swan Island, at the upper End of Merry-meeting-Bay-where we Run on Shore and Came to an Anchor,¹⁰ I went on Shore with some of my officiers, and Stay'd all Night.

Septemʳ 22ᵈ:

Proceeded, up the River, We pass'd Fort Richmond¹¹ at 11: O Clock where there are but few Settlements at Present,   this afternoon we pass'd Pownalborough,¹² Where there is a Court-House and Goal—and some very good Settlements,   This day at 4. O Clock we arrived at the place where our Batteaus were Built.¹³

We were order'd to Leave one Sergeant, one Corporal and Thirteen men here to take a Long the Batteau's, they embark'd on Board the Batteaus, and we all proceeded up the River to Cabisaconty, or Gardners

anchored at Parker's Flats, four miles from the river mouth. Justin Smith, *Arnold's March From Cambridge to Quebec* (New York, 1903), 69.

9. Arrowsic Island, about 1 mile above Parker's Flats.

10. Swan Island, about 3½ miles in length, is five miles above Merrymeeting Bay. It splits the river. The bay is formed by the junction of the Androscoggin River with the Kennebec; it is about twenty miles from the sea.

11. Fort Richmond was occupied in 1720-1721, but was dismantled in 1754. The expedition passed the remains of this fort, located on the west side of the river a little above the present village of Richmond. Smith, *op. cit.*, 72.

12. Pownalborough was situated on the east side of the Kennebec, on the present site of Dresden, Lincoln co., Maine.

13. The batteaux were built at Maj. Reuben Colburn's ship-yard, at what is now Pittston, Kennebec co., Maine, on the east side of the Kennebec River. Arnold had ordered 200 batteaux large enough to carry six or seven men with provisions and luggage. The boats were to be fitted with 4 oars, 2 paddles and 2 setting poles. Smith, *op. cit.*, 74-8.

Dearborn was so impressed by the beauty of the country in this vicinity that he moved his family to Pittston in 1784. Daniel Goodwin, *The Dearborns* . . . (Chicago, 1884), 21.

Town,[14] Where Doctor Gardner of Boston owns a Large Tract of Land and Some Mills, & a Number of very good dwelling Houses, where we Stayed Last night, on Shore.

23^d We put up the River, and before Night, we arrived at Fort Western[15] which is 50 Miles from the Mouth of the River, this evening a very unhappy accident happen'd, a Number of Soldiers being in a Private-house, some warm words Produced a quarrel and one McCormick being Turned out of the House, Soon after discharged his Gun into the House, and Shot a Man thro' the Body of which wound he Soon Expired.

McCormick was Try'd by a Court Martial and Condemn'd to be hanged, He abstinately denyed the fact until he was Brought under the Gallows where Confess'd the Crime—but for Some reasons was reprieved, until the pleasure of Genl Washington could be known.[16]

24th 25th 26th We lay at Fort Western preparing for our March— Fort Western Stands on the East side of the River and Consists of two Block Houses, and a Large House 100 feet Long which are Inclos'd only with Picquets, this House is now the property of one Howard Esqr where we were well entertained.

25 Captains Morgan, Smith, and Hendrick,[17] with their Companies of Rifle, Men embarked on Board their

14. Gardinerston comprised the vast estate of Sylvester Gardiner. Until 1803 it included Pittston, Gardiner, West Gardiner, Farmingdale, Chelsea and Randolph. Smith, *op. cit.*, 74, *passim*.

15. Fort Western, on the east bank of the Kennebec, was about 9 miles above Colburn's ship-yard, in the present town of Augusta. Built in 1754, it had been a strong, well-defended frontier post, marking the head of navigation in the Kennebec. *Ibid.*, 77, *ff.*

16. According to Arnold, James McCormick had been condemned for the murder of Reuben Bishop on board the schooner *Broad Bay*. The prisoner had been drafted for the expedition out of Col. Scammon's regiment. In sending him to Gen. Washington for approval of the sentence, Arnold called him a simple, ignorant fellow and recommended him for mercy. Arnold to Washington, Sept. 27, 1775, Kenneth Roberts, *March to Quebec* (New York, 1938), 67.

17. Captain Daniel Morgan (1736-1802) commanded a company of Virginia riflemen noted for their marksmanship. He volunteered for Arnold's expedition. When

Batteaus, with orders to proceed up the River as far as the great Carrying place, there to Clear a Road a Cross the Carrying place, while the other divisions were geting up.[18]

26... Colo: Green[19] embark'd on Board the Batteaus with three Company's of Musketmen to proceed for Canada.

27... at 3.. O:Clock P..M: Major Meigs[20] embarked on Board the Batteaus with four Companies of men, my

Arnold was wounded in the attack on Quebec, Morgan assumed command and penetrated far into the lower town, but was forced to surrender when he was not supported. He was not released from prison until the fall of 1776, when he was commissioned a colonel. Morgan raised a corps of 500 sharpshooters that was conspicuous in defeating Burgoyne in 1777. He resigned from service in July, 1779, but re-entered the war in the southern campaign, winning a brilliant victory at Cowpens in 1781. Ill health forced him to retire to his Virginia home. *Dict. Am. Biog.*, XIII, 166–7.

Capt. Matthew Smith (d. 1794) of Pennsylvania commanded the Lancaster County riflemen. In 1765, as one of the "Paxton Boys" he had led a mob which destroyed trade goods going to the western Indians, and massacred a group of Conestoga Indians. Smith was the only officer who failed to take part in the assault on Quebec; his company was led by Lt. Archibald Steele. Smith was made a captain in the 1st Continental Infantry in 1776, but resigned and was appointed major in the 9th Pennsylvania regiment the next year. He left the army early in 1778. F. B. Heitman, *Historical Register of Officers of the Continental Army* . . . (Washington, 1914), 505.

Capt. William Hendricks was an officer in Thompson's Pennsylvania Rifle battalion. He seems to have been a hardy, courageous and well-liked officer. In the assault on Quebec his company was placed in the rear, but under his direction his men pushed to the front to storm the barrier; there Capt. Hendricks was killed. *Ibid.*, 285.

18. On September 25 at Fort Western, the battalions and riflemen were divided into four divisions. Three companies of riflemen under Capt. Morgan composed the first division and led the expedition. Lt. Col. Greene and Maj. Bigelow led the second division comprised of three companies under Thayer, Topham and Hubbard. The third division, under Maj. Meigs, was made up of four companies under Dearborn, Ward, Hanchet and Goodrich. The companies of McCobb, Smith and Williams brought up the rear under Col. Enos.

19. Lt. Col. Christopher Greene (1737–1781) was a lieutenant of Rhode Island's Kentish Guards, and marched to Boston at the Lexington alarm. A month later he was appointed major in Col. Varnum's Rhode Island regiment. Greene volunteered for the Quebec expedition and commanded the second division. He was taken prisoner at Quebec and held until August, 1777. Appointed colonel of the 1st Rhode Island regiment, he held Fort Mercer against a Hessian attack and later was active in the Rhode Island campaign. Surprised at his headquarters in Westchester County, New York, he was killed May 14, 1781. *Dict. Am. Biog.*, VII, 563.

20. Return Jonathan Meigs (1740–1823) marched a company of Connecticut volunteers to Boston after the Lexington alarm. There he was commissioned a major in the 2nd Connecticut regiment. He joined Arnold and kept a journal of the Quebec

Company being One of them) With 45 days Provisions proceeded up the River four miles, and encampt, the [water?] not very rapid.

28 Procee'd up the River four miles, the Water exceeding Rapid, some bad falls and encampt.

29 Proceeded up the River four miles to Fort Hallifax[21] against a very rapid stream, where we arrived at 11-O Clock A.. M.   this Fort stands on a point of Land, Between the Rivers Kenebeck and Sabastacook. It Consists of Two Large Block-Houses and a Large Barrack which is Inclosed by Picquet Fort. after Staying half an hour at the Fort I Cross'd the River to a Carrying place, which is 97 Rods,   We carry'd a Cross our Batteaus and Baggage and Encampt.

30 Proceeded up the River this Morning, found it exceeding rapid and rocky for five miles, so that any man would think, at its first appearance, that it was impossible to get Boats up it, I fill'd my Battoe to day, and wet all my Baggage, but with the greatest difficulty, we got over what is call'd the 5 mile ripples, and then encampt, and dryed my Cloathing as well as I could.

Octo: 1 Proceeded up the River 3 miles, the Stream was very rapid,   here Major Meigs had Bought an Ox, and had him dress'd for us when we came up,   we eat what we could and took the remainder into our Batteaus, and proceeded up the River four miles further and encampt,

campaign. He was captured at Quebec and exchanged in 1777, after which he was promoted to the rank of lieutenant-colonel. He retired a colonel at the end of 1781 when the Connecticut troops were reorganized. He was a leader in the establishment of Marietta, Ohio, in 1788 and later became an Indian agent. *Ibid.*, XII, 508-9.

21. Fort Halifax stood about ¾ of a mile below the present city of Waterville, at the junction of the Sebasticook and the Kennebec. It was built in 1754 under the direction of Gen. John Winslow. The fort accommodated 100 men on the point, and a redoubt on the tip of the tongue of land projecting into the river could accommodate a dozen men as well as 2 two-pounders and a swivel. Smith. *op. cit.*, 94-9, *passim.*

the Water not so rapid as before,   the Land here on the Shores very good in General.

2 Procee'd up the River Nine miles, the Water not very rapid intil towards Night, We encampt, it Rained very fast the most part of the night.

3 proceeded up the River over very bad falls and Shoals such as seem'd almost Impossible to Cross, But after much fatigue, and a Bundance of difficulty we arrived at Schouhega^n-falls,[22] where there is a Carrying place of 60 rods, here we hall'd up our Batteaus and Caulk'd them, as well as we could they being very leaky, by being knocked a Bout a Mong the Rocks, and not being well Built at first, we Carryed a Cross and loaded our Batteaus, and put a Cross the River, and encampt, this days March was not a Bove 3 Miles, from here I sent Back two Sick men.

4 Our Course in general from the Mouth of the river to this place, has been from North, to North East, from here we Steer N: W.. to Norrigwalk,[23] which is Twelve miles to where we arrived to night, the River here is not very rapid. Except Two bad falls, the Land on the North side of the river is very good, where there are 2 or 3 families settled, at Norrigwalk, is to be seen the ruins of an Indian Town, also a fort, a Chapel, and a Large Tract of Clear Land but not very good, there is but one family here at present   Half a Mile above this old fort, is a Great fall, where there is a Carrying place of one Mile and a Quarter.

5 We haled up our Batteaus, and Clear'd them for over-hauling, and repacked all our pork, and Bread, several

22. Skowhegan Falls were about 3 miles above the present town of the same name and 21 miles above the Sebasticook. The approach to the falls included a sharp bend in the river, fast water and whirlpools. *Ibid.*, 102, ff.

23. What Dearborn describes is *Old* Norridgewock, at the mouth of the Sandy River, in the present town of Starks and about 2¾ miles above the present town of Norridgewock, Somerset co., Maine. *Ibid.*, 105, ff.

Barrels of Bread was Spoiled, here we found Colo. Greens Division.

6... After our Batteaus were repair'd, we Carry'd them a Cross the Carrying place, and Loaded them again, we put up the River two Miles and Encampt.

7 We proceeded up the river nine miles and encampt. the Land we pass'd to day, was exceeding good, the Stream not very rapid, it rained very heavy all Night.

8 It rain'd some part of this morning, But we proceeded up the river Seven miles to Carritunkus-falls,[24] where we arriv'd at 1 O Clock, P: M: the Weather proved very rainy, here is a Carrying place of 95 Rods, we Carry'd a Cross and put up the river 3 miles, the water was very rapid, and encampt.

9 We proceeded up the River, 9 miles the Water was very Rapid, the river is divided here into a Number of Channels, occasion'd by small Islands, which Channels are Shoal and rapid, it rain'd the Bigest part of this day, We encamp'd at dusk, and I Catched Some fish before Supper.

10 We proceeded up the River, I march'd by Land, the Weather Severely Cold, in Crossing a Small River on a Logg I slipt off and fell flat on my Back in the river, the Water not being more than four feet deep I waded out, But was obliged to Stop and Strike up a fire, to dry me, at 2.. O..Clock we arrived at the great Carrying place,[25] Where we found the three Rifle Companies, and Colo:

24. Carritunk Falls, about 18 miles above Norridgewock Falls, are at present a drop of 21 feet. Arnold estimated the drop as 15 feet, but a dam has increased the drop. *Ibid.*, 337, *passim.*

25. The Great Carrying Place, also called Twelve Mile Carry, began about 17½ miles above Carritunk Falls. It was about 12½ miles in length and consisted of a chain of three ponds and four portages by means of which it was possible to cross from the Kennebec to Dead River ten miles below their junction. By cutting off ten miles of shallow, unnavigable river, the Great Carrying Place was an important segment in the trail through the wilderness to the Chaudière River.

Green's Division we Carryed one Turn a Cross the Carrying place which is four miles, to a Pond.[26]

11 Lieu.t Hutchins[27] and Ten of my men were order'd to assist Cap.t M.cCob[28] in Building a Block-House, here to-day, Our last Division has now arrived, Commanded by Colo.. Enos.[29] We carryed the Chief of our Baggage and Boats To-day.

12 This morning we took the remainder of our Baggage and march.d a Cross the Car'ying place to the pond. which is one mile wide But we Cannot Cross it today by reason of the winds blowing very hard, here we Catch'd plenty of trout.

13 We Cross'd the pond and Came to another Carrying Place half a mile a Cross, where our first division had Built a Block-house and left some Sick men under the Care of Doctor Erving.[30] We Carryed over the Carrying place to a pond,[31] We Cross'd the pond, 1½ Miles and Came to a Carrying place, one mile and three Quarters, We Carry'd half a mile and encampt.

26. The distance from the Kennebec to East Carry Pond, the first in the chain, is closer to 3¼ miles. Smith, *op. cit.*, 346, *ff.*

27. Lt. Nathaniel Hutchins (d. 1832) was a second lieutenant in Capt. Dearborn's company. He was captured at Quebec, and on his release was given a captain's commission. Hutchins left the army at the end of 1780. Heitman, *op. cit.*, 312.

28. Captain Samuel McCobb (d. 1791) was a captain of Minute Men who joined Nixon's Massachusetts regiment. On the march to Quebec he traveled with Col. Enos' division and voted to abandon the expedition. Later he transferred to the 5th Continental infantry, and later was a colonel of the Massachusetts Militia. *Ibid.*, 366.

29. Col. Roger Enos (1729–1808) had served in the French and Indian War and was a lieutenant-colonel of the 1st Connecticut regiment on the march to Quebec. At Dead River his captains voted to abandon the expedition and Enos joined his men in the return march. Accounts of his behavior at the time differ. Washington ordered him courtmartialed, and although he was acquitted, he was never promoted, and in 1779 he resigned. In 1781 he moved to Vermont and was put in command of the Vermont militia. Smith, *op. cit.*, 161–3; *Cyclopedia of Am. Biog.*, (Boston, 1897), II, 667.

30. Dr. Matthew Irvine (d. 1827) was surgeon's mate in Thompson's Pennsylvania Rifle Battalion. He later served as surgeon to Lee's battalion of Light Dragoons. The log hospital or block house built for the wounded was called Arnold's hospital; also Fort Meigs. Heitman, *op. cit.*, 314; Smith, *op. cit.*, 129.

31. Little Carry Pond.

14... We Carry'd a Cross the Carrying Place, to a Pond three miles over,[32] we Cross'd the pond and Came to a Carrying place,[33] four miles over a Very-high-Hill, and the last mile a Spruce Swamp Knee deep in mire all the way, We Carry'd one mile over this Carrying place and then Encampt, from here I sent three sick-men Back.

15 We Carry'd a Cross the Carrying place to a Small Stream[34] within half a mile of the dead River,[35] we went down this Stream into the River, and proceeded one Mile up said River and then encampt, the water here very deep and Still, the Land where we Encampt was very good.

16 At 12.. Clock we proceeded up the River ten miles to a Small Carrying place 7 Rods a Cross and then encampt.[36]

17 We proceeded up the River 10 miles and Came to an Indian Wig-Wam, Said to belong to an old Indian Called Nattannas[37] it Stands on a Point of Land Beautifully situated, there is a Number of acres of Clear'd Land a Bout it—the river is very Still, and good Land on each side of it a Considerable part of the way, To day we proceeded up the River 5 miles farther, and found Colo: Arnold, and Colo: Green with their Divisions, making up Cartri^dges, here we Encampt.

32. West Carry Pond, which Arnold's surveyors called 3 miles long and 2 miles wide. Smith, *op. cit.*, 126.

33. The last portage was over Carrying-Place Mountain to Bog Brook. The length of the portage has been estimated as between 3 and 5 miles. *Ibid.*, 126, *passim*.

34. The stream was Bog Brook. The spruce swamp and mire may have been the east branch of Bog Brook or the lowlands around it.

35. Dead River or West Branch is formed by a chain of ponds extending westward to the "height of land." This river meets the East Branch, formed by the outlet of Moosehead Lake by way of Indian Pond, to form the Kennebec.

36. This camp has been identified as Hurricane Falls, located about 8 miles up Dead River from Bog Brook. Smith, *op. cit.*, 139, 362.

37. Natanis, a Norridgewock Indian, had a cabin on the present site of Flagstaff, Maine. Arnold was first given to understand that he was employed by Carleton as a spy, and ordered him killed. Later Natanis showed himself to be a helpful friend and guide. He fought with the Americans at Quebec and was wounded. *Ibid.*, *passim*.

18.. The weather is very rainy To day. My men had their Powder-Horns filled with Powder. Joseph Thomas[38] is appointed my Ensign, By Colo: Arnold this day, I had a ½ Quarter of Beef Served to my Company today.

19.. The weather Rainy, at 2.. O.. Clock A: M: We Set off: from this place proceeded up the River five miles, pass'd several Small falls and then Encampt.

20 Proceeded up the River, pass'd by Several small falls, one Carrying place, thirteen rods, the Weather rainy all day we Suppose this days March to be 13 Miles.

21 We proceeded up the River 3 Miles to a Carrying place 35 Rods Carry'd a Cross and Continued our Rout up the River two miles to a Porlag[39] 30 Rods a Cross and Encampt. it Rained very fast all Night, the River rose fast.

22.. The River has Risen eight or Nine feet, Which renders it very bad getting up, We pass'd three Carrying places To'day 74 Rods Each, our whole March To-day is not more than four miles, the River Rising so much, fills the Low ground so full of Water, that our Men on Shore have found it very difficult and Tedious Marching.

23 We Continued our March, tho. very slow by reason of the Rapidity of the Stream, a very unlucky accident happen'd to us today, the most of our men by land miss'd their way and marched up a Small river,[40] Which Comes into the Dead River, a few Miles a Bove where we encampt last night. We fancied they took a Wrong Course, I Sent my Batteau up that four miles (where they that went in it) found the foot people had Cross'd

---

38. Joseph Thomas of Deerfield, N. H., was an ensign in the 1st New Hampshire regiment. He was taken prisoner at Quebec, at which time Dearborn referred to him as a lieutenant. Heitman, *op. cit.*, 539.

39. Portage.

40. Alder Stream, at its junction with the Dead River. Here Alder Stream is about the same size as Dead River. Smith, *op. cit.*, 155, 373.

the River on a Tree, and had Struck a Cross for the dead River, my Batteau Came Back, and we proceeded up the River to a Carrying place, where we found our foot-men at the foot of these Falls,[41] Several Batteaus overset, which were entirely lost, a Considerable quantity of Cloathing, Guns, and Provisions, our march to-day we Judge, to be, about 8 miles. here we held a Counsel, in Consequence of which we Sent Cap.[t] Hanchet[42] and 50 Men forward to Shadear[43] as an advanced party, and Sent Back 26.. Sick-men under the Command, or Care of an officer and Doctor.

24 At 10.. O, Clock, we proceeded up the River, tho with a great deal of difficulty, the River being very rapid, This days march don't exceed four miles.

25 Continued our Rout up the River, the Stream very rapid, We pass'd three Carrying places, Two of them four Rods and the other 90, our march to day 6 miles and then Encampt,— This Night I was Seized with a Violent Head-Ach and fever, Charles[44] gather'd me some herbs in the woods, and made me Tea of them, I drank very Hearty of it and next morning felt much Better.

26 Continued our Rout and Came to a Pond 2 miles a Cross[45] and then Came to a narrow gut 2 Rod wide, and four rod Long, and then to a nother Pond one mile over,[46] then to a narrow Streight, 1½ miles Long, Then a third

41. Upper Shadagee Falls, about 2 miles above the mouth of Alder Stream. *Ibid.*, 156.

42. Capt. Oliver Hanchet (1741–1816) had been a lieutenant of Minute Men. He later received a captain's commission in the 2nd Connecticut regiment. After a quarrel with Arnold, and after objecting to Montgomery's plan of attacking Quebec, he joined in the assault and was captured. He was paroled in 1776 but was not exchanged until early in 1777. Heitman. *op. cit.*, 271.

43. Chaudière Valley. Here the expedition hoped to obtain provisions from the French settlers.

44. Charles Burget, a French youth who enlisted in Dearborn's company at Fort Western and acted as his orderly. Burget was taken prisoner at Quebec.

45. Lower Pond, the first of a series of ponds. Here, above Sarampus Falls, the trail left Dead River. Smith, *op. cit.*, *passim.*

46. Bag Pond. *Ibid.*, 165.

Pond 3 Miles over,[47] Then pass'd another Streight half a Mile Long, and then enter'd a fourth Pond a Bout a quarter of a Mile Wide,[48] then entered a Narrow gut 4 Miles in Length,[49] and then Came to a Carrying place 15 Rods a Cross, Here we Encampt.

27... Cross'd the Carrying Place to a pond half a mile over,[50] Came to a Carrying Place, one Mile, also to a Pond ¼ Mile Wide,[51] then to a Carrying place 44 Rod, to a Pond 2 Miles Wide and Cross'd it.[52]—and Came to the Carrying place into Chaudear pond 4½ Miles a Cross,[53] we received orders here to Leave our Batteaus, and all march by Land, We here Divided our Provisions and gave every man his part, we march'd a Bout half a mile, and then encampt. Here I found a fine Birch Canoe Carefully Laid up, I Suppose by the Indian's.

Here a Very unhappy Circumstance happen'd to us, in our March, Which proved very fatal and Mortifying to us all, Viz^t—

When we were at the great Carrying place (just mention^d) from the Dead River to Shodeer Pond we had the unhappy News of Colo. Enos, and the three Company's in his Division, being so Imprudent as to return back Two or three days before which disheartned and discouraged our men very much, as they Carri'd Back more than their part, or quota of Provision, and Ammunition, and our Detachment, before being but Small, and now loosing

47. Long Pond. *Ibid.*, 165.
48. Natanis Pond. *Ibid.*, *passim.*
49. Horse Shoe Stream, which Arnold estimated as 5 miles in length. *Ibid.*, *passim.*
50. A small lake which empties into Horse Shoe Stream (or river), named Lost Lake by Justin Smith. It is practically unknown to sportsmen and guides in the region. *Ibid.*, *passim.*
51. Horseshoe Pond. *Ibid.*, 165.
52. Arnold Pond, formerly called Moosehorn Pond. *Ibid.*, *passim.*
53. Dearborn refers to Boundary Portage leading to Arnold River, then called Seven Mile Stream. *Ibid.*, *passim.*

these three Companies, We were Small, indeed, to think of entering such a place as Quebec. But being now almost out of Provisions we were Sure to die if we attempted to Return Back.—and We Could be in no Worse Situation if we proceeded on our rout. Our men made a General Prayer, that Colo: Enos and all his men, might die by the way, or meet with some disaster, Equal to the Cowardly dastardly and unfriendly Spirit they discover'd in returning Back without orders, in such a manner as they had done, And then we proceeded forward.

28 Very early in the morning my Company marched one M.[r] Ayres,[54] the Cap.[t] of our Pioneers a Gree'd to go with me in the Canoe, We took it on our Backs, and Car'y'd it a Cross the Carrying place, to a Small Stream, which led into Shodeer Pond,[55] we put our Canoe in, Went down the Stream, my men marched down by Land. When we Came to the Pond, I found Cap.[t] Goodrich's[56] Company, who Could not proceed by reason of finding a River which leads into the Pond,[57] which they

54. Pioneers were military laborers employed to build roads, dig trenches, make bridges and keep camps clean. Although today they form a part of the corps of engineers and are attached to every division, formerly they were local civilian laborers impressed into military service. They carried tools as well as weapons. Capt. Ayres, who did not hold a regular commission, doubtless was given brevet rank to command the needed trail blazers on this expedition. E. S. Farrow, *Farrow's Military Encyclopedia* . . . (New York, 1895), II, 528.

55. Probably Mud Brook which flows into Arnold River, which in turn flows into Lake Megantic or Chaudière Pond, as Dearborn calls it. Smith, *op. cit., passim.*

56. Capt. William Goodrich had commanded a company of Minute Men and now was in Glover's Massachusetts regiment. On the march to Quebec his company and Dearborn's missed their way by reason of setting off a few hours before a letter from Arnold was received warning the troops to avoid the river route to Lake Megantic. Their mistake threw them into a swamp and so increased their suffering that Goodrich's company was reduced to eating dog meat. Goodrich was captured at Quebec. After his exchange he became a brigade major in Putnam's brigade. Later he was in the Massachusetts militia. Heitman, *op. cit.,* 252; Smith, *op. cit.,* 200, 225.

57. The men who marched overland probably came up against either the sweep of the Arnold River, which crosses the trail, or what is called the Dead Arnold, a branch of the Arnold which empties into the lake. The land between the men and the lake, as a matter of fact, was a series of bogs and swamps and small streams lying south of Rush Lake. Smith, *op. cit.,* 203, *ff.*

Could find no way to Cross,   my Company Came up and
had thoughts of Building a raft. I told them I would go
with my Canoe, and See if I could not find some place to
Cross the River, going into the Pond and round an Island,
where Cap.ᵗ Goodrich was with Some of his Men who had
Waded on, He informed me that he had made a thorough
Search, and that there was no way to pass the River without Boats, the Land round here was all a Sunken Swamp
for a Great distance, Cap.ᵗ Goodrich, informed me also,
that one of his Sergeants and another man, who were not
well, had gone forward with a Batteau, and he did not
doubt but I could find it not far off it now Began to be
Dark, We discover'd a Light on Shore which Seem'd to
be 3 Miles from us, Cap.ᵗ Goodrich was almost perished
with the Cold, having Waded Several Miles Backwards,
and forwards, Sometimes to his Arm-pits in Water & Ice,
endeavouring to find some place to Cross this River, I
took him into my Canoe, and Carryed him over, and
When we arrived where we Discover'd the Light, we
found a good Bark-House with one man in it who was
Left by our advanced Party for want of Provision to join
his Company, We warmed ourselves but not finding Cap.ᵗ
Goodrich's Batteau here, we Sent my Canoe farther on to
find it, if Possible,   after being gone an Hour and a half,
they return'd but had not found the Batteau, Cap.ᵗ Goodrich and I were very uneasy all Night a Bout our men.

29 As Soon as it was Light we went to our Men and
Began to Carry them over in my Canoe, But Lucky for us
Capᵗ Smiths Batteau arrived which we hired to Carry
our Men over, But after we had got them over this river,
we had not marched above 50 Rod before we Came to
Another River,⁵⁸ Geting a Cross these Two rivers took

58. Another branch of the Arnold River, probably near the point where the Arnold
and Rush rivers flow together. *Ibid., passim.*

up the Chief of the day, Before Sun Set we all arrived at the Bark-House Safe, where I slept last Night, But the men were very much fatigued here we encampt.

30 We Marched very early in the Morning, our Provisions [torn] to be very Scant, Some Companies had but one pint of Flour for Each Man and no Meat at all, M.r Ayres and I went down the Pond, in our Canoe, this Pond is 13 Miles Long. at the Lower end of the Pond, I met my Company where we found the Mouth of Shodeer River,[59] Which Looked very wild, Here I Choose to walk by Land, and accordingly did a Bout Eight Miles, I was at this time very unwell, we encamp'd near a fall,[60] where all the Boats that had attempted to Come down had overset except Colo, Arnolds, and mine, The Number of Boats that was overset here was Ten, one man was Drown'd, and a great Quantity of Baggage and Guns were lost.

31 We Started very early this morning, I am Still more unwell, than I was yesterday, We Carry'd our Canoe over a Carrying place of a Bout Half a mile, and put it into the River, the Same is very Rapid, Shole and Rocky, We pass'd another Carrying place to-day, we went down about 28 miles, then went on shore and Enca'p'd, I saw Some of the men on foot to-night who I find are almost famished for want of Provisions.

Nov. 1 This morning we Pitched our Canoe she being Somewhat Leaky, we have run several times on the

59. Chaudière River, meaning cauldron, rises at the northern end of Lake Megantic and follows a north-northwest course of 102 miles between high, sometimes precipitous, banks into the St. Lawrence River. The falls near its mouth are more than 100 feet high. Lake Megantic lies almost 1100 feet above the level of the St. Lawrence; thus the river is very turbulent, and filled with rapids. Dearborn should have said the outlet of Lake Megantic or the source of the Chaudière. The *mouth* of the river is at the St. Lawrence River.

60. This point was the Devil's Rapids. The boats which met with an accident were swamped in the less violent rapids above. Smith says the accident probably saved the party—they never would have survived the treacherous water of the Devil's Rapids just below. Smith, *op. cit.*, 432.

Rocks going down falls, where I expected to have Stove her to pieces, we put her in and proceeded down the river, which Remains very rapid, and a Bounding in falls, we got down a Bout 30 Miles, by which time our Canoe got to be worn out, we went on shore and Encamp'd, Here I saw Some of the foot-men who were almost Starved, This day Cap.[t] Goodrich's Company Kill'd my Dog, and another dog, and Eat them, I remain very unwell.

2 M.[r] Ayres my Shipmate, Said he would Try to go down a Little further, in the Canoe and Carry our Baggage, I conclud.[d] to march by Land, I set out and marched a bout four miles and met some French-men with 5 oxen & Two Horses going to meet our People, although, I wanted no Provision myself, yet knowing, how the Poor men were suffering for want & seeing we were like, to Come to some Inhabitants, it Caus.[d] the Tears to Start from my Eyes, before I was apprized, I proceeded about four miles farther, and Came to a Large fall,[61] where we found a good Canoe, Here was a Carrying place one Mile long, We Carryed a Cross the Carrying place, and put in. below the falls, where we found Two Indians with Some Provisions for our men, they left their Provision with some of our men, and went down with us, I got into their Canoe, and one of them into our's, the river being very rapid, & Shoal, we found it very difficult to pass.—we run down a bout eight miles, and to our Great Joy Espy'd a House,[62] where we arrived at 4.. O..Clock P..M: at 5 O Clock Lieu.[t] Hutchins, Ensign. Thomas and 50 of my men arriv'd, with Cap.[t] Smith's Company which were the first Company that

61. The Greater and Lesser Falls. The first was a drop of about 20 feet. Arnold, with the help of two Indians, paddled the half mile between the two falls, but Dearborn portaged around both of them. *Ibid.*, 432, *ff.*

62. About 4 miles below the mouth of the Rivière du Loup, and about 64 miles from Lake Megantic. *Ibid.*, *passim.*

arrived, Here, 3 Colo- Arnold had Provided provisions for us against we arriv^d We Stay'd here one night, this morning our men proceed'd down the River, tho, in poor Circumstances, for Travelling, a Great Number of them being Barefoot, and the Weather Cold and Snowy, many of our men died within the last three days, from here to Quebec, is Seventy miles, I hir'd an Indian to Carry me down the River 6 miles to where Colo: Arnold was, where I found 22 Indians who Engaged with Colo: Arnold for 40/ a month, here I Stay'd all night, By Colo: Arnolds advice being Snowy, I took a Puke this night which did not operate much.

4 The Weather Snowy I Stay'd here to-day, Major Biggellow,[63] Doctor Senter,[64] and some others stay'd here Likewise all night.

5 The Weather is very Clear and pleasant for this season of the year, Major Biggaloe, and I hir'd each of us a Horse to go down the River 6 miles, and Came to a Tavern, where we had Provisions Served out for the Men, the Country here is Tolerable good Land, and Considerably Settled on Both sides of the River, the People are very Ignorant, but seem to be very kind to us, at evening Charles Hilton,[65] and Charles Burget, a French Lad, Inlisted, at

63. Maj. Timothy Bigelow (1739–1790) had been a captain of Minute Men before joining Ward's Massachusetts regiment, in which he was commissioned a major. He volunteered for Arnold's expedition. Mount Bigelow in Maine is supposed to have been named for him because he is said to have climbed it. Captured at Quebec, he was exchanged in May, 1776. He became colonel of the 15th Massachusetts regiment and saw service at Saratoga, Valley Forge and around the Hudson. He retired Jan. 1, 1781 and died in debtor's jail. *Cyclopedia of Am. Biog.*, I, 294; Heitman, *op. cit.*, 102.

64. Dr. Isaac Senter (1753–1799) was studying medicine in Newport, R. I., with Dr. Thomas Moffat, when the Revolution began. He joined the 3rd Rhode Island regiment as surgeon and went to Cambridge, where he was later assigned to Arnold's expedition. He remained with the American forces until June, 1776, when he returned southward. Senter kept a journal of his adventures. He retired from the army in 1779 and became surgeon-general of the Rhode Island militia. Smith, *op. cit.*, 266; Heitman, *op. cit.*, 489.

65. Charles Hilton, a private in Dearborn's company, helped take care of his commander for the next few days. Hilton was taken prisoner at Quebec.

Fort Western, who was a native of Canady, Came back for me with Two Horses, we Stay'd here all night.

6 I hir'd an Indian to Carry me down the River, 9 Miles, to one Sonsosees, a French-mans, one of Charles Burgets relations, where I hir'd Lodgings and took my Bed Immediately, I was this time in a High fever. I kept the Two Charles's to take Care of me— I will now with my Pen follow our Main Body,[66] they have now proceeded as far as S.t Mary's the middle Parish of what is Commonly Call'd Sattagan,[67] here is a very good Church, and a pleasant Country— our people are Supply'd with provisions at Several places By the way, but being in Great Hurry, and having but Little time to provide, necessaries, our men were but Very poorly supply'd in General, the Inhabitants appears to be very kind, but ask a very Great price for their Victuals.

7 Our Troops Proceeded as fast as possible, they followed the river Shodear down from the first Inhabitants a bout 36 miles, and then Turn'd to the Eastward, and left the river, had to pass thro, a wood 15 Miles where there is no Inhabitants, and at this time of the year it is Terrible Traveling, by reason of its being Low Swampy land, our people Carry'd Twenty Birch Canoes a Cross these woods, in order to Cross the River S.t Laurence in. —[68] as we Suppos'd the Boats near Quebec, would be in

66. Dearborn was in bed from this date to Nov. 28; his entries made in the interim, therefore, do not contain first-hand information as to what was going on. From a comparison of texts, it is probable that Dearborn obtained his information from the journal of Maj. Return J. Meigs.

67. Ste. Marie de la Beauce. Sattigan or Sartigan or Sertigan "meant the region (St. Egan) watered by the Chaudière, from the Du Loup to St. Isodore de Lauzon,— that is to say, almost to the St. Lawrence." At. Ste. Marie was the manor-house of Gabriel Elzéar Taschereau, a gentleman and landed proprietor of considerable importance. Smith, *op. cit.*, 247, 447.

68. From Ste. Marie the expedition followed the Chaudière to a point a little beyond the present village of Scotts. Here the road left the river, turning sharply to the right through the "forest of Sertigan." This road formed the boundary between the seigneurie of Beauce and of Lauzon; it is known as the Route Justinienne. *Ibid.*, 249.

the Hands of our Enemies after we had got thro, these Woods, we arrived at S.t Henry's,[69] a Considerable Parish with a Church, we pass'd several other Small parishes, before we arrived at Point, Levi,[70] where the main Body of our Detachment, arrived the 9.th Day of November, But so fatigued, that they were very unfit for action, a Considerable number of our men are left on the road Sick or woren out with fatigue & hunger.

On our arrival we found Two Men of war Lying in the river Between Point-Levi, and Quebec, and Guard Boats passing all Night, up and Down the River.

10 Our men lay at Point Levi, Nothing extraordinary 11 happen'd except that a Deserter[71] from Quebec Came 12 to us who Inform'd us that Colo: M.cLane[72] had 13 arrived from Sorrell, with his Regiment, and our men made A prisoner of a young Man, by the Name of M.cKensey,[73] Midshipman of the Hunter Sloop [of] War. On the evening of the 13.th Our men Embarked on Board 35 Canoes, and by four of the Clock, in the morning we had Landed all our men that were fit for duty which was about 500.. at Woolfs Cove,[74] entirely undiscover'd, altho, we pass'd Between Two Men of War, who had

69. At the end of the Route Justinienne the troops crossed the River Etchemin and entered the village of St. Henry (St. Henri) about 20 miles from Ste. Marie. Ibid., 249.

70. Point Levis. The exact location of this point in the different journals, accounts, and on contemporary maps, varies. The name was usually applied (in 1775) loosely to the great promontory across the river from and a little below Quebec.

71. The deserter's name was Halstead or Haulstead. He had come, originally, from New Jersey, and had been working as a merchant in Quebec. Ibid, 456, 457.

72. Col. Allan MacLean (1725-1784) had remained in America after serving in the French and Indian War with a Scots regiment. In June, 1775, he was commissioned to raise a regiment of highland emigrants in Canada to augment Carleton's army. His corps was sent up the St. Lawrence, but returned on the night of Nov. 13. Carleton entrusted the command of Quebec to MacLean, who was responsible for resisting the American attack. Dict. Nat. Biog., XII, 643-4.

73. Midshipman McKenzie was a brother of Capt. Thomas McKenzie of the Hunter, British sloop-of-war. Smith, op. cit., 456.

74. Wolfe's Cove is on the Quebec side of the river just above the Plains of Abraham which faced the fortified city on the land side.

Guard Boats Cruising all Night, after Parading our men, and sending a Reconitring party towards the City, and placing Some Small Guards, we marched a Cross the plains of Abraham,[75] and took possession of a Large-House formerly own'd by General Murray,[76] Now by Mg.ᵣ Codlwell, and some Houses adjacent which made fine quarters.

14 After reconitring, proper Guards being placed to Cut off all Communication from Between the Town and Country, at 12... O..Clock the Enemy surprized one of our Centinels, and made him Prisoner, soon after our Main Body, Turn'd out and march'd within Half a mile of the Walls on the Height of Abraham, Immediately after being full in the'r view, we gave them Three Huzza's, but they did not Chuse to Come out to meet us, this afternoon, the Enemy set fire to Several Houses in the Suburbs, at Sun set Colo: Arnold sent a Flag to Town Demanding the Possession of the Garrison in the Name, and in behalf of the united American Colonies, But the Flag being fired upon was obliged to Return, We lay Constantly upon our Arms to prevent a Surprize, We are by a Gentleman from Quebec inform'd, that we may expect an attack very soon from the Garrison.

15 Colo: Arnold sent a flag to Demand the Town again this morning, thinking the Flag's being fir'd upon

75. The Plains or Heights of Abraham commanded the land side of the city of Quebec, which was well protected by strong walls. From a rising ground about a hundred yards from the walls it was possible to bombard the upper town. Three important approaches to the city by land ran across the Plains; a road from Lorette, one from Ste. Foy, and one from Three Rivers and Sillery.

76. Gen. James Murray (1719?-1794) had been governor of Canada, 1763-66. His large house was more than a mile outside the city of Quebec. Maj. Henry Caldwell (1738-1810) had leased the estate. He was commander of the Canadian militia during the siege of Quebec and was selected to carry the announcement of Arnold's defeat to London. For this service the king made him a baronet, a lieutenant-colonel and a councillor of Quebec. Royal Society of Canada: *Proceedings and Transactions* (Ottawa, 1903), Series 2, IX, 27-39.

Yesterday was done thro. mistake, but was Treated in the Same manner, as yesterday, This morning an express was sent off to General Montgomery,[77] at 12... O Clock we were alarmed by a report that the Troops in the Garrison Were Coming out to attack us, we Turn'd out to meet them, but it Proved to be a false report.

16 This Morning it is reported that Montreal surrendred to Gen[l] Montgomery last Sabbath, and that he had taken a Number of the enemys Ships, One of our Rifle Serg[ts] was kill'd to day by a Cannon shot from the Town, we sent a Company of men To,day to take possession of the General Hospital,[78] which is a very large Pile of Building a Bout three Quarters of a mile from the Walls of Qebec, in this Building is a Nunnery of the first order in Canada, where at present there are a Bout Thirty fine nuns— The Canadians are Constantly Coming to us, and are expressing the Greatest satisfaction at our Coming into the Country.

17 A Soldier Came to us from Quebec, But brings no Extraordinary Intelligence, a Party of our men are gone over the River, to Bring over some of our men, who were not Come over before, also to bring some provisions,— The Weather is very pleasant for this Country, and the Season.

77. Brig. Gen. Richard Montgomery (1738-1775) was born in Dublin and educated at Trinity College. He served in America during the French and Indian War, returned to England a captain in 1765, sold out of the army in 1772 and came back to New York to farm. Elected to the Provincial Congress in 1775, he was commissioned a brigadier-general and reluctantly took up arms against England. He was second in command to Maj. Gen. Schuyler on the expedition into Canada, but because of the latter's illness Montgomery was in full charge. His forces took Chambly, St. Johns and Montreal. He joined Arnold at Pointe aux Trembles and assumed full command. He was killed at the beginning of the assault on Quebec. *Dict. Am. Biog.*, XIII, 98-9.

78. The General Hospital was situated on the north side of the upper town on the right bank of the St. Charles River (Little River) and about a mile from the Porte du Palais or Palace Gate.

18 Nothing Extraordinary To,day, the evening orders that are given is to Parade To-morrow Morning at 3 of the Clock.

19.. Very early this morning we Decamp'd, and March'd up to Point Aux-Tremble,[79] a Bout Seven Leagues from Quebec, the Country thro, which we marched is thick settled and pleasant, there are a Number of Handsome Chapels by the way, we find the people very kind to us.

20... An Express arrived this morning from Genl. Montgomery, The Contents of which is that he's in full possession of Montreal, also of the shipping that are there, and that he intends to join us very Soon... We have sent an Express to Montreal To-day.

21 The Curate of the Parish Dines at Head-quarters To-day.

22 An Express arrived this day from Montreal, which informs that Genl. Montgomery's Army had taken 13 Vessels with a Large Quantity of Cloathing and provisions and that the General was a Bout Marching for Quebec.

23... This Morning an express arrived from Montreal which Inform, that Genl. Montgomery is on his March for this place, And that he has sent Cloathing forwd. for our Men.

24 This Morning the Hunter Sloop of War, and three other Arm'd vessels appear'd in sight;— An express is sent from us to meet the Troops from Montreal.

25 The Hunter Sloop, a Large Snow, and an Arm'd Schooner Came to an Anchor Opposite our Quarters this Morning. Some of our men were sent up the River in a boat to meet the Troops which were Coming down from Montreal.

79. Pointe aux Trembles en Bas is on the north side of the St. Lawrence River 19 miles above Quebec.

26 A Number of Gentlemen Came in this morning from Quebec.

27 We are inform'd that the House belonging formerly to Maj^r Coldwell, in which our Troops were Quarter'd before Quebec, is Burn't down.

28 Colo: Arnold is gone up to Jackerty,[80] about 12 Miles above Point Aux-Tremble, to hasten down the Ammunitio^n

29.. Capt Morgan who had been sent down Near Quebec, sent up Two Prisoners which he took in the Suburbs.

30 Capt Duggan,[81] has arrived from Montreal with Provis'ens and Ammunition.

Decr 1 Genl Montgomery, arriv'd this day at 10.. O Clock with Three Arm'd Schooners, with men, Artillery, Ammunition, Provision & Cloathing, to the Great Joy of our Men,   Towards evening our Detachment turn'd out & march'd to the Gen^{ls} Quarters, where we were Rec^d by the General, who Complimented us on the Goodness of our appearance.

2 This morning our field Artillery was sent down by Land and our Large Cannon by Water Near Quebec.— the Boats when they had Landed the Cannon were to go to Point Levi for the Ladders.

3 Our men are drawing Cloathing this day, the General has made a present of a Suit of Cloaths to all our Detachment which they were in great need of.

---

80. Jacques Cartier, sometimes spelled Jackerty, Jackurté or Iaques Quartier, was a small stockaded settlement on the north shore of the St. Lawrence River above Pointe aux Trembles, at the mouth of the Jacques Cartier River.

81. Capt. John Dugan, with Col. Livingston, had been influential in raising the Canadians against the British. He obtained a commission from Congress to raise three companies of rangers among the Canadians. Col. Hazen's jealousy drove Dugan out of the service in 1776, but he raised some Canadian troops to help Gen. Sullivan just before the retreat from Canada was ordered. J. H. Smith, *Our Struggle for the Fourteenth Colony* . . . (New York, 1907), *passim.*

4 At 12-O Clock we marched for S.t Foys[82] before Quebec, We March'd as far as Augustine,[83] where we Tarry'd all Night.

5 In the Morning we proceeded on our March and about noon arrived at S.t Foys— my Company were order'd into the General Hospital for quarters.

6 Nothing extraordinary or remarkable to-day, the weather is attended with Snow Squalls.

7 We are inform'd that a Company of our[s] took a sloop with Provisions and Some quantity of Cash, not far from the Island of Orlean's.[84]

8 We receiv'd Some shot from the enemy to-day but no person Injur'd thereby.

9 Now I will give Some account of Matters respecting myself I Still remain sick at Sattagan at the House which I heretofore mention'd taking up Lodging at, from the 6.th Day of November to the 28.th before I went out of the House, the first Ten days I had a Violent Fever, and was Delirious the Chief of the time, I had nothing to assist Nature with, but a Tea of Piggen plumb Roots, and Spruce,[85] as there are no Doctors in these parts nor any Garden Herbs, my fever abated in some degree, but did not leave me, I had a violent Cough, and lost my flesh to that Degree, that I was almost Reduced to a perfect Skeleton, and so very Weak that when I first began to set up for Several days, I could not go from the bed to

82. St. Foy or St. Foix, about 4 miles above Quebec and 12½ miles from Pointe aux Trembles.

83. St. Augustine—half way between Pointe aux Trembles and St. Foy on the north shore of the St. Lawrence River.

84. Isle of Orleans divides the St. Lawrence River into the north and south channels 4 miles northeast of the city of Quebec. It is 20 miles long and 6 miles across.

85. Probably the *Mitchella*, which has 16 local or popular names, two of which are "pigeon berry" and "squaw plum." This shrub is found in woods from Nova Scotia to Florida and was used for a tea. The spruce was added for flavoring; spruce beer was a well known fermented beverage. Britton and Brown, *An Illustrated Flora of the Northern United States* . . . (New York, 1896–98), III, 255.

the fire with a Staff without being held up,   I heard that
our people had got Possession of Quebec, and as I could
not perceive that I gain'd any Strength, and my fever remain'd upon me very high, at this time I concluded to
send Charles Burget, my french Lad to Quebec, to see if
he could procure me something from an Apothecary to
help my Cough and to assist nature, in Carrying off my
fever,   he went and in four days return'd, but to my
great mortification Brought nothing for me but bad
News, which was, that our people had not got Possession of Quebec, but had March'd from Quebec up the
River, towards Montreal,   hearing this, Struck a damp
upon my Spirits which reduced them something Low,
But through the kind hand of Providence, I amend'd
tho, very Slowly,   the first day of December I rode out in
a Carry'al with my Landlard, and found myself much
The better for it, tho, I was so weak now that I Could
not walk from the Carriall into the House without help,
I now began to be very uneasy and wanted to be with the
Army and the Seventh day I set out in a Carriall to Quebec, and the 9.th day I Cross'd the River S.[t] Laurence,   I
join'd my Company who Seem'd very Glad to see me,
they told me that they had been inform'd by one of our
men that Came not many days since from Sattagan that
I was Dead, and that he saw Charles Hilton, and Charles
Burget making a Coffin for me.

I will now return to Matters respecting our Army, We
had a body of men that began to build a battery Last
night on the height of Abraham about half a mile from
S.[t] Johns Gate,[86] and we had five small mortars order'd
into S.[t] Roach's[87] near the Walls of Quebec, to Heave

86. St. John's Gate faces a commanding height to the north of the plains and west
of the upper town.

87. St. Rochs, a suburb of the city of Quebec located 1½ miles northwest of the
Quebec post-office.

Shells into the City To-Night the Artillery are to be Cover'd with 100 Men, they Threw about 30 Shells this Night.

10 The enemy began a heavy Cannonade upon our Camp this morning and Continued it all day, our people hove shells this Night from St Rock's, & a party was to work on the Battery— The enemy return'd a few Shells to us last Night & Some Cannon Balls, but no person received any hurt except an old Canadian Woman who was shot thro: the Body with a 24^{lb} Shot.

11 This morning one of our men lost his way in the Storm and had got under the Walls and was fir'd upon by the Centinel before he knew where he was, and had received a Shott through the thigh, but got away and is in a fair way to recover. The enemy has kept up a faint Cannonading all this day, this night our Train of Artillery Threw 45 Shells into the Town, and had a party to work on the Battery, the Enemy hove a few shot and Some shells at our people who were to work on the Battery, but did no damage, the Weather now is Exceeding Cold.

12 The Platforms are almost ready for the Guns at the Battery, the Weather Still remains very Cold.

13...14 We hove open our Battery, have several men kill'd & wound.^d This morning before sun rise, our Battery, Began to Play upon the Town, we had 5 .. 12 Pounders and a Howeteer[88] Mounted, all very well attended, there was a very heavy fire from the Town upon our Battery— after our Battery had play'd one hour they Ceas'd and General Montgomery sent a flag to the Town but it was refus'd admittance, But after some discourse with some officiers upon the Rampart return.^d at 2.

88. A howitzer, a short and comparatively light cannon which fires a heavy shell by means of a high angle of elevation. It was and still is a favorite siege gun.

O Clock P: M: our Battery began to play, again and our Mortars at the same time were at work in S: Rock's, we hove 50. Shells into the Town to-day, there was a very heavy Cannonading kept up from the Town, we had Two men kill'd To-day at our Battery, and one of our Guns damaged and our Howeteers dismounted, it is now in agitation to Storm the Town, which if resolved upon I hope will be undertaken, with a proper sense of the nature and Importance of such an attack and vigorously Executed—

16 In the evening began to Cannonade, Colo: Arnold's quarters were Struck by Several Cannon shot, upon which he thought it best to remove to other quarters, one of our men was Shot through the body with a grape shot— to-day his life is dispair'd of, a Counsel was held this evening by all the Commission'd officers belonging to Colo: Arnolds detachment.—A majority of which was for Storming the Garrison of Quebec as soon as the men are well equip'd with good arms, Spears, hatchets, Hand, granades...&c.

17 Nothing extraordina'y or remarkable, to-day the weather is very Cold and Snowy.

18 Nothing extraordinary to-day the weather Still remains very Cold, my Company are order'd out of the Hospital, the room is wanted for a Hospital for the use of the sick, we took our quarters on the opposite side of the River S: Charles, at one M: Henry's, a presbyterian minister which place is about one mile from the Hospital.

19 I began to recover my Strength again & have a fine appetite.

20 The weather Continues Still Cold, preparation is making for the intended Storm, several of our men have the small Pox.

21 We are order'd every man of us to wear a hemblock sprig in his Hat, to distinguish us from the enemy in the attack upon Quebeck.

22 Matters seem ripening fast for a storm, may the blessing of Heaven attend the enterprize— —

23 This evening all the officers of our detachment met at and are visited by the Gen! at Colo: Arnolds Quarters.

24 This evening the Revd Mr Spring[89] preach'd a sermon in the Chapel in the Gen! Hospital, which is exceeding elegant inside, is Richly decorated with Carved and guilt work.

25 Colo: Arnolds detachment is Paraded at 4 Clock P: M: Gen! Montgomery attended and address'd us on the Subject of making the attack upon the Walls of Quebec, in a very sensible Spirit'd manner—which greatly animated our men.

26 Nothing Material happen'd to day the weather is Still cold.

27 This morning the Troops assembled by order of the General, with a design to attack the Town of Quebec, and were about to march, when there Came an order from the Gen! to return to our quarters by reason of the weather's clearing up which render'd it improper for the attack—

28 The following Came out in Gen! orders this day— Viz^t

The Gen! had the most Sensible pleasure in seeing the good disposition with which the Troops last night moved to the attack, it was with the greatest reluctance he found himself Call'd upon by his duty to repress their

---

89. Rev. Samuel Spring (1746–1819) was chaplain of Arnold's expedition. He left the army at the end of 1776 and became pastor of the Congregational Church at Newburyport, Mass., where he spent the rest of his life. *Dict. Am. Biog.*, XVII, 481.

ardor, but should hold himself answerable for the loss of those brave men whose lives might be Saved by waiting for a favourable opportunity— —

29 . . . Nothing remarkable or extraordinary to-day—

30 I have the Main-guard in S<u>t</u> Rock's, I came on last evening   our Artillery hove 30 Shells last night into Quebeck, which were answer'd by a few shells and Some Grape shott,   early this morning the Garrison began a very heavy Cannonade upon all parts of our Camp within their Reach, Particularly on those quarter'd in S<u>t</u> Rock's, and upon the Guard-House which is within musquet Shott of the Walls, but partly under the Cover of a hill— about sun'set this afternoon, the Garrison brought a gun to bear upon the Guard-house much more exact, and better level'd, than any that they shott heretofore, and within the Space of 15 minutes they knocked down the three Chimneys of the Guard-house over our heads, but could not get a shot into the lower Rooms where the Guard kept,   at 10.. O Clock this evening I went home to my quarters—

31 This morning at 4.. O Clock I was inform'd by one of my men that there was orders from the Gen<u>l</u> for making the attack upon Quebec this morning,   I was surprized that I had not been inform'd or notified Sooner, But afterwards found it was owing to the neglect of the Serg<u>t</u> Major, who excus'd himself by saying he could not get across the River, by reason of the Tides being so exceeding High,   however I gave orders to my men to prepare themselves immediately to March, but my Company being quarter'd in three different Houses, and the farthest a mile from my Quarters, and the weather very Stormy and the Snow deep, it was near an hour before I could get them all Paraded & Ready to March, at which

time I found the attack was began by the Gen! party, near Cape Diamond,⁹⁰ I had now two miles to March, before we Came to the place where the attack was made, The moment I march'd I met the Serg! Major who inform'd me that Colo: Arnold, had march'd, and that he cou'd not Convey intelligence to me Sooner, as there was no possibility of Crossing the River, we now march'd or rather ran as fast as we could, when I arrived at S! Rock's I met Colo: Arnold Wounded⁹¹ Borne, and brought away by Two men, he Spoke to me and desir'd me to push on forward, and said our people had possession of a 4 Gun Battery.—and that we should Carry the Town, our Artillery were Incessantly heaving shells, with 5 Mortars from S! Rock's, and the Garrison were heaving shells and Balls of all sorts from every part of the Town, my men seem'd to be in high Spirits, we push'd forward as fast as possible, we met the wounded men very thick,— —

We Soon found ourselves under a very brisk fire from the walls & Picketts, but it being very dark & Stormy, and the way we had to pass very Intricate & I an utter Stranger to the way we got bewilder'd, an altho, I met Several men, and Some officiers who said they knew where our people were, yet none of them would pilot us untill I met one of Colo: Arnolds Waiters who was endeavouring to forward some ladders who said he would shew me the way, and altho, he was well acquainted with the way,

90. Cape Diamond is on the southwest corner of the fortified city of Quebec. The vulnerability of this point had been brought out by British engineers shortly after the city was captured from the French, and an elaborate, heavily-fortified citadel had been projected for this spot, but had not been built.

91. Arnold was wounded in the left leg by a piece of musket ball which entered below the knee and passed downward, lodging above the ankle. It gave Arnold great pain and occasioned a loss of much blood. Dr. Senter removed the ball, but it was late in February before Arnold could hobble around. Dr. Senter's Journal, in Roberts, *op. cit.*, 234, 123.

RIVER St CHARLES or THE LITTLE

RIVER

HEIGHTS OF ABRAHAM

London, Published as the Act directs in Septemr 1776. by Wm

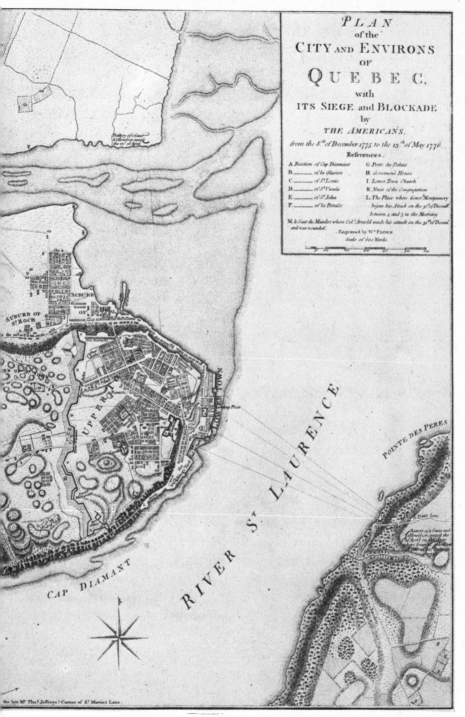

he having lived some years in Quebec, he miss'd it and
Carry'd us quite wrong, but when he found his mistake
he declared he did not know, where we were, and he immediately left us, we were all this time harrass'd with a
brisk fire from the Picketts, which we were Sometimes
within a stones throw of, I now thought it best to retreat a little and then make a new attempt to find the
way, I accordingly order'd Lieu.^t Hutchins who was in
the Rear to retreat, to a Certain place a few rods back,
he accordingly retreated, and in retreating he had to pass
very near the Picket, under a very brisk fire, it now began to grow a little light, the Garrison had discover'd
us and Sent out Two hundred men, who took possession
of Some houses which we had to pass before we could
discover them, and as Lieu.^t Hutchins retreated they Sallied down in a lane from the Wall, I divided my Company about the middle, I now again attempt.^d to find the
way to the main body, It being now so light that I
thought I could find the way, I order'd that part of my
men that were with me, to follow me, we pushed on as
fast as possible, but the enemy took some of my rear, and
kept a brisk fire upon us from the Houses, which we had
pass'd, when I Came to a place where I could Cover my
men a little, while I could discover where our main body
was, I heard a shout in Town, which made me think
that our people had got possession of the Same, the men
were so thick within the Picketts, I was at a Stand to
know whether They were our men, or the enemy, as they
were dress'd like us,^92 I was Just about to Hail them,
when one of them hail'd me, he asked who I was (I was
now within Six rods of the Picketts) I answer'd a friend;

92. Arnold's troops were dressed wholly or in part in British uniforms captured
by Montgomery at Montreal, welcome replacements for the rags they had been
wearing. See Dearborn's entries for Nov. 22 and 23.

he asked me who I was a friend to, I answer'd to liberty,
he then reply'd God-damn you, and then rais'd himself
partly above the Pickets, I Clapt up my Piece which
was Charged with a ball and Ten Buck shott Certainly to
give him his due, But to my great mortification my Gun
did not go off, I new prim'd her, and flushed and Try'd
her again, but neither I, nor one in Ten of my men could
get off our Guns they being so exceeding wet, They
fired very briskly upon us from the Picketts, here we
found a great number of wounded men, and some dead,
which did belong to our main body; I order'd my men to
go into a lower room of an house, and new Prime their
Guns, and prick dry Powder into the Touch-holes, we
Now found ourselves surrounded by Six to one, I now
finding no possibility of getting away, my Company
were divided, and our arms being in such bad order, I
thought it best to Surrender after being promis'd good
quarters and Tender usuage, I told my men, to make
their escape, as many as possibly could, and in the Confusion a considerable Number did effect the Same, Some
of them after they had given up their arms, we were
now marched to Palace Gate,[93] on my way there to my
Surprize, I found Lieu.^t Hutchins, Ensign Thomas, &
about 15 or 20 of my men under Guard, who were march'd
to Palace-gate with me, we were Carried to a Large
Convent and put under the Care of a strong Guard, on
my way to this House I was inform'd that our people had
got possession of the Lower Town[94]

It appears at this time, according to the following
Arrangement, that my Comp'y which may be seen

93. The Palace Gate into the city was on the north side, opposite the suburb of
Palais. The large hospital inside the gate was the Hotel Dieu.

94. The upper and lower towns were so named by virtue of the physical features of
the two divisions. The upper town comprised the streets and habitations built on the
high, rocky bluff. The lower town was built on the low shelf facing the east.

hereafter, in the attack upon the Town was intended to be the second to the front.

The Gen! gave orders last evening for the Troops to assemble at Two O:Clock this morning in order to make the attack, at 5.. O..Clock in the following manner viz!

The Gen! with the first.. 2.. & 3.. Battalians of New-york Troops was to attack the Southerly part of the Lower Town, at a place Call'd the Pot-ash— —95

Colo: Arnold with his detachment and part of Cap! Lambs96 Company of Artillery, with one Field-piece, was to march through S! Rock's down between the river Saint Charles, and the Picket of the Garrison to the North part of the Lower Town Call'd the South-ax-Matillo,97 and there attack a 4 Gun Barrier in the following order, a Subaltern with 24 Men was to be an advanced party, Cap! Lambs Artillery next with a six pounder mounted on a Sled, then the main-body, Cap! Morgan first, my Company next, Then Cap! Smith's, then Captain Hanchet's, then Cap! Hubbard's,98

95. The Potash, also called Près de Ville, was a natural point of defence, being the southern pass into the Lower Town. Above this point on Cape Diamond was a redoubt, which, if manned with gunners, could command the pass.

96. Capt. John Lamb (1735-1800) was a radical agitator from the passage of the Stamp Act until the battle of Lexington afforded him the opportunity to seize the Customs House and military stores in New York. Then he became captain of an artillery company and joined Montgomery's expedition into Canada. Lamb lost an eye and was captured at Quebec. Paroled, he was not exchanged until January, 1777, when he was appointed colonel of the 2nd Continental Artillery. He commanded the artillery at West Point in 1779 and 1780 and was ranked as brigadier-general at the close of the war. *Dict. Am. Biog.*, X, 555-6.

97. Sault au Matelot or Sailor's Leap, a high precipice at the edge of the Upper Town.

98. Capt. Jonas Hubbard of Worcester, Mass., had been a lieutenant of Minute Men and was now a captain in Ward's Massachusetts regiment. In the attack on Quebec he was wounded and captured, and Dearborn reports that he died of his wound. Nevertheless, Simon Fobes, a private in Hubbard's company who dictated a journal of his experiences on the expedition, relates meeting Hubbard again in the summer of 1776 near Worcester where he was working on a farm. Fobe's journal is printed in Roberts, *op. cit.*, 575-613.

Then Cap[t] Topham's,[99] then Cap[t] Thayer,[100] then Cap[t] Ward's,[101] then Cap[t] Goodrich's, & then Cap[t] Hendrick's, Colo: Arnold in the Front Colo: Green and Maj[r] Biggellow in the Centre, and Maj[r] Meigs in the Rear— — Colo: Levingston,[102] & Maj[r] Brown[103] with some of Maj[r] Browns men & some Canadians were to make a feint upon the upper Town & at the Same time, were to Set fire to S[t] John's Gate with a Certain quantity of Cumbustibles prepar'd for that purpose— The Gen[l] with his Party began the attack, the Gen[l] with his Aid-de-camp,[104] and Cap[t] Shearman[105] & the Carpenters, who served as

99. Capt. John Topham (d.1793) was a captain-lieutenant in the 3rd Rhode Island regiment. Wounded and captured at Quebec, he was exchanged and was made a colonel in 1778. Heitman, *op. cit.*, 545.

100. Capt. Simeon Thayer (1737-1800) was a peruke maker in Providence who had served in the French and Indian War. He was made a captain-lieutenant in the 2nd Rhode Island regiment in May, 1775, and his company was the first to arrive at Cambridge from that state. Taken prisoner at Quebec, he was not exchanged until July, 1777, when he was given the rank of major. He lost an eye at Monmouth, 1778, and retired from the army in May, 1781. Smith, *Arnold's March* . . . 267; Heitman, *op. cit.*, 538.

101. Capt. Samuel Ward (1756-1832) was the son of the governor of Rhode Island and belonged to the 1st Rhode Island regiment. Taken prisoner at Quebec, he was exchanged in 1776 and rose to be lieutenant-colonel in 1778. Ward retired from the army at the end of 1780. Heitman, *op. cit.*, 568.

102. Col. James Livingston (1747-1832) joined Montgomery's expedition and raised and commanded a regiment of Canadians. With Major John Brown he captured Fort Chambly and helped besiege St. Johns. He went on to Quebec with Montgomery where he took part in the assault, but was not captured. Subsequently he served at Saratoga under Arnold and was in command of Stony Point in 1780. He resigned his commission on Jan. 1, 1781. *Dict. Am. Biog.*, XI, 313-4; Smith, *Our Struggle* . . . *passim*.

103. Maj. John Brown (1744-1780) was a lawyer until he volunteered in February, 1775, to go to Montreal to seek rebel sympathizers. He took part in the capture of Ticonderoga, was commissioned a major, and led the detachment which began the invasion of Canada. With Ethan Allen he tried to take Montreal and failed, but he helped Maj. Livingston take Fort Chambly. Brown joined the assault on Quebec and afterward quarrelled with Arnold. He was promoted to lieutenant-colonel, but resigned in 1777. As a colonel of militia he captured Fort George that fall, then returned to the practice of law. In 1780 he took the field again with militia in the Mohawk valley and was killed Oct. 19. *Dict. Am. Biog.*, III, 129-30.

104. Capt. John Macpherson (1754-1775) of Pennsylvania was an aide-de-camp to Montgomery. He was killed by the latter's side in leading the assault on Quebec. Smith, *Our Struggle* . . . II, 125, 142.

105. As no Capt. Shearman appears on any of the casualty lists, and as Capt. Cheeseman (see Note 110) was killed at the side of Montgomery, it seems probable that the person who copied this journal from Dearborn's original misread the name.

Pioneers advanced in the front, The Carpenters Cut the Picketts, the Gen! with his own hands pull'd them down & enter'd.—after the Gen! had enter'd, he Call'd to his men to Come on, they did not advance as quick as he thought they might, he Spoke to them again in the following moving Terms, saying come on my good soldiers, your Gen! Calls upon you to Come on, The Gen! was now very near a Battery of Several Cannon Loaded with grape shott, some of which were unfortunately discharged, and which Cut down our Brave Gen!, his Aiddecamp, Cap! M<u>c</u>Ferson, Cap! Shearman, & three or four Privates—

The Guards immediately after firing the first Cannon quited their post and Ran, which gave our Troops a fair opportunity to enter, But instead of entering Colonel Campbell,[106] who now took Command, order'd a retreat, which was a very unlucky retreat for us,— A few minutes after the Gen! made the attack on his part, Col: Arnold made an attack with his party, but instead of making the attack in the manner proposed, which was, when the advanced party had got within musket shot of the Barrier,[107] they were to Halt and then open to the right and left, and the Artillery to fire three shott, upon the Barrier and then the advanced party were to fire into the Port Holes, Cap! Morgan's Company to pass round a wharf on which the Barrier was Built, and Come in upon

106. Col. Donald Campbell, formerly in the British army, was now Deputy Quartermaster General of the New York department, which office he held until 1784. He was known for his profanity, and Justin Smith calls him a "pictorial fraud." Smith, Our Struggle . . . II, 115-6.

107. Arnold's detachment had passed around the north side of Quebec, following the narrow shore between the bluff of the Upper Town and the St. Lawrence, which led into the Lower Town at the eastern extremity of the city. Blocking this pass were two barriers about 12 feet high, presumably made of pickets, with loopholes for cannon and muskets. The first extended from a wharf across the shore road to the bluff. With scaling ladders Morgan's men were the first over the barrier; Arnold was wounded soon after coming up to it. Most of the Americans lost their lives between the first and second barriers. Morgan and some of his men got over the second barrier, but lacking support they were soon forced to surrender. Ibid., II, 131-40.

the back of the Guard, while we Scall'd the Barrier with
Ladders, but the Snow being so deep and the way so difficult to pass—The Artillery were obliged to leave the
Field piece behind, & Colo: Arnold, with the advanced
party rushed up to the Barrier and kept such a hot fire in
at the Port-holes, that the enemy Could fire but one of
their Cannon, before Cap.[t] Morgan and some of his Company, and some others Scaled the Barrier, and took the
Guards Prisoners Consisting of a Cap.[t] & 30 men,   Colo:
Arnold was wounded in the Legg in the first of the attack
and was Carried Back,   our men enter'd the Barrier as
fast as possible.—But the Main body had not come up
yet by reason of missing their way, and were obliged to
Counter-march twice before they could get right,   there
was now a second Barrier to force, where there ⌈were⌉
two Cannon placed, Charged with Grape' shott, our
men who had enter'd the first Barrier, were now waiting
for the main-body to come up, but before the main-body
had got into the first Barrier, the enemy found that the
Gen.[l] Party had retreated, and the whole Garrison had
Turn'd their attention upon our party, and had taken
possession of the Houses almost all round us, and had
mann'd the Barrier so strong that when our people made
an attempt to force it, we were repulsed, and obliged to
shelter ourselves in the Houses, as well as we could,   I
say, we altho, I was not at this place, but in order to distinguish our Troops from the Enemy,   our people being
Surround'd By Treble their Number, and was under a very
hot fire, it was now Motion'd by some, whether or no, it
would not be most advisable to retreat,   others immediately repli'd who knows but our Gen.[l] with his party, is
in some part of the Town, and if we go, and leave him
behind, he and his party will most certainly be Cut off, It
was then concluded upon to send somebody off in order

to learn what was become of our Gen! and his party, and agreed to make a stand while [!] night, Immediately after entering the Barrier, Cap: Hendrick, Lieu: Humphrey's and Lieu: Cooper,[108] together with a number of Privates was kill'd Just as this resolution took place, the same party that took me followed after our main-body, and Came upon their Rear, but our people finding the impracticability of a retreat, and hearing nothing from our Gen!'s party, & having lost about one hundred men out of less than five hundred, it was thought it most prudent to surrender, upon the encouragement of being promis'd good quarters and Tender usage, It was by this time 10:O Clock A:M:... The officiers were Carried to the main Guard house and the Soldiers to the House where I was Carried first, I with my other officiers, ware Carry'd to the main, guard-House to the other officiers, where we had a good Dinner, and aplenty of several sorts of wine, in the afternoon we were Carry'd to a Large Seminary,[109] and put into a large room in the fourth Story from the ground,———

A List of the officiers that were killed.

Brigad: Gen! Montgomery
M: John M:pherson Aid-decamp to the Gen!
Cap: Cheasman[110]   .   .   .   .   . of New-york
Cap: W:m Hendrick   .   .   .   .   . of Pensilvania
Lieu: Humphry .   .   .   .   .   . of Virginia
Lieu: Sam! Cooper   .   .   .   .   . of Connecticut

108. Lt. John Humphries of Capt. Morgan's company of Virginia riflemen; not to be confused with Lt. William Humphrey of Capt. Thayer's company, who was taken prisoner. Lt. Samuel Cooper belonged to the 2nd Connecticut regiment. Heitman, *op. cit.*, 170, 309.

109. The Seminary of Quebec.

110. Capt. Jacob Cheeseman belonged to the 1st New York regiment and was aide-de-camp to Montgomery. He had raised two sunken British vessels after the capture of St. Johns. In the attack on Quebec he fell by his commander's side. Smith *Our Struggle* . . . , I, 468; II, 142.

A list of the wouned officiers that was in the engag[t]

Colo, Benedict Arnold shot thro one of his Leggs—
Cap[t] John Lamb of New york shot in the Cheeck bone by
which the sight of one of his Eyes . . . . . . [was lost]
Cap[t] Jonas Hubbard of Worcester shot thro, the ancle of
which he died.
Lieu[t] Archibald Steel[111] of Pensilvania two of his fingers
shot off—
Lieu[t] Jam[s] Tindal[112] of the Massachusetts Bay shot thro.
his right shoulder

The Sergeants, Corporals, and privates, kill'd &
wounded according to the best accounts I could obtain,
Amounted to a bout one Hundred men, the number kill'd
on the Spot, about 40[113]

A list of the officiers taken, but not wounded.

Names	Provinces	Towns
Cap[t] Daniel Morgan		
Lieu[t] William Heath		Frederick
Lieu[t] Peter Brewin	Virginia	County
M[r] John M[c]Guyer Volunteer		
M[r] Char[s] Porterfield..do..		

111. Lt. Archibald Steele (d. 1822) was in Capt. Matthew Smith's company of
Pennsylvania riflemen. He had been sent on ahead to reconnoitre the Quebec route
as far as Chaudière Pond, before reporting to Arnold on Oct. 12. He led Smith's company in the attack on Quebec and was wounded and captured. Exchanged in August,
1776, Steele became Deputy Quartermaster General in 1777 and served until October,
1781. He was military storekeeper in 1816 and was finally discharged in 1821. Heitman, op. cit., 517.

112. This was James Tisdale, a 2nd lieutenant in Heath's Massachusetts regiment.
After his exchange he was made a captain in the 3rd Massachusetts regiment and
served to the end of the war. Ibid., 544.

113. According to the casualty lists, 35 officers and men of Arnold's force were
killed and 33 were wounded; 13 of Montgomery's force were killed and one was
wounded. See Roberts, op. cit., 40.

Names	Provinces	Towns
Lieu: Archibold Steel		Lancaster
Lieu: Francis Nichols	Pensilvania	Carlisle
M: Mathew Duncan Volunteer		Philadelphia
M: John Henry Volunteer		Lancaster
Lieu: Andrew Moody	New-york	
Maj: Return Jona. Meigs		Middletown
Cap: Oliver Hanchet.		Suffield
Cap: Sam: Lockwood	Connecticut	Hamford
Lieu: Abijah Savage		Middletown
Cap: Aliezer Aswald Vol:		New-Haven
Quar: Mas: Ben: Catlin...		Weathersfield
L: Col? Cristopher Green		Greenwich
Cap: John Topham	Rhode-Island	Newport
Cap: Sam: Ward		Westerly
Cap: Simeon Thayer		Providence
Lieu: James Webb		Newport
Lieu: William Humphrys	Rode Island	Providence
Lieu: Edw. Slocam		Tivertown
Lieu: Silvanus Shaw		New-port
Maj: Timothy Bigellow		Worchester
Cap: Wᵐ Goodrich		Stockbridge
Lieu: Sam: Brown	Massachusets Bay	Acton
Lieu: John Cumston		Sacho
Lieu: John Clark		Hadley
Cap: Henry Dearborn		Nottingham
Lieu: Nathan: Hutchins	Hampshire	Dunbarton
Lieu: Ammi Andrews		Hilsborough
Lieu: Joseph Thomas		Deerfield

Adju.^t Christian Febeger { The Number of Serg.^{ts} Corpor.^{ls}
a deanish officier...   { & Privates Taken, but not
                            { wounded, are about 300[114]

1776

January 1 I begun this year in very disagreeable Circumstances, it being the first day I ever Spent in Confinement except by sickness, but I hope I shall be enabled to bare it with a becoming fortitude. Considering it to be the fortune of War.

2 Gen! Montgomery's body was taken up to day, and brought into Town— —

3 Gen! Carlton[115] gave Major Meigs Leave to go out after our Baggage to-day— —

As the Small pox is prevalent in this Town, it is thought best for as many of us, as had not had the Small Pox to be Innoculated immediately— Accordingly sixteen of us Concluded to apply to some physician to innoculate us, Doct.^r Bullen was recommended to us as being a skilful in Innoculation, whom we apply'd to, to day, & he engag.^d to Innoculate us, and gave us some preparatory Medicines to day.—

114. There were 372 men taken. Roberts, *op. cit.*, 40.

115. Guy Carleton (1724–1808) began his army career in 1742 and served in Canada and the West Indies during the French and Indian War. He was appointed lieutenant-governor of Quebec in 1766 and held the office for four years. At the end of 1774 he was sent back to Canada as governor of Quebec. When Gage was recalled, the command of the British troops was divided; those in Canada were placed under Carleton and those in the American colonies under Howe. Having only two regiments of regulars to depend on, Carleton narrowly escaped capture when Montgomery took Montreal on Nov. 12, 1775. He moved on to Quebec and successfully resisted the assault led by Montgomery and Arnold. In the summer of 1776 he followed the retreating Arnold up Lake Champlain, but winter forced him to withdraw before he had established himself. In 1777 a second attempt was made to invade New York state, this time under Burgoyne, who replaced Carleton as commander, much to the latter's disgust. The next year Carleton returned to England, but was sent back as commander-in-chief in 1782. His main task was to get the defeated British army back to England. Later he was created Baron Dorchester and served as governor of Canada. *Dict. Nat. Biog.*, III, 1002–4.

4—We were this day Innoculated,... Gen! Montgomery's body Was Interr⁴ to-day,[116] in a very decent manner by order of Gen! Carlton—

5 We that have been innoculated, are removed to-day into another Room, & have the liberty of walking into another room adjoining to that we Lodge in.

6... Maj. Meigs return'd to-day, with some part of our Baggage but a Considerable part of it is not Brought in— four of our men are tolerated to wait upon us.

7... We purchas'd some poor mutton to make Soop of at one Pistereen[117] p⁵ pound.

8 We had a very good Collection of Books sent us by several friends in Town, in the perusal of which, we pass many of of our dull hours—

9 To,day I wrote a letter to send to my wife, but find no opportunity of sending it.

10 This day M⁵ Levius,[118] who was formerly a Judge of our Court, came to see me, and offer'd to supply me with any thing I stood in need of, that was in his power, he furnish'd me with some Cash, and Two shirts, and said he would have me let him know, if I should hereafter be in want of any thing, as he would be ready to oblige me therewith if within the Sphere of his Influence—

11..12...13 Nothing extraordinary. The Field officier of each day, Generally visits us, the Guard that is set over us, is a subaltern and Twelve men— Our mens Baggage is sent for to-day—

116. Montgomery's body was buried within the city of Quebec. It was removed in 1818 to St. Paul's churchyard, New York. *Dict. Am. Biog.*, XIII, 99.

117. A pistareen was a small Spanish silver coin current in America and the West Indies at this time.

118. Peter Livius (1727?–1795), formerly a member of the council and chief justice of New Hampshire, was transferred to Quebec as a justice in 1775, and two years later became chief justice. He held this office until 1786. He was of German-Portuguese extraction. L. J. Burpee and A. G. Doughty, eds., *Index and Dictionary of Canadian History* (Toronto, 1911), 221.

also I begin to feel the simptoms of the small Pox.

Lieu.^t Savage,[119] who was one that was Innoculated with me, for the Small pox, has it the natural way, he having taken it before he Came into Quebec, & is very bad—

14 I begin to break out with the Small Pox—

15..16..17..18: 19 Nothing extraordinary the Small Pox is Turning, the greatest of my suffering is hunger since I was Innoculated, one of our Waiters who was Innoculated after he Came to wait upon us has had it the Natural way, he having had it before and broke out with it in two days, after he was Innoculated.—and is dead, Lieu.^t Savage is getting better, Nothing very extraordinary happens from this time to the 10th of February— when Major Meigs is Carried to the Hottel-dieu—which is a nunnery & a Hospital, he having a swelling under his arm, and the remainder of us who have had the small pox are removed into the room which we were first put into with the other officiers, we spend our time in reading in the forenoon, and at Cards in the afternoon, and endeavour to make ourselves as happy as possible under our present disagreeable Circumstances, We hear a great deal of bad News, but none that's good— We are told that General Washington, with his army made an attempt to Storm Boston, but had lost 4000 men, some kill'd and the rest were drown'd, we have been inform'd of Montreal's being retaken by the Canadians four or five times— We are told that Genl Lee, in marching to New:york with 3000 men lost them all to 300, by dissertion for want of Cloathing.

We are inform'd that Genl Amherst is arrived at Newyork with 12000 Troops, we are likewis^e told that the

---

119. Lt. Abijah Savage (d. 1825) belonged to the 2nd Connecticut regiment. He was exchanged in October, 1776, and rose to the rank of captain. He retired from the army Jan. 1, 1781. Heitman, *op. cit.*, 582.

paper Currency has lost its value, and that the Congress is impeached with dishonesty by the people, but we give no Credit to any such Rumours—[120]

March 10 We had a square of Glass put into the door that opens into our room, and two Centinels stands looking in all the time, and a lamp is kept burning all night —in our room, and Two Centinels stands under our window who are order'd to fire upon any of us who attempted to open either of the windows in the night, no person is allowed to come into our room but the Field offic. of the day, and the officier of the Guard—not even our washer-woman—

16 Being indispos'd I got liberty to go to the Hotteldieu to day—

I remain'd at the Hottel-dieu, until the 31st day of March nothing very extraordinary happen'd during this time, I recover'd my health in a few days after I got here, I saw one of my men here who inform'd me that all my Company has had the Small Pox, and not one of them died with it, which I think is something remarkable, we are all, now order'd to the Seminary, we are told for want of wood in the Garrison.

April 1 We are informd that our men who are prisoners in this Town, were last night detected in the execution of a plan in order to make their Escape, for which reason, they are all put in Irons. We have two Small Bed-rooms allow'd us to sleep in, being too: much Crouded in one room—

4 This day our people open'd a four Gun-Battery, at Point Levi and play'd upon the Town. there was now a very heavy Cannonading from the Town, upon our Battery every day, there was six or seven Balls shot from our Battery into the Garden under our

120. And quite rightly, because none of the rumors was true.

window, & three or 4 of them struck against the Seminary.

25 In the Course of this month there has been two or three alarms in Town, the Garrison thought that our people were about making an attack.

Cap[t] Thayer was detected by the officier of the guard to-day in attempting to open a door that led from the Passage to the necessary, into an upper loft, and was Carried on board a vessel and put in Irons there is Bolts & Locks put upon our doors and we are order'd not to go out of our respective Lodging Rooms after dark until sometime after sun-rise—

28 This day Colo: M[c]Lane, M[r] Lanodear[121] the Gen[l] Aid-decamp and several other officiers, Came into our room & took Cap[t] Lockwood,[122] & Cap[t] Hanchet and Carried them off, witho't saying any thing to them, but we heard since it was reported that they had Tamper'd with a Cintinel, they were likewise put in Irons on Board the Vessel where Cap[t] Thayer was—

29 Our people open'd a Two Gun Battery to-day upon the opposite side of the Town from Point Levi a Cross the river St Charles and play'd upon the Town, we are likewise inform'd that they are about opening another Battery on the height of Abraham, there is a Constant Cannonading on both sides every day.

May 4 As I was laying down my book this evening about Ten of the Clock, preparing for bed, I heard a

121. François de Lanaudière was a member of the first legislative council under the Quebec Act. He had tried to enlist some Canadians to aid the British, but his company was dispersed on the way to Montreal. However, Lanaudière joined Carleton and escaped with him to Quebec. From Dearborn's entry it would appear that he was now Carleton's aide-de-camp. W. Kingsford, *History of Canada* (Toronto, 1892), V, 422, 445, 463.

122. Capt. Samuel Lockwood was an assistant engineer. On his release from capture he became captain in the 2nd Continental artillery, but resigned early in 1779. Heitman, *op. cit.*, 355.

Centinel hale a ship, which very much surprized me, as
I expected some relief had arrived, But I soon was unde-
ceived by a brisk fire of Cannon, and Small arms, & the
ringing of the alarm Bell, as also hearing a great confusion
in all parts of the Town, we now Concluded, that our people made an attack upon the Town, we soon discover'd
a fire-ship in the River, near the Lower Town, which was
sent as we since heard, in order to set fire to the shi'ping
in the Lower Town, & which must Consequently set fire
to the Lower Town, & at the same time we heard Gen!
Worster[123] with his Troops had drawn up near the Town,
with their Ladders ready to Scale the walls, when ever
the Lower Town was on fire, but as the fireship fail'd the
attack was not made.

6 This day forenoon, three ships arrived from England
to the Great Joy of the Garrison, but much to our mortification as we now gave over all hopes of being retaken,
and Consequently of seeing our families again until we
had first taken a Voyage to England and there Tryed for
rebels, as we have often been told by the officiers of the
Garrison, that, that, would be the case.

The ships that have arrived Brought the 29th Regiment with them, who landed, and at 12.. O Clock, this
Regim! with 5..or 6 Hundred of the Garrison marched
out of Town, and two of the Frigates which arrived to-
day put up the River, and an arm'd Schooner. Towards
Night, the Troops return'd back to Town, and said they
drove all the yankees off.—and took a large quantity of

123. Brig. Gen. David Wooster (1711–1777) had served in King George's War and
the French and Indian War. In April, 1775, he was appointed major-general of 6 Continental regiments and served in New York that summer. Congress named him brigadier-general rather than give him his provincial rank. He accompanied Montgomery into Canada and was left in command at Montreal when the latter went on to
Quebec. After Montgomery's death he became commander of the American forces in
Canada, but was superseded in May because of incompetence. He was killed in action
during Tryon's raid on Danbury, Connecticut. *Dict. Am. Biog.*, XX, 524–5.

Cannon, ammunition, and Baggage from the Americans, which indeed proved too True,   But from the accounts we have had since from Lieuten! M!Dougle,[124] who was taken in a schooner at Point Aux Tremble by the Two Frigates & an armed Schooner, that went up the River the day they arrived, we find that Gen! Woosters Troops began to decamp, the day before the Troops arrived, by hearing there was a Large Fleet in the river, but what Baggage they left was not very Considerable,   there are more or less ships coming in daily, we are inform'd that there are 15000 Men destin'd for Canada,   the 47 Regiment has arrived here from Boston, who bring Acc! that Gen! Howe,[125] with his Troops has evacuated Boston & Came to Hallifax, pursuant to orders received from home.

10 A party marched out to day towards Montreal,   we have Liberty to walk the Seminary Garden for our recreation to-day, which is a very excellent Garden for Canada.

Maj! Meigs has obtain'd Liberty of the Gen! to go home to New-Eng! on his Parole.

13 M! Levius Came to see me to-day, & informed me, that if I would endeavour to assist him, in getting his family to him from Portsmouth, he would use his influence w!ʰ the Gen! to get leave for me to go home with Maj! Meigs On Parole, but he told me I must not depend

124. Lt. Ronald T. McDougall belonged to the 1st New York regiment, which had invaded Canada under Montgomery. Heitman, *op. cit.*, 368.

125. Sir William Howe (1729–1814) had distinguished himself in America during the French and Indian War. As a major-general he was sent over to aid Gen. Gage as commander-in-chief of the American colonies in October. After spending the winter in besieged Boston he evacuated the city in March, 1776, and moved his army to Halifax, from whence he descended on New York in August. He defeated Washington in their first encounters, but failed to follow up his victories. Refusing to co-operate with Gen. Burgoyne in the campaign plan of 1777, Howe instead moved on to Philadelphia and spent an inactive winter. In the spring of 1778 he was recalled and was succeeded by Sir Henry Clinton. *Dict. Nat. Biog.*, X, 102–5.

much upon going as he thought it very uncertain whether he should succeed or not, notwithstanding I depended much upon going, as I thought his influence with the Gen! would be great, he being one of the Counsel, Judge of the Admiralty, & Judge of the Superior Court at Montreal—

14 Major Meigs was sent for to wait upon the Gen! who inform'd him the Vessel would sail in a day or Two, in which he was to go to Hallifax, when the Major Came back, & I hearing nothing of M! Levius's obtaining leave for me to go home, I then began to dispair, and accordingly wrote a letter to my wife to send by the Major—

16 At one O Clock P: M: M! Levius Came to see me, & to my great Joy, inform'd me that the Gen! had given his Consent for me to go home, on Parole, & that we should sail this afternoon,— at 5: of the Clock the Town Major Came for Major Meigs & myself, to go to the Lieu! Governor, to give our Parole, the verbal agreement we made was, that if ever there was an exchange of Prisoners, we were to have the benefit of it, and until then we were not, to take up arms against the King. after giving our Paroles from under our hands, we were Carried before the Gen! who appear'd to be a very humane tender-hearted man. after wishing us a good Voyage, & Saying he hoped to give the remainder of our officiers the Same Liberty, he desir'd the Town Major to Conduct us on Board, we desir'd leave to visit our men in prison but could not obtain it.

after getting our baggage & taking leave of our fellow prisoners we went on board a schooner, which we are to go to Hallifax in, but as she did not sail to day, we were invited on Board the Admirals ship, where we were very genteely used, and Tarried all night—

17 We Sail'd this morning, 10..O..Clock,   we fell down
to the lower end of the Island, of Orleans,   the wind being a head we were obliged to Cast Anchor, at Two of
the Clock P: M: we went on shore upon Orleans, bought
some Fowl & eggs,   Orleans is a very pleasant Island,
but the Inhabitants are extremely Ignorant—

18 We weighed Anchor at 4 this morning, & had a fine
breeze. at 2 Clock we Struck on the Rocks off against the
Isle of Caudre,[126] which is eighteen Leagues from Quebec.
we ware in great danger of staving to pieces. But Lucky
for us we got off,   here we Saw a great many white Por-
puses which were very large— We came to an Anchor this
Night by Hare-Island, which is 36 Leagues from Quebec.

19 We hove up at 4 this morning,   we have but very
little wind the River here is 5 Leagues in Weadth,   we
fell down to the Isle of Beak,[127] which is 50 Leagues from
Quebec, where we found his Majesty's Ship Niger, which
is a 32 Gun Frigate, and an arm'd schooner lying at Anchor,   we cast our anchor here at sunset.

20 We weighed anchor here this morning at 4..   we
had a small Breeze & some rain, and a very large sea. at
six a Clock we had both our Masts sprung, which were
barely saved from going overboard,   we made a signal of
distress to the above mention'd Vessels, which we were
in sight of.—who gave us immediate relief,   we put back
to the ship as fast & well as we could, and after the
Schooner was examin'd by the Carpenters, it was order'd
back to Quebec, and we were put on Board the Niger,
which was now going to sail, bound for Hallifax. at
10..O Clock this evening we met with Two Men of war
and several Transports—

126. Isle aux Coudres, 12 miles southeast of St. Paul's Bay in the St. Lawrence
River.

127. Bic, or l'Islet au Massacre, near the south shore of the St. Lawrence opposite
the village of Bic. The island is 3 miles long by ¾ of a mile broad.

21 This morning we met 32 Transports with Troops on Board under Command of Gen! Burgoyne, said to be 6000 Troops in the whole on Board this Fleet—[128]

22 We enter'd the Gulph of S! Laurence this afternoon, at 5 in the afternon we pass'd Bonaventura—[129]

23 at Twelve of the Clock we pass'd the Magdolen Islands.[130]

24 This morning we made the Isle of S! Johns, this afternoon we made the Isle of Cape Briton—[131]

25 at 2-Clock P: M: we enter'd the gut of Canso,[132] pass'd half way through it, having no wind we Cast anchor—

26 Having no wind we Catched plenty of fish—

27 We hove up this morning at 9 O Clock, & had a fresh breeze, at 12..O..Clock we enter'd the Atlantick.

28 This day we have a fair wind, but a very thick fogg.

29 We made Land within 15 Leagues of Hallifax, the wind is Contrary—

30 This morning we enter'd the mouth of Hallifax, Harbour, as we pass'd up the Bay [the] Town has a very handsome appearance, at 12..O..Clock we Came to Anchor, near the Town & at Two We went on shore, the Land on which this Town is Built rises Gradually until

128. Maj. Gen. John Burgoyne (1722–1792) had been sent to America to assist Gage in the spring of 1775, but had returned to England in disgust over his inactivity. On this second arrival he was to serve as second in command to Carleton on a campaign designed to take New York and split the colonies. Carleton's forces were held back on Lake Champlain by Arnold in the summer and fall of 1776 and gave up the expedition as winter set in. Again Burgoyne returned to England. *Dict. Nat. Biog.*, III, 340–2.

129. Bonaventura—a small island at the mouth of the St. Lawrence River south of the Bay of Gaspé.

130. Magdalen Islands—a group near the center of the Gulf of St. Lawrence.

131. Cape Breton Island, off the extreme northeast tip of the peninsula of Nova Scotia. It is 100 miles long and 85 miles across. The Island of St. Johns is now Prince Edward Island.

132. The Gut of Canso, about 17 miles long, separates the Island of Cape Breton from the peninsula of Nova Scotia. It averages 2½ miles in width.

it forms a beautiful eminence, Call'd the Citadel-Hill. the Town is handsomely laid out, the Building are but small, in general, at the upper end of the Town there is a very good Dock-yard, handsomely built with Stone and Lime, in which there are some handsome buildings. Major Meigs & I waited on his Excellency Gen! How this afternoon, with some dispatches from Gen! Carlton.

June..1 Gen! Howe after some Conversation desir'd us to wait on him again, on Monday Next, & he promis'd us he would inform us when and how we should have a passage to New England, I visited some officiers, and others who were prisoners in Hallifax. Viz! Cap! Mortingdell, of Rhode, Island who was taken in a privateer, Lieu! Scott[133] who was taken at Bunker Hill, the 17.th of June last and a number of others amounting in the whole to 20.. persons— this day we took Lodgings at one Riders Tavern.

2..3..4..5 We remained on shore, untill 3..O..Clock this afternoon, then we embark'd on Board his Majesties Ship Scarborough.

6 Lord Piercy[134] din'd on board the Scarborough, at his Coming on Board he was saluted by 13 Guns from this ship, & the same number from several ships that lay near us, I went ashore to-day and found an opportunity of writing to my fellow prisoners in Quebec, which I gladly embraced—

133. This is probably 2nd Lt. William Scott (d. 1796) of Sargent's Massachusetts regiment. After his exchange he attained the rank of captain. He retired from the army at the end of 1780, but served later in the navy. Heitman, *op. cit.*, 486.

134. Sir Hugh Percy (1742–1817) came to America in 1774 as a colonel, although opposed to the King's colonial policy. He commanded the re-enforcements sent to Lexington, April 19, 1775, to cover the British retreat; soon after he received the rank of major-general. He went to Halifax with the army when Boston was evacuated in March, 1776. Later he moved to New York. After several disputes with Howe, Lord Percy returned to England. He succeeded his father as second Duke of Northumberland in 1786. *Dict. Nat. Biog.*, XV, 865–7.

7..8..9 We Still remain here expecting every day to sail.

10 at 10..O..Clock this morning we sail'd, we had a fair brisk Breeze.

11 Little wind to day—

12 The wind is not fair, we are beating of[f] Cape Sables—[135]

13 The wind is Contrary we are beating off..d°—

14 This morning we enter'd the Bay Fundy, at 3.. O..Clock P: M: we pass'd Falmouth,[136] a small Village I am inform'd 15..or 18..sail of Vessels own'd at six o..Clock we were abreast of Long Island,[137] the wind is fair & fresh, we pass'd a number of small Islands, & Rocks to day, particularly Gannets Rock, which was Cover'd with white Fowl in such Numbers, that at a distance it looks like a small Hill, Cover'd with Snow, These Fowl are Call'd Gannets or Solen Geese, they are almost as large as our Common Geese—

15 The wind N: E.. we pass'd Peteet, Passage, to day.[138]

16 We pass'd high Islands the wind is fair for us to go to Cumberland, where we are order'd—

17 At 10..Clock A..M: we Came to Anchor in Cumberland Bay[139] about 4 Miles from the Town. the Country has a very pleasant appearance from where we lye, I am in a disagreeable Situation to-day, but there is not such a

135. Cape Sable Island, at the southwestern tip of Nova Scotia, not to be confused with Sable Island.

136. Falmouth—probably Yarmouth, on a small bay about 35 miles northwest of Cape Sable.

137. Long Island—between St. Mary's Bay and the Bay of Fundy.

138. Petit Passage separates Long Island from the peninsula which forms St. Mary's Bay.

139. Cumberland Basin—the northeast arm of Chignecto Bay, which communicates on the southwest with the Bay of Fundy. The town and Fort Cumberland were on the present site of Amherst.

scence of Slaughter, and Blood shed, as I was in this day
12 Months—

18 This day we apply'd to the Capt for leave to go on
shore but were refus'd.

19 We sent on Shore, & Bought 2..Fowl at 3.^s Lawful,
dear indeed—

20 We understand we are to sail the first fair wind, we
had a fine dinner to-day, one Fowl roasted, and another
Boil'd, with some pork and Potatoes, I made the best
meal that I had made for about six-months past, some
of the Inhabitants Brought some sheep along side to-day
for which they asked 48/p.^r piece for— New: England
Rum here is 21^s/4^d Lawful p Gallon.

21 This is the first day that has looked like Summer
since I came to Hallifax, we expect to sail from here to-
morrow, if the wind do favour us, every day seems a
month to me, I am very anxious to see my dear family
once more.

22 We hove up to day, and attempted to go down the
Bay, but the wind was so fresh against us that we were
obliged to come to anchor again, after falling down about
2.. Leagues.

23 The wind blows very Strong & Contrary against us.

24 We had a heavy gale of wind at S..W..last night,
it was suppos'd that we were in great danger, of driving
on shore, but by letting go another anchor, we Rode it
out without any damage, the wind remains Still Contrary—

25 At 12..O..Clock to,day we sail'd from Cumberland
with a fresh Breeze—

26 at 8..O Clock this morning we came to anchor at
the mouth of Anapolis Harbour,¹⁴⁰ seven Leagues from

140. An inlet of the Bay of Fundy, formerly Port Royal, at the mouth of the river
Annapolis.

the Town. from Fort Cumberland to this place is 30 Leagues, Anapolis lays on the east side of the Bay of Fundy, the Land at the Mouth of the Harbour, is very Mountanious, and Barren, as is almost all the Land on this Coast which I have seen,— at 3.. O.. Clock P: M: we weighed anchor and put up the River, and at 6..of the Clock, Came to Anchor at Anoplis Town, which appears to have 50..or 60 Houses in it, and a fortification; several miles before we come to the Town, there are some Inhabitants, On both sides the River, where there is several very good Orchards, the Land in general, is Cold, spruce bad looking Land, but there is very fine Marshes here, which makes a very pretty appearance, as we Sailed up the River—

27 We apply'd for leave to go ashore to-day, but was refus'd the weather is very pleasant— This afternoon I was seized with a violent pain in my head, and soon afterwards, I was seized with a sickness in my Stomach, after vomiting very heartily, I felt some rilief at my stomach, but the pain in my head increas'd, I was visited by the Surgeon of the ship, who said I was in a high fever, & urged me to take a puke, which Operated very well upon me, after heaving up a large quantity of Bile, I found myself much better, and a tolerable Nights Rest.

28 I find myself very weak and something feverish, I have had blood let, after which I felt much better, I am now in hopes of escaping a fever, which last Night I was much afraid of.

29 The weather is very fine, we heard to day, that the Milford ship of 28 Guns, has taken a Privateer of 18 Guns, belonging to Newbury Port, Commanded by one Tracy, we Bought some Veal to-day at 6ᵈ Sterling pᵣ pound, which is very Cheap, call'd here, at 7 O Clock

we left the Scarborough (P..M)   This morning we come to Sail with a good Breeze,   we are extremely well Treated by Capt Graves,[141] and the other officiers on Board   at 7 O Clock this evening we are abreast of Grand Manan.[142]

July 1 We have very little wind, the weather is very Cloudy,   at 12..O..Clock We have a brisk Breeze and a thick Fogg.

2 The weather remains Foggy,   we have a light Breeze; our General Course is S..S..W..but as the weather is thick, and we not willing to fall in with the Land, untill it is Clearer, we keep running off and on waiting for the weather to Clear up—

3 The weather is Clear,   we are in sight of Mount desert,[143] we have a fresh Breeze at N: W.. We are Stearing for Machias,[144]   at 3..O..Clock, as we were about entering Machias harbour, we espied three small sail to windward,   the Capt sent a Barge after them, at 6..O Clock the Barge Return'd with a small fishing Schooner as a prize,   they inform'd the Capt that there was a small privateer along shore, which fired several shot at them,   at seven O Clock the Capt order.^d about 20.. hands   on   board   the Schooner—Which they had taken, with some Blunder-Busses and ther arms, and sent them off, after the Privateer, which was in sight when the Schooner left the ship, which was about sun'set—

141. Doubtless this officer belonged to the famous naval family of Graves, but whether he was Sir Samuel Graves (1747?–1814) or one of his three brothers is uncertain. See *Dict. Nat. Biog.*, VIII, 440–1.

142. Grand Manan Island, about 20 miles long with an average width of 5 miles, lies due east of Annapolis harbor near the west coast of the Bay of Fundy.

143. Mount Desert Island lies about one mile off the Maine coast, about 75 miles from Grand Manan Island.

144. Machias bay or harbor is at the mouth of the Machias River. The town, a port of entry of Maine and the capital of Washington county, is situated 10 miles up the river.

4 We are Cruising up and down from Mount Desart to Machias waiting for the Schooner which went after the Privateer last Night, the weather is very fine— at 2.. O..Clock P: M: the Boats return'd with Two small fishing boats and two men we Anchor'd this Night by an Island, Called Mespecky[145]

5 about three Leagues from Machias Harbour, the boats were sent out this morning, and took a Small fishing schooner Laded with fish belonging to Portsmouth, one Fumell Master, by the writing found on Board, the people all left her, and went off in a Canoe, when they found they were like to be taken, we lay at anchor here all day.

6 This morning Cap.ᵗ Graves gave two of the men, who were taken in some of the fishing Boats, liberty to take one of the Same, (by the name of Wallas: & Dyer) belonging to Narriguagos,[146] a few leagues below Mount Desart; upon their promising to Carry Major Meigs, & myself to Casco, Bay, and at 10.. O..Clock, we left the ship and went up as far as Narriguagos, which is about 5 Leagues, and went on shore, to one Cap.ᵗ Wallas's where we were very genteelly entertained.

7 This day being Sunday, we went to meeting, the weather is very warm, we found the people all in arms, to oppose any boats from the men of War, that attempted to land—as they were apprehensive of their Coming to plunder for fresh Meat,—

145. Probably one of the islands off the coast of Maine between Indian River and Englishman Bay. An 18th century chart names the stretch of shoreline between these two points "Moose À Becky's Beach." Osgood Carleton's map of Maine, 1795, names the *channel* between this beach and the islands "Mispeckey Channel."

146. Narraguagus here refers to a settlement near the mouth of the Narraguagus River, indicated on Des Barres' chart of the coast of Maine, 1776. On this chart the river empties into what was called Naragnagus Bay, now a part of Pleasant Bay. Dearborn should have located Narraguagus *above* "Mount Desart" (Mount Desert Island) instead of a few leagues below it. By water, the distance from Pleasant Bay to Casco Bay is about 100 miles.

8 At seven O..Clock in the morning we sailed for Casco: Bay, we made no Harbour this Night, we are off, abreast of Mount Desart,.

9 We have a light Breeze this morning at S..W.. we pass'd the Bay, of Jericho this forenoon, this afternoon, we pass'd the Isle, of Holt,[147] we saw a Number of very Large whales to day, at 5..O..Clock this afternoon, we pass'd Ponabscutt Harbour,[148] a few Leagues without this Harbour, is a number of small Islands, Call'd the Silley Islands,[149] at 9..O..Clock this evening, we came to an Anchor in a small bay—Called Talland Harbour,[150] where there are several families— it is on the West side of Ponobscut Bay—

10 This morning we set sail at Sun-rise, but the Fogg being very thick we were obliged to put back to the same Harbour again— we went on shore and got some milk and Greens, at 9..O..Clock the weather Cleared up a little and we put to sea, but soon after we put out, it came on very foggy again, it was so Foggy and Calm, that we concluded to go back into the Harbour again—where we came to Anchor at 2..O..Clock P: M: Maj.ʳ Meigs & I agree'd to take our Land-Tacks on board and quit the Boat— We walked 2 miles & Came to a river, Called George's River, we Cross'd the same and Came, to a Village Called George's Town,[151] we walked Two Miles, and Came to a river Call'd Madamcook, which we Cross'd and Came to a Village call'd Madamcook,[152]

147. Isle au Haut, opposite Deer Island.

148. Penobscot Bay.

149. Probably the group including Seal, Wooden Ball, Matinicus, Criehaven and Green islands.

150. Tenants Harbor—about 12 miles south-southwest of Rockland, Maine.

151. St. George's River opens into Muscongus Bay. The village is about 9 miles southwest of Rockland, Maine.

152. Madam Cook—Madumcook or Medumcook—between St. George's River and Broad Cove.

where there lives 40 families, we Tarried here one Night.

11 We started this morning for Broad Bay,[153] which is six miles distant from here, at 9 O..Clock we arrived at said Bay—where there is fine settlements, the inhabitants seems to live very well; we were very Genteely Treated by Esq: Thomas, of said place, who I found was Nephew to Gen! Thomas[154] in the Continental Army, said Thomas favour'd us with his Horse to Carry our Packs as far as Damascoty[155] which is eight Miles, we Cross'd Demoscoty River & walked Two miles to one Barkers Tavern, in a place Called Newcastle,[156] here Stayed all night,.

12 We hired Horses to go to Sheepscutt River,[157] where we arrived at 9 O..Clock; we sent the Horses back again and Cross'd the River called Sheepscut, and walked one mile, and met some people to work on the High:way, we were asked into a house to eat some dinner, here we hired Two Horses to go to Kennebeck River, which is 15 miles, we Cross'd Kennebeck River, at sun-set & walked one mile, then Lodged at M: Lamberts Tavern,—[158]

13 We hired said Lamberts Brother & Horses to Carry us to Falmouth, at 9..O..Clock we Started, at 11..

153. Now called Broad Cove.

154. Maj. Gen. John Thomas (1724-1776) of Massachusetts. He was sent north to replace Wooster as commander of the Canada expedition, but died during the retreat. Dict. Am. Biog., XVIII, 438.

155. Damariscotta, on the east bank of the Damariscotta River opposite Newcastle, Maine.

156. Newcastle, Lincoln co., Maine, on the west bank of the Damariscotta River about 15 miles from the sea.

157. The Sheepscott River enters the ocean about 10 miles southeast of Bath, Maine.

158. Lambert's tavern is located on High Street, Bath, Maine. It was built in 1762 by Joseph Lambert who occupied it and kept a tavern. The Lambert property was sold to Jonas Hagan whose descendents now occupy it as a farm.

O..Clock, we Cross'd Browns Ferry on Stephen's River,[159] at 12..O..Clock we arrived at Brumswick[160] which is 30 Miles from Casco, he[re] we dined, here are a number of elegant Buildings, & the ruin of an old Fort, Called Brumswick Fort, at 4..O..Clock PM.. we left Brumswick, after passing thro, Yarmouth woods, which is 10 Miles, we pass'd through North-Yarmouth,[161] and at Sun'set we arrived at Nights Tavern, which is 5 Miles to the eastward of Falmouth, and there put up and Tarryed all night—

14 We started early this morning for Falmouth,[162] when we arrived at Falmouth, there we found a sloop ready to sail, in which several Masters of Vessels belonging to New England, who came from Hallifax, were going Passengers   We also embarked on Board said sloop, & at 10..O..Clock sailed for Portsmouth, having but very little wind & that quite Contrary, we made but small headway—

15 This morning we are a Breast of Wood-Island,[163] at 5..O..Clock P..M: we are abreast of old York, and the wind ahead—

159. Stevens River was the name applied to the head of New Meadows River, an arm of the sea reaching north from Small Point to within a mile and a half of Merry-meeting Bay. The old road from Bath to Brunswick crossed the river (at Brown's Ferry) close to the site of the Penobscot Shore Line R. R. The ferry was about 2½ miles from Bath; here the river was about 40 rods wide. W. D. Williamson, *The History of the State of Maine*, (Hallowell, 1832), I., 33.

160. Brunswick, Cumberland co., Maine is on the right bank of the Andro-scoggin River 9 miles west of Bath and about 29 miles from Portland. The fort was old Fort George, also called Pejepscot, built on the remains of Fort Andros. The fort was dismantled in 1737. H. E. Dunnack, *Maine Forts* (Augusta, Me., 1924), 232.

161. Probably Yarmouthville, Cumberland co., Maine, about a mile up the Royal River from Casco Bay.

162. That part of Falmouth which Dearborn mentions is now a part of the city of Portland. In 1776 the town was located on the south side of the peninsula. Portland harbor was called Falmouth harbor. The present town of Falmouth is five miles north of Portland.

163. Wood Island—at the entrance of Saco River in Maine.

16 This morning we are a Breast of the Isle-of Shoals,[164] we have a small Breeze and are Running for the Lighthouse in Portsmouth-Harbour, which place rejoiced me very much to see once more, at 10..O..Clock, A: M: I arrived at Portsmouth[165] to my Great joy, and at sunset arrived safe at my own House, at Nottingham,[166] & found my wife well, my Children alive, & my friends in General, well.

Finis.

March 25.th 1777—[167]

164. The Isles of Shoals are eight small islands 10 miles south-southeast of Portsmouth, New Hampshire.

165. Portsmouth, Rockingham co., New Hampshire, on the right bank of the Piscataqua River about 3 miles from the ocean.

166. Nottingham, Rockingham co., New Hampshire, about 18 miles northwest of Portsmouth.

167. This date may indicate the completion of this journal by the copyist.

The Burgoyne Campaign

IN *1777 a reinforced British army launched a vigorous offensive into New York from Canada. The first force, under Burgoyne, followed the Lake Champlain route. The second, under St. Leger, entered the state by way of Lake Ontario. At Albany the two commanders were to meet and plan further moves after consulting Howe, whose army was then in possession of New York City. St. Leger was stopped at Fort Stanwix; and as Burgoyne marched slowly southward, he met with a determined resistance which increased steadily as homesteads and farms were laid waste. Meanwhile, Howe had sailed off to take Philadelphia, leaving too small a force behind him to relieve the pressure on Burgoyne. The American army under Gates and Arnold, its numbers swelled by an aroused militia, halted the invasion. After repeated skirmishes and two pitched battles, Burgoyne's army was cut off from its supplies, surrounded, and forced to surrender at Saratoga.*

[1776] JULY 25 I set out for New york where our main army then lay, to settle my accounts, I remaind at N york until the enimy took possession of Long Island,[1] & our army was about quiting the City, & then returnd home:—

1. The battle of Long Island, in which the British under Gen. Sir William Howe defeated the Continental Army under Washington, took place on August 27, 1776. By the middle of September the British were in possession of New York City. Washington fell back to White Plains and later crossed the Hudson into New Jersey.

Decem[r] 30th I set out for Philadelphia to settle some accounts with congress, I was obliged to go to Baltimore in Maryland, Congress having retreeted from Philadelphia to that place.[2]—I stayd there 10 days & returnd home.

[1777] 24th of March I was Exchanged[3] & appointed Maj[r] to the third N: H. Reg[t] Commanded by Col[o] Scammell.[4]

10th of May I set out for, & the 20th ariv'd at Ticonderoga[5]— the first of July Gen[l] Burguoyn[6] came against Ticonderoga with a Learge fleet & Army, & began to erect batteries against several parts of our works, the

2. The Continental Congress adjourned in Philadelphia on Dec. 12 and reconvened in Baltimore on the 20th. *Journals of the Continental Congress* (Washington, 1906), VI, 1015, 1027-8.

3. In 18th century warfare officers usually were paroled soon after being captured. They were allowed to return home free men, but could not engage in any activity against the enemy until they had been exchanged, i.e., until their respective commanders had agreed to cancel the parole obligation of paroled officers of equal rank from either side. Paroles usually were strictly observed. In this instance Washington had exchanged a paroled British captain for Capt. Dearborn, and both officers were able to resume military activity. Dearborn's promotion was dated March 19, 1777, according to Heitman, to rank from Nov. 8, 1776.

4. Col. Alexander Scammell (d. 1781) had been a major of New Hampshire militia and aide-de-camp to Gen. Sullivan before he was given a regiment in November, 1776. He became adjutant-general of the Continental Army early in 1778 and held the post three years. He was in command of the 1st New Hampshire Regiment at Yorktown when he was wounded and captured. See Dearborn's entry for Oct. 1, 1781. Heitman, *op. cit.*, 483-4.

5. Fort Ticonderoga occupied a point of land on the west bank of Lake Champlain at the outlet of Lake George. It was built by the French in the 1750's and was captured by the British under Amherst in 1759. At the beginning of the War of Independence it was in a dilapidated state of repair and fortified by a very small garrison; it fell an easy victim to the Continentals under Ethan Allen and Benedict Arnold. When Dearborn reached there in 1777 the old French works had been repaired and re-enforced with new earthworks and blockhouses. The garrison consisted of about 2,500 poorly armed Continentals and 900 raw Militia. Justin Winsor, ed., *Narrative and Critical History of America* (Boston & New York, 1889), VI, 295, ff.

6. His first expedition from Canada southward having failed in 1776, Burgoyne planned a new one for 1777. Commanding a force of about 10,000, he left St. Johns in June and moved up Lake Champlain and took Ticonderoga. After a long delay he advanced uncertainly towards Albany. Howe failed to co-operate with him and at the same time left Clinton in New York with too small a force to risk a march up the Hudson. The American army meanwhile grew steadily until it numbered 17,000. After

5th a councel of war was held in which it was determind
to Evacuate the post next morning before day brake,—
early on the morning of the 6th we left the place, the Enimies pursued us by land & water, destroyd all our baggage that was sent to Skeensborouh[7] by water.—a learge
body of Light troops pursued by land, & early on the
morning of the 7th fell in with our rear guard & after an
action of half an hour, in which they met with considerable loss our troops ware obliged to retreet— our Loss
was about 300 kill'd & taken— our main body was at
two great a distance from the rear guard to go to their
relief in season— our main Army now found themselves
obliged to perform a Circuitus march of about 150 miles
thro what is calld the Green Mountains to Saratogia,[8]
almost totally destitute of any kind of provisions or any
other necessaries of life:[9]— that part of our army that
went by water, by the way of Skeensborough with the
baggage, after loosing the baggage ware pursued by a
body of the Enemy to fort Ann[10] where two or three severe scurmishes happn'd, in which the Enimy went of [f]
second best, in one of these scurmishes the brave Capt

suffering heavy losses in men and provisions at Bennington and at Freeman's Farm,
Burgoyne began to retreat. At Saratoga he was surrounded and forced to surrender.
He returned to England at once where he faced a Parliamentary inquiry. *Dict. Nat.
Biog.*, III, 340-2.

7. Skenesboro (now Whitehall, New York) stood on the west bank of Wood Creek
near its junction with the Poultney River. The latter empties into Lake Champlain.
Here the passage was navigable for batteaux.

8. Saratoga stood on the present site of Schuylerville, New York, on the west bank
of the Hudson River near the mouth of the Fishkill River or Creek.

9. The garrison at Ticonderoga, about 3,000 effectives under Maj. Gen. Arthur St.
Clair, lacked provisions to withstand a siege, so a retreat southward was ordered.
The main body marched by way of Hubbardton and Castleton; about 500 went by boat
to Skenesboro and beyond. The rear guard action took place between three American
regiments which had stopped at Hubbardton contrary to orders and British detachments under Generals Fraser and Riedesel. H. Nickerson, *The Turning Point of the Revolution* (Boston, 1928), 144-54.

10. Fort Anne, on the line of march to the Hudson, was 11 miles below Skenesboro
on the west bank of Wood Creek.

Weare[11] of the third N. H. Reg[t] received a wound of which he afterwards died.

the 12 of July our main body ariv'd at Hudson river oposite Saratogia, ware there reinforc'd by several Reg[t] of Continental troops & a considerable body of Millitia, some part of our army march'd up the river as far as fort Edward,[12] after remaining there several days finding the Enimy ware advancing, our whole force was Collected at a place called Moses creek[13] about five miles below fort Edward, where we remaind a number of days & then retreeted to Saratogea, had several scurmishes with the Enimies advanc'd parties, consisting mostly of Indians & their more savage brothers, the tories   after remaining two days at Saratogea we retreeted to Stillwater[14] where we ariv'd the 3[d] of August.

August 3[d] 1777—

this morning our army ariv'd at Stillwater & Incamp'd

4th we are Begining to Erect some fortifycations to Day.

5th I am on the advanced Piquit to Day.

6th it is in Genr! Orders for a Company of Light Infantry to be form'd from Each Continental Regiment Immediately.

7th Nothing New to Day.

8th an Indian Scalp was Brought in to Day By a Party of our men which is a Rareety with us—   Genr! Arnold march'd this Day with Genr! Larnerds[15] Brigade for fort

---

11. Capt. Richard Weare died August 2, 1777, of the wound he received on July 8 at Fort Anne. Heitman, *op. cit.*, 577.

12. Fort Edward stood on the east bank of the Hudson River 16 miles south of Fort Anne. It was built in 1755.

13. Moses Creek or Mosses Creek, also called Mosses Kill on contemporary maps, flows into the Hudson from the northeast about 5 miles south of Fort Edward.

14. Stillwater is on the west side of the Champlain Canal about 23 miles above Albany.

15. Ebenezer Learned (1728–1801) of Massachusetts was commissioned a brigadier-general in April, 1777. After relieving Fort Stanwix, his brigade was active in the

Stanwix[16] which has Been Beseiged some time By a Party [of] British Troops & their Brothers the Savages under Command of Genr! S! Ledger[17]—

9th Nothing New—

10th from the appearences of thing[s] we are about to Retreet further Down the River—

11th D°—D°—

12th D°—D°—

13th the Army is ordered to march to morrow morning at 4 O Clock, the Tents to Be Struck at 2. this Evining the Above order was Countermanded.

14th the army is ordered to march to morrow morning at gun fire tomorrow morning—

15th we march'd this morning about 6 miles to a Place Call'd fort Abraham[18] & incamp'd & Drew Tents for the New hamps! Battallions which are the first we have had Since we Left Ty[19]—

16th we Lay still to Day.

17th we are Ordered to march to morrow morning—

18th the army march'd this morning,— Genr! Poors Brigade[20] march'd up mohawke River about 7 miles

battles of Sept. 19 and Oct. 7, as well as in the final capture of Burgoyne's army. Learned resigned from the army in March, 1778, because of ill health. *Dict. Am. Biog.*, XI, 77.

16. Fort Stanwix, later named Fort Schuyler, was built on the right bank of the Mohawk River in 1758, near the present site of Rome, New York.

17. Lt. Col. Barry St. Leger (*c.*1737–1789) was brevetted a brigadier-general for the command of an expedition designed to co-operate with Burgoyne's advance on Albany. St. Leger, with British regulars, Tories and Indians marched by way of the St. Lawrence, Oswego and the Mohawk River. He was unable to take Fort Stanwix, although at Oriskany he succeeded in cutting off reinforcements sent out to strengthen the post, and was forced to retreat to Canada. Nickerson, *op. cit.*, 194, *ff.*

18. Fort Abraham probably refers to a small stockaded Indian settlement in the vicinity of Albany, named after Abraham, a chief of the upper Mohawk Castle. *Docs. Rel. to the Col. Hist. of . . . New-York* (Albany 1855), VI, 870, *passim.*

19. Ticonderoga.

20. Enoch Poor (1736–1780) of New Hampshire became a brigadier-general in February, 1777. His brigade suffered heavy losses at Saratoga. After wintering at Valley Forge, he accompanied Sullivan on his Indian expedition of 1779. *Dict. Am. Biog.*, XV, 69.

& Cross'd it at a Place Call'd Lowdens ferry[21] & incamp'd. the other Part of the army incamp'd at what is Call'd the sprouts, which is the Place where Mohawk River Emties into Hudsons River in three Different Branches. this Place is about 9 miles from Albany—

19th Genr! Gates[22] takes Command of the Northern army this Day which I think will Put a New face upon our affairs.

20th we have the Glorious News this Day of the Signal victory that Genr! Stark[23] has Obtain'd over the Enimy at Benington Where he has kill'd & taken about 1200

21. Loudon's Ferry, named after the British commander Earl Loudon, was built under the direction of Maj. Gen. William Johnson in 1755 five miles from the mouth of the Mohawk River. The site is now a part of the Erie barge canal. The original military route from Albany to Montreal, which crossed the Mohawk at "the sprouts," included four fords, all of which were dangerous during high water, and sometimes impassable. The British under Johnson established Loudon's Ferry and fortified it from 1755 to 1768. The Continental army occupied the old British fortifications at the ferry from 1775 to 1782. A bridge replaced the ferry in 1795.

22. Horatio Gates (c.1728/29–1806) had served in the British army from an early age until 1765, when he retired a major. In 1772 he settled in Virginia. Espousing the rebel cause, he was commissioned adjutant-general of the Continental army with the rank of brigadier-general. In 1776 he was made a major-general to take command of the troops retreating from Canada, but he acted under Schuyler. The next spring he was ordered to replace Schuyler in command of the northern department, but did not finally relieve him until August, 1777. He quarrelled with the abler Arnold who actually led the troops against Burgoyne and forced his surrender to Gates. Congress elected Gates to the Board of War, where he became involved in the Conway cabal against Washington. In 1778 he again commanded the northern department, but was transferred to the eastern department. He retired in 1780, but in June of that year he was ordered to take command of the southern department. His defeat at Camden caused him to be replaced by Greene. He again retired until 1782, when he joined Washington at Newburgh. *Dict. Am. Biog.*, VII, 184–8.

23. John Stark (1728–1822) had served in the French and Indian War as an officer of rangers. He was appointed colonel of a regiment of New Hampshire patriots (in which Dearborn was a captain) that converged on Boston in 1775. Sent to Canada in May, 1776, he accompanied the American retreat that summer. He resigned his commission in March, 1777, but the New Hampshire General Court soon asked Stark to lead a brigade of militia to defend Vermont against Burgoyne's invasion. He attacked Col. Baum near Bennington and captured almost his whole detachment of 800. Stark then was made a brigadier-general in the Continental Army. He captured Fort Edward and blocked Burgoyne's retreat. Twice he commanded the northern department. *Ibid.* XVII, 530–1.

men— Besides a Large Quantity of Baggage & 4 Brass field Peices.[24]

21[t] I went to Albany this Day to take Care of the Effects of the Brave Cap[t] Weare who Died a few Days since of the wound he Receivd in the action at fort ann the 8th of July—

22[d] I returned to Camp from albany this Day— this afternoon we are Join'd By 2 N. york Regiments. Van Courtlandts & Livingstanes.[25]

23[d] the two Regiments that Join'd us yesterday are ordered to march to fort Stanwix to Join Genr[l] Arnold—

24th Nothing New to Day—

25 this Day we are Informed that the Enimy made an attempt to storm fort Stanwix But ware Repuls'd with Considerable Loss in Concequence of which they Immediately Raisd the seage.[26]

the 26th 27th 28th Nothing New—

29th the two N. york Regiments above mentioned Returnd this Day & Join'd our Brigade.

30th Col[o] Morgan from Virginia with 400 Riflemen Join'd us to Day—

31[t] Genr[l] Arnold with Genr[l] Larnards Brigade Returnd from fort Stanwix & Joind us this Day.

24. The battle of Bennington took place about 5 miles south of that hamlet. Burgoyne had sent out a foraging party of 800 men under Col. Baum to capture rebel supplies at Bennington. On August 16, Gen. Stark met the party with 2,000 men and all but annihilated it. Reinforcements which Baum had ordered on first learning of Stark's presence came up later in the day under Col. von Breymann. But Stark, too, had been strengthened with a fresh regiment under Col. Seth Warner, and von Breymann's force of about 650 was routed. The American casualties were about 30 killed and 40 wounded. This battle was the first real check which Burgoyne had received. Nickerson, *op. cit.*, 233–63 .

25. Col. Philip Van Cortlandt commanded the 2nd New York regiment, and Col. Henry Beekman Livingston commanded the 4th. Heitman, *op. cit.*, 354, 555.

26. The determination and courage of the garrison of Fort Stanwix under Col. Peter Gansevoort held off St. Leger's siege until a relief detachment could be sent out. Arnold, in command of the party, sent on ahead a half-wit and a friendly Indian to inform St. Leger's Indians that he was coming with a great army. The ruse worked, the British were unable to hold their allies together, and St. Leger was obliged to retreat towards Canada. Nickerson, *op. cit.*, 270–5.

Septem^r 1^t 2^d 3^d Nothing New—

4th a Scout of 40 men under Command of Capt fry^{27} of Col^o Scammels Regi^t was Surpris'd By a Body of Indians & others Consisting in the whole of about 300. we Lost out [of] our scout 9 men kild & taken—

5th we are makeing all Possible Preparation to meet the Enimy, our Brigad is mustered to Day By Col^o Varrick^{28}—

6th we are Ordered to hold our Selves in Rediness to march at a munites warning to meet the Enimy. we are Joind By a Conciderable Body of Millitia from Connecticut, Both foot & horse.—

7th we Expect Every hour to have orders for marching — this Evining we Receivd orders to Strike our Tents at gun fire to morrow morning & march towards the Enimy—

8th we Cross'd the River & march'd about 8 miles to Day & Incamp'd—

9th we march'd about 10 miles this morning to Stillwater & Incamp'd on the Hights— a flag Came to Genr^l Gates to Day from Genr^l Burguoyn with a Doct^r & some Baggage & Nessesaries for their sick & wounded taken at Benington.

10 we are Begining to fortify on the hights—

11th the army is as yesterday. I am appointed to the Command of 300 Light Infantry who are Draughted from the Several Regements in the Northern army & to act in Conjunction with Col^o Morgan's Corps of Riflemen.

27. Capt. Isaac Frye of the 3rd New Hampshire regiment, formerly a regimental quartermaster. Later he was transferred to the 1st New Hampshire regiment and was brevetted a major at the close of the war. Heitman, *op. cit.*, 239.

28. Lt. Col. Richard Varick (d. 1831) had been aide-de-camp to Gen. Schuyler and was now deputy commissary-general of musters. He became an aide-de-camp to Gen. Arnold in 1780, then joined Washington's staff as private secretary to the commander-in-chief, which position he retained until Washington's death. *Ibid.*, 559.

12th I Join'd the Light Infantry this morning which with the Rifle men are incamp'd about 2 miles advanc'd of the Main army.

13th this morning the whole army advanc'd about 4 miles to a Place Call'd Beemes's Hights[29] a very advantageous Post & incamp'd.

14th L[t] Col? Butler[30] of the Riflemen & myself with 200 men went out as a scout Near to Saratoga to Indevour to find out the situation of the Enimy But Being misled By Our guide we made No great Discoveries, & tarried all Night.

15th After Reconoyrtering the woods Round Saratoga we Returnd to Camp—

16th from some Intiligence we Receivd Last Night we Expected to have been Attacted this morning, But ware Disappointed—Genr! Stark Joind us to Day with his Brigade from Benington.

17th the Enimy are advancing towards us.

18th we march'd with 3000 men to attact the Enimy— we fell in with some small Parties & took about 30 Prison[rs]

19th hereing this morning that the Enimy ware advancing, the Rifle & Light Infantry Corps turnd out to meet the Enimy & about 2 miles from our Camp we fell in with their advanced Guard & attacted them[31] about 12

29. After Arnold and Learned had joined Gates, and Morgan had come in with 400 riflemen, Gates was encouraged to advance his army. He first moved to Stillwater, 13 miles north of the Mohawk River. Entrenchments were begun, but it was decided that the terrain was not suitable for a strong defence. The army was therefore moved 3 miles north to Bemis Heights, named for a tavern keeper who lived on the spot. New fortifications were immediately begun under the direction of Kosciusko, the Polish engineer.

30. Lt. Col. Richard Butler (1743–1791) belonged to Morgan's riflemen. Later he served under Wayne, and after the war became an Indian agent. Dict. Am. Biog., III, 366.

31. The first battle of Freeman's Farm took place on the plain between the American defences and those of the opposing forces; the British had occupied Wilbur's Basin 2 miles to the north. Freeman's Farm lay to the left of the American position, and was defended by Arnold with Dearborn's detachment and Morgan's riflemen.

O Clock,   after fighting about half an hour Being over
Powerd with Numbers we ware Obliged to Retire to A
height, about 50 rods & there weare Reinforc'd With
Col? Cilleys Regiment³², who attacted a Body of the
Enimy with a great Deal of Spirit,   I Ran to his assist-
ance with the Light Infantry, But he was Obliged to Retreet Before I Came up.—Col? Scammells & Hales³³ Regiments then Came to our Assistence   it was Now about 2
O Clock P. M. when a very Heavy fire Commenced on
both Sides, which Continued until Dark.   the Enimy
Brought almost their whole force against us, together
with 8 Peices of Artilery. But we who had Something
more at Stake than fighting for six Pence Pʳ Day kept our
ground til Night, Closed the scene, & then Both Parties
Retire'd.³⁴   our Loss was about 180 kill'd 250 wounded &
20 taken Prisoners.   among the Dead was the Brave Lͭ
Col?s Colborn & Adams & Capͭ Bell Lͭ Thomas³⁵ all of
Newhampshire,   the Loss of those Brave men are very
greatly Lamented in the Army, But as it was a Debt that
they & Every one owe their Country I Beleave they Paid
it with Cherefullness.—the Loss the Enimy Sustaind this
Day from Best Accounts, was about 300 kill'd & 500
wounded & about 20 Prisoners.³⁶   on this Day has Been

32. Col. Joseph Cilley (d. 1799) commanded the 1st New Hampshire regiment.
Heitman, *op. cit.*, 155.

33. Col. Nathan Hale (d. 1780) commanded the 2nd New Hampshire regiment.
He had been captured at Hubbardton on July 7, and he died in prison. *Ibid.*, 267.

34. Although the British had been driven back through the woods by Dearborn
and Morgan, Burgoyne rallied them and made a second attack, reinforced by Riedesel
with fresh troops. The Continentals were finally driven in towards their center, only
after they had taken a heavy toll with their superior marksmanship. Nickerson,
op. cit., 307–19.

35. Lt. Col. Andrew Colburn of the 3rd New Hampshire regiment; Lt. Col. Winborn
Adams of the 2nd New Hampshire regiment; Capt. Frederick M. Bell of the same, who
is reported as having died of his wounds on Oct. 9; Lt. Joseph M. Thomas (not Dearborn's ensign on the Quebec expedition) of the 3rd regiment. Heitman, *op. cit.*, *passim*.

36. Nickerson's figures are nearly 600 British killed, wounded, or taken, and 320
Americans similarly lost. Nickerson, *op. cit.*, 319.

fought one of the Greatest Battles that Ever was fought in Amarrca, & I Trust we have Convincd the British Butchers that the Cowardly yankees Can & when their is a Call for it, will, fight—

20th We Expect a General Battle this Day,—but No fighting, to Day—

21^t the Enimy have Retired about 1 mile from the field of Battle & are fortifying. our army are also for- tifying—

22^d we hourly Expect a General Battle.

23^d about 100 Onyda Indians who Joind us the Next Day after the Battle, have Brought in more or Less Pris- oners Every Day—

24th A Conciderable Body of Millitia have Joind us to Day from Different Parts—

25th we supprisd a Small Piquit of the Enimies—

26th we toock 18 Prisoners this Day—

27th Nothing New to Day—

28th Several Deserters Came in from the Enemy.

29th 10 Deserters Came in—

30th 7 Prisoners Ware Brought in this morning— Our Camp was Allarm'd this morning By hearing that the Enimy ware Comeing out in three Collums to attact us, our army in General seem anxious for an other Battle. No fighting to Day— our army has Been Reinforcd since the Battle of the 19th Ins^t with at Least 3000 Millitia who appear in high spirits.[37]

Octob^r 1^t 1777 this month Begins with Pleasant weather & a fine Prospect Before us, & if Mr Burguoyne & his army are Not subdued this month, it will [not] be for want of spirit in us, or for the want of that Divine Assistence which has Not faild us heretofore.

37. Of this number 2,000 were the troops under Gen. Lincoln who joined Gates; the others were militia coming in from New England and New York. *Ibid.*, 326.

2^d we toock about 40 Prisoners. we had also a Body of Millitia Joind in.

3^d we toock several Prisoners.

4th Several Deserters Came to us.

5 we toock a Number of Prisoners.

6 I went out a scout with Col? Morgan & 800 men. we went in the Rear of the Enimy toock 7 Prisoners & as we Returnd, Night Comeing on, together with a heavy Rain, we got Bewildered in the woods & Stayd all Night.

7th we Came in this morning from our scout & By the Time we had Refresh'd our Selves, which was about 12 O Clock we found a Body of the Enimy ware Advancing towards our Lines. the Rifle men & Light Infantry ware sent Immediately Round upon their Right flank. Some other Regiments ware sent out to meet them. a scattering fire Commencd of Both Cannon & musketry, & about 3 O Clock Scammells Cilleys & Hales Rigements formed a line at ½ after 3 & about 4 O Clock the Battle Began Between the 3 Last mentioned Regime^{nts} & the Enimys main Body— we with the Rifle men & Light Infantry fell on upon the Enimys Right flank & Partly in their Rear, which soon Obliged them to Quit their heavy Artillery & a Conciderable Number of waggons with Amonition & other stores & at the same time finding us in their Rear, their main Body Gave way, Leaving several other Peices of Cannon. they then all Retreeted with great Precepitation & Confusion, we followed them about ¾ of a mile in which they attempted several times to make a stand But Could Not until they got within their out Lines. in this time we ware Reinforcd By several Regiments, Immediately after the Enimy got into their out works we attackd & Carried them, found their Tents standing & several Peices of Artillery in their Lines, & several field officers & a Number of officers &

soldiers. the Enimy Retired Down Near the River into their strongest works:[38]—we toock to Day Si[r] Frances Clark wounded, Adedecamp to Genr[l] Burguoyn, Maj[r] Aclan[39] of the granedeers, Maj[r] Williams of the artillery, & several Hushen field Officers & several other officers of Different Rank. & about 240 Rank & file. their loss in kill'd was very Conciderable, among which was Genr[l] Fraser[40]— Our Loss was very inconsiderable Except that of Genr[l] Arnold's Receiveing a wound in his Leg in forceing the Enemies Lines.[41] we Remain'd all Night in their Lines. we toock 8 Peices of Brass Cannon to Day in the whole 2 of which ware Double fortify'd 12 Pounds.

8th this morning the Rifle men & Light Infantry & several other Rigements march'd in the Rear of the Enimy Expecting they ware Retreeting But found they ware Not. there has Been scurmishing all Day in which Genr[l] Lincoln[42] got wounded in the Leg. a Large Number of the Enimy Deserted to us to Day—

38. In this second battle of Freeman's Farm, Dearborn played an important part. Morgan's riflemen had struck first at the British right flank and routed it. Then they moved around to the enemy's rear. The British right began changing front to oppose them when Dearborn's riflemen broke up this counter move and drove them back. Meanwhile the British left had given way, and Arnold was leading a brigade against the center. In less than an hour Burgoyne's advance detachment of 1500 was in wild flight back to their breastworks, and during the night the British began a general retreat. *Ibid.*, 361–70.

39. Sir Francis Clarke died of his wounds; he was shot while carrying Burgoyne's order to retreat, and the order did not get through. Major John Dyke Acland, who had commanded the grenadiers on the British left, was captured; he died the following year as a result of a duel. *Ibid.*, 361, 364.

40. Brig. Gen. Simon Fraser (*c.*1729–1777) had served with the Scots brigade in Holland, and with other regiments at Louisburg and Quebec. He was a close friend of Burgoyne and one of his ablest officers. His effectiveness in this battle was such that Arnold asked Morgan to order his best sharpshooters to pick him off. One of them succeeded, and Fraser died the next morning. *Ibid.*, 116–7, 363.

41. Arnold had his horse killed under him and his leg broken by the last volley fired by the Germans as they retreated. This was the same leg that had been wounded at Quebec. Arnold was carried back to the American camp. *Ibid.*, 367.

42. Benjamin Lincoln (1733–1810) had been a militia officer in Massachusetts and a member of the Provincial Congress before the Revolution. Appointed a brigadier-general early in 1776, he commanded the militia regiments supporting Washington

9th this morning we found the Enimy had Evaquated the whole of their Lines & had Left about 500 Sick & wounded on the ground & a Considerable Quantity of Provisions. the Rifle men & Light Infantry ware sent Immediately to take Possession of their works we march.d about one mile above their Lines & a heavy Rain Comeing on we Stay.d all Night. the Enimy March.d about 4 miles & Incampd Near Saratoga, where they found Genr! Fellows[43] with a body of Millitia in their front—

10th there is some Cannonadeing at Saratoga this morning Between M! Burguoyn & Genr! Fellows. our army march.d this morning for Saratoga where we found the Enimy in great Confusion. they had Left Large Quantity of Baggage Scattered along the Rode & 1 Brass 12 Pounder which they Had Buried in the ground— But was found A heavy Cannonadeing was kept up all Day — & a scattering fire of musketry—

11th this morning at Day Break the Rifle men & Light Infantry, march.d over fish Creek,[44] & fell in with the Enimys guards in a thick fogg, who kill.d 1 L! of ours & 2 men, we then found our selves Close to the Enimy works where their whole Army Lay & we about 400 strong. the Enimy on one side & a River which we had Cross.d on scattering Logs on the other side. we Remain.d in this situation about 2 hours Before we ware Reinforc.d. we

around New York. The next year he was made a major-general in the Continental service and commanded the Vermont militia that attacked Burgoyne's detachment near Bennington. The wound here mentioned kept him out of service for ten months; then he was given command of the army in the southern department. In May, 1780, he and his army were captured at Charleston, S. C. Exchanged in November, he rejoined Washington and participated in the siege of Yorktown. From 1781 to 1783 he was Secretary of War. *Dict. Am. Biog.*, XI, 259–61.

43. Gates had posted two bodies of militia to block Burgoyne's northward retreat. The Massachusetts contingent of 1300 was under Brig. Gen. John Fellows (d. 1808), who was ordered to march down the Hudson and post his troops at Saratoga. When Burgoyne approached the latter place, Fellows crossed the river and took up a stronger position.

44. Fish Creek was just below the British defences at Saratoga.

Ware then Reinforcd with Genr! Larnards Brigade, the
Enimy Began a Brisk Canonade upon us, kill.d Several
men But we held the ground & Began to heave up up
some works, we toock a Number of Prisoners to Day—
this afternoon Genr! Poors & Patterson's Brigade[45] Came
over fish Creek with some field Peices & Joind us—

12ᵗʰ Matters Stand much as they Did yesterday. about
20 Deserters Came in to Day,— the Rifle men & Light Infantry toock Post in the Rear of the Enimy & incamp.d—

13ᵗʰ the Light Troops mooved to the main River[46] in
the Rear of the Enimy, Left some small Parties to watch
the Roads & paths while the Remainder of Light Troops
Reconoytered the Enimys Camp. we toock 15 Prisoners
and went to what is Call.d Jones.s mill, & Eat. Breakfast, & then moovd Down Near Genr! Poors Brigade
who Lay on the Enimys Right wing & Partly in their
rear & incamp.d. A heavy Cannonade is kept up on Both
sides [to] Day & a scattering fire of muskettry—

14ᵗʰ at 10 O Clock to Day a flag Came from Genr! Burguoyn with some Proposels of Caputilation in Consiquence of which a Sessation of armes was agree.d on until Sun Set in which Time Several flags Pass.d Between
Genr! Gates & Burguoyne—

15ᵗʰ in Consiquence of the flags yesterday, a Sessation
of Arms is agreed on to Day—

16ᵗʰ there is a Caputilation agreed on—.

17ᵗʰ this Day the Great M! Burguoyn with his whole
Army Surrendered themselves as Prisoners of war with
all their Publick Stores, & after Grounding their armes,
march.d of[f] for New England, the greatest Conquest
Ever known.

45. John Paterson (1744–1808) was appointed a brigadier-general in February, 1777.
After the Saratoga campaign, he rejoined Washington at Valley Forge and spent most
of the rest of the war on the Hudson. *Dict. Am. Biog.*, XIV, 292–3.

46. Hudson River.

the following is a True account of Britons Loss in the Northern Department in america this year at huberton,[47] fort Ann, Benington, fort Stanwix, Still water & Saratoga &c &c in kill.d wounded & taken in the whole 10250 men & 47 Peices of Brass Artillery Besides a vast Quantity of Stores Baggag &c.

18th the whole Army are Ordered to march Down the River towards Albany to Day, & Haveing Intiligence on the Rode that Genr! Clinton[48] was Indeavouring to git up to Albany & Burn it as he has Assopus[49] & other Places, we ware ordered to march to Albany to Night which is 38 miles where we arivd at 12 O Clock At Night but Did Not see Mr Clinton—

19th we incamp.d on the hights about Albany to Day.

20th Nothing Extreordinery to Day—

21t 22d 23d there is Some Cloathing Drawing for the men.

24th Col? Morgan march.d this Day with the Rifle men for the Southward & Genr! Poors Brigade Cross.d the River & march.d Down toward fish kill[50]—

25 & 26 I Lay at Albany with the Light Infantry Nothing Extreordinery happened Except that of gitting some Cloaths.

47. Hubbardton, Rutland co., Vermont. This engagement took place on July 7, 1777, between the British forces under Fraser and Riedesel and the Continentals under St. Clair, during which the latter were defeated. Nickerson, *op. cit.*, 149, *ff.*

48. Sir Henry Clinton (1738–1795) had come to America a major-general with Howe and Burgoyne to assist Gage. After seeing action at Bunker Hill, he attempted to capture Charleston, S. C., but failed. He participated in the battle of Long Island. Left in command at New York when Howe sailed off to Philadelphia in 1777, he was without sufficient strength to help Burgoyne in his plight at Saratoga, although he did capture the forts up the Hudson early in October. He sent a force to Esopus, New York, which threatened Albany, but was too late to aid Burgoyne, who had already begun negotiations for a surrender. Clinton succeeded Howe as commander-in-chief in May, 1778. He resigned his command early in 1782. *Dict. Nat. Biog.*, IV, 551–2.

49. Esopus, Ulster co., N. Y., stood about 5 miles west of the Hudson River on the left bank of Esopus Kill and about 3 miles southwest of Kingston.

50. Fish Kill, Dutchess co., N. Y., is 5 miles east of the Hudson River on a creek of the same name. It is 7 miles northeast of Newburgh and about 84 miles south of

27th this Day a very heavy Rain Came on which continued until the 29th it is Said So heavy a Rain was Never known here Before—

30th this Day I march.d with the Light Infantry Down the River 12 miles to a Place Call.d Quemens[51] & incamp.d—

31t this Day Genr! Glover.s,[52] & Genr! Pattessons Brigades march.d Down & incamp.d at Quemens—

Novem! 1t I have fine weather, good Quarters & good Liveing which is Something New to me—

2d as yesterday—

3 D°—

4 D°—

5 D°—

6 D°—

7 I went to albany to Day to See Genr! Gates. the Light Infantry under my Command are Dismisd this Day & I Set Sail for fish kill—

8th on my way to fish kill—

9th D°—

10th ariv.d at fish kill & Joind my Regiment—

11th we are Prepareing to march for Philadelphia.

12 as yesterday.

13 we march.d to Pecks kill.[53]

14 we Crossd kings ferry & incamp'd.[54]

Albany. This place should not be confused with Fish Kill Creek near Saratoga (Schuylerville), New York.

51. Coeymans, Albany co., N. Y., on the west bank of the Hudson River, 13 miles below Albany.

52. John Glover (1732–1797) of Massachusetts was commissioned a brigadier-general in February, 1777. After Burgoyne's surrender Glover conducted the British prisoners to Cambridge. He served in Rhode Island and was later stationed at West Point. Dict. Am. Biog., VII, 331–2.

53. Peekskill, Westchester co., N. Y., on the east bank of the Hudson River, 17 miles below Fishkill and about 42 miles from New York City.

54. Kings Ferry operated between Verplank's Point on the east bank of the Hudson, 3 miles below Peekskill, to Stony Point on the opposite side.

15 march.d to Suffinene[55] 18 miles & incampd.

16th march.d 18 miles & incampd.

17th marchd to Morristown.

18th march.d 12 miles.

19th march.d 16 miles.

20th Cross.d the River Dilaware.[56]

21 march.d 14 miles.

22 we Joind the main army at white marsh.[57]

23[d] Nothing New.

24 Nothing Extrordinery.

25 D[o]

26 D[o]

27 D[o]

28 D[o]

29 D[o]

30 D[o]

Decem[r] 1 we have very Poor Living.

2[d] Nothing New.

3[d] D[o]

4 D[o]

55. Suffern, southwest of Stony Point, near the Jersey boundary.

56. Dearborn's regiment probably crossed the Delaware near the mouth of Smith Creek, either by Coxe's Ferry or by way of the ford just below Smith Creek.

57. White Marsh, 11 miles north by west of Philadelphia, the site of Washington's encampment.

Operations in the Middle Colonies

LEAVING *Burgoyne to face alone the disgrace of surrender at Saratoga, Howe embarked his army from New York and sailed for the Delaware River. He captured Philadelphia and thereafter repulsed Washington's efforts to dislodge him from the city. The Continental army went into camp at Valley Forge poorly equipped and underfed; but early in the spring of 1778 it was cheered by the news that France had joined the American colonies against Great Britain. Howe was replaced as commander-in-chief by Clinton, who ordered the army back to New York. Washington followed the British troops as they marched across New Jersey and engaged them in an indecisive action at Freehold, or Monmouth Court House.*

The British moved into New York City and Washington went into camp in the vicinity of White Plains. Later that summer an unsuccessful attempt was made to drive the British garrison out of Newport, Rhode Island. Clinton next dispatched an expedition to invade the South. In the winter of 1779 Washington stationed his army in camps extending from the Connecticut River, through the highlands of the Hudson, to the New Jersey coast.

D ECEM.^r 5th 1777
this morning we ware allarm'd at 4 O clock by hearing that the Enemy ware advancing, in consiquince of which the whole army Turnd out, & form'd

the Lines of battle, & Sent the baggage of the army back out of Camp.— at 9 O Clock some scurmishing hapened at Chesnut Hill[1] 3 miles from our front between the Enimys advanc'd Party & a Party of Millitia in which we Lost Genr! Arving[2] who was taken Prisoner— the Enimy advanc'd no further we Remaind all Day on our Posts. at Evining we Shifted our ground a Little & Incamp'd—

6th we Lay all Day Loocking at one or the other

7th we form'd our Lines at 6 O Clock & at 7 the allarm guns ware fir'd by finding that the Enimy ware advancing very Rapedly upon our Left wing, but at 8 O Clock Several deserters came in who inform'd us that the Enimy ware Retreeting towards Germantown.[3] this after noon we found that the Retreet which we heard the Enimy ware making this morning was in fact Shifting their ground from our Right wing to our Left & advanc'd within ¾ of a mile of our front Line in Consequence of which Some Scurmish hapened, when our Rifle men gave a Party of them a Severe Drubing— we hourly Expect a General Ingagement.— Near Night I was ordered out with our Regiment to attact the Enimys Cavelry, but found them so strongly Posted that I Could Not attack[t] them without too great a Resk— the whole army Lay to Night upon their arms.

1. On the night of December 4, Howe moved out of Philadelphia with most of his army. His intention was to drive Washington out of his lines at White Marsh and force him beyond the hills. Howe was met by Washington's advance under Gen. Irvine at Chestnut Hill, 10 miles out of Philadelphia. But Irvine's Pennsylvania militia were driven back to the army's main lines. After looking things over, Howe decided that Washington's position was too strong to attack, and after spending four days trying to lure him into the open, he gave up and returned to Philadelphia.

2. James Irvine (d. 1819), colonel of the 2nd Pennsylvania regiment, had been brigadier-general of the Pennsylvania militia since August. He was captured during Howe's advance on Chestnut Hill and not exchanged until June 1, 1781, when he was made major-general of the Pennsylvania Militia. Heitman, op. cit., 314.

3. Germantown lay six miles north northwest of Independence Hall, between Philadelphia and Washington's position at White Marsh.

Expecting that they would attact us in the Night with fix'd bayonets—

8th the Two armies Lay this morning as yesterday this after noon the Enimy began to Retreet we at first supposed they ware only indeavouring to Draw us off of our ground. but at Dark we found they had Retreeted into Philadelphia,—which must Convince the world that M[r] How[4] Did not Dare to fight us unless he Could have the advantage of the ground—

9th we are all Quiet to Day & our Tents are Ordered into Camp.—

10th as yesterday—

11th This morning at 4 O Clock the whole army ware Ordered to Strike Tents & Parade Redy to march when Ordered— at 6-O Clock We march'd & at 9 we begun to cross the Schuylkill on a Bridg about 14 miles from Philadelphia, & when Genr[l] Wain's[5] Division had Cross'd we found the Enimy had got Possession of the heights Near the bridg & ware so strongly Posted that it was Thought best for Genr[l] Wain to Retreet back over the bridg. the whole Army form'd in Lines of Battle & Remain'd so untill Near Night & then march'd about five miles up the River to a Place Calld Sweeds ford.[6] & incamp'd—

12 this fournoon we built a bridg with waggons across the Schuylkill for the army to Cross on but Near Night finding the Enimy had moov'd from the Ground they

4. Sir William Howe, the British commander-in-chief.

5. Anthony Wayne (1745–1796) had supported the American retreat from Canada in 1776 and then commanded the garrison at Fort Ticonderoga. Appointed a brigadier-general in 1777, he took command of the Pennsylvania line. He was active in the battles of Brandywine and Germantown. At the battle of Monmouth, Wayne led the advance attack. Transferred to the command of a corps of light infantry, Wayne captured Stony Point in July, 1779. In 1781 he served under Lafayette in Virginia. After Yorktown, Wayne went to Georgia with Greene for the final hostilities of the war. He again took the field in 1793 to defeat the Indians in the Northwest. *Dict. Am. Biog.*, XIX, 563–5.

6. Swedes Ford was at or near the site of Swedes Ford bridge at Swedeland Station, 15 miles from Philadelphia.

had Lately Occupied the whole army march'd Down to the bridg which we began to Cross yesterday & Cross'd over & toock Possession of some Heights & incamp'd— 11 heshins ware taken to Day

13th we Lay still to Day— the Enimy have Retreeted into Philadelphia—

14 this fournoon we are all Quiet— this after Noon a Party of the Enemys Light Horse & some Light Troops Came with in 3 or 4 miles of us & Carried off some Liquers from a Tavern.

15 we have fine weather for the season.

16th the weather is Cold & wet which renders our Living in Tents very uncomfortable. 11 Prisoners ware Brought in to Day.—

17th the weather Remains very uncomfortable— our General Officers are Consulting what winter Quarters we are to have which I fear will be very Poor—

18th the weather still Remains uncomfortable— this is Thanksgiving Day thro the whole Continent of America[7]—but god knows We have very Little to keep it with this being the third Day we have been without flouer or bread—& are Living on a high uncultivated hill, in huts & tents Laying on the Cold Ground, upon the whole I think all we have to be thankful for is that we are alive & not in the Grave with many of our friends— we had for thanksgiving breakfast some Exceeding Poor beef which has been boil.d & Now warm.d in an old short handled frying Pan in which we ware Obliged to Eat it haveing No other Platter— I Dined & sup.d at Genr! Sulivans[8] to Day & so Ended thanksgiving—.

7. A resolution recommending that the states set apart December 18 for a day of thanksgiving was passed by the Continental Congress on November 1, in consequence of the victory over Burgoyne. *Journals of the Continental Congress*, IX, 854.

8. John Sullivan (1740-1795) was commissioned a brigadier-general in 1775. He served in the siege of Boston and for a short while commanded the American forces

19 the army marched about 5 mile & incamp.d Near a height where we are to build huts to Live in this winter.[9] 20th we are making Preperation for huting.

21t as yesterday—

22d Nothing New—

23d we have began to build huts—

24 a Party of our Light hors & some Rifle men toock 10 of the Enimies Light hors men & 13 horses to Day—

25th we have Not so mery a Crismus as I have seen— the weather warm & Rayny.

26 the whole army are very busy in building huts—

27 as yesterday—

28th Snowey Last night & to Day—

29th the weather is very Cold & we have not Done building Huts yet—

30th I think the weather is as Cold here as it is in New England—

31t Nothing Extreordinery to Day: we are Still Living in Tents, Covered with Snow. this year 1777 has not Closed without somthing very Extreordinery.s Turning up— having Obtaind Leave from Genr! Washington I intend to set out for home Next Sunday. God Grant me a happy sight of my friends—

January 1t 1778 this year begins with Pleasant Weather. may it Prove Ominus of a Happy year for America—

retreating from Canada. Promoted to the rank of major-general in August, 1776, he was captured by the British at Long Island, but was soon exchanged. He was with Washington in the attacks on Trenton and Princeton. Active in opposing Howe before Philadelphia in 1777, he spent the winter at Valley Forge. In 1779 he took command of the drive against the British at Newport. He began the siege, but D'Estaing's supporting fleet was dispersed by a storm. Sullivan led an expedition into western New York against the Indians and Loyalists in 1779. On his return eastward he had to resign because of ill health. *Dict. Am. Biog.*, XVIII, 192-3.

9. The encampment at Valley Forge was bounded on the north by the Schuylkill River and on the west by Valley Creek. The only approaches, from the south and east, were protected by strong lines of entrenchments. The strength of Washington's position was such that no attempt was made against it during the entire winter, even though Howe was aware of the impoverished condition of the Continental army.

2^d the weather Remains Pleasent. our Brigade is Mustered to Day—

3^d I Receivd my Commission this Day as Lt Col^{o10} to Col^o Scammell—

4th I set out for home the weather very moderate—

5th the Traviling is Exceeding bad—

6th 7th 8th 9th the weather & Traviling Remains as it was—

10 I am at Danbury.^{11} about 6 inches of Snow fell to Day

11th the Traviling is better, the weather cold.

12th I Bought a Slay to-Day & have very good Traviling—

13th 14th 15th 16th 17th have fine slaying—

18th at 2 O Clock P. M. I arivd safe home,^{12} & found all well.

―――――――   ―――――――――――   ―――――――

Aprill 22^d 1778 Set out for Camp & ariv'd there the 12 Day of May at valey Forge—

[May] 15th I am P[residen]^t of a Brigade Coart Marc^l for the Tryal of Capt Clays^{13} he was aquited with Honour

16 I am Field Officer of the Day

17th I Dined at Genr^l Washingtons

18 Nothing New—

10. Although Dearborn did not receive his commission as lieutenant-colonel of the 3rd New Hampshire regiment until this day, his promotion dated from September 19, 1777. He succeeded Lt. Col. Andrew Colburn, who was mortally wounded on September 19, 1777. Heitman, *op. cit.*, 41, 190.

11. Danbury, Connecticut, about 30 miles west northwest of New Haven.

12. His home was still in Nottingham, Rockingham co., New Hampshire.

13. Capt. Elijah Clayes of the 2nd New Hampshire regiment. He died in 1779. No mention of Clayes or his court-martial is made in Washington's correspondence or general orders. Heitman, *op. cit.*, 159.

19 a Detatchment of 2000 men march'd out to Day Commanded by Marques Le fiete.[14] this day we are assured of Receiving 7 years Half Pay.[15]

20th this morning at 8 o Clock we ware alarmd & the whole army Turnd out—in Consequence of hearing that the Detatchment that march'd yesterday are Surrounded by 7000 brittish Troops & no other way for them to Escape but by fording the Schuylkill which was Perform.d in Sight of the Enimy. the army Lay under armes until night When finding that the Enimy after a small scurmish with a Party of our Anydo Indions[16] Retired into Philadelphia it was a very Luckey afair on our side, that we Did not Loose our whole Detatchment, our only Loss was 6 of my frenchmen.—

21[t] Nothing very Extreordinery Except that Genr.[l] Lee[17] & Genr.[l] Arnold have both arivd in Camp to the great joy of the army.—

14. Marie Joseph Paul Yves Roch Gilbert du Motier, Marquis de Lafayette (1757–1834), although from a titled and wealthy family and a captain in the French army, became so enthusiastic over the American cause that he volunteered his services and arrived in this country in June, 1777. Commissioned a major-general, but given no command, he joined Washington's staff. He was wounded at Brandywine, and after recovering was given command of the Virginia light troops. He spent the winter at Valley Forge. His sortie on May 19, 1778, resulted only in his escaping capture by a larger British force. He returned to France early in 1779, but came back the next year and rejoined Washington. In 1781 he acted with Gen. Greene in the southern campaign that ended the war. *Dict. Am. Biog.*, X, 535–9.

15. On May 15, 1778, the Continental Congress unanimously resolved that all commissioned officers should receive half pay for the first seven years after the war. Non-commissioned officers and privates were to be awarded $80 bonus at the end of the war. *Journals of the Continental Congress*, XI, 502.

16. The Oneidas and Tuscaroras, thanks to their personal attachment to the Rev. Samuel Kirkland, were for the most part friendly to the American cause. Many of the former volunteered to act as scouts for the Continental army. Winsor, *op. cit.*, VI, 623, *ff*.

17. Charles Lee (1731–1782) joined the British army in 1747 and fought in America during the French and Indian War. Later he served in the Polish army, but returned to America in 1773 and supported the American cause. At the outbreak of war he was appointed major-general, and served at Boston and in Charleston, S. C. In December, 1776, he was captured by a British patrol in New Jersey and seems to have given Howe information about the American army. Exchanged in 1778, he rejoined the army. His conduct at Monmouth brought to an end his military career. He was court-

22^{d} the Marquis with his Detatchm^{t} Returnd to Camp this afternoon.

23^{d} Nothing New to Day.

24th we here from Philadelphia to Day that a Frigate arivd there yesterday in 21 Days from Britan which brings News of a battle fought at sea between the French & English in which the English Came of[f] second best in Loosing two 60 gun ships;—& that the Troops are ordered to hold them selves Redy to Imbark at a munites warning.—

25th Nothing New.—

26th we Hourly Expect to Hear that the Enimy have Lift Philadelphia. I have the fever & ague to Day.

27th Nothing New.—

28 I am very Sick—

29 I take a Puke to Day.—

30th I am better.

31^{t} we are yet in suspence Respecting the Enimy.s going from Philadelphia

June 1^{t} more or Less Deserters from the Enimy Every Day.—

2^{d} Nothing New.—

3^{d} D^{o}

4 D^{o}

5 I have got the better of the fever & ague.—

6 the Enimy have sent of[f] the most of their baggage down the River.

7 Lord Cornwallis[18] with the Cormissioners for making Peace between Great Brittan & America have ariv.d in Philadelphia.—

martialed, found guilty, but was only suspended from the army. *Dict. Am. Biog.*, XI, 98–101.

18. Charles Cornwallis, 1st Marquis and 2nd Earl Cornwallis (1738–1805), had been a Whig in Parliament. He came to America a major-general in 1776 and joined Howe at Halifax. He took part in the operations around Long Island, White Plains and New

8 Nothing New.—

9th the New arangement of the army has ariv'd from Congress.[19]

10th the whole army moov'd out of Huts into tents to Day, about one Mile in front of our old incampment, for the sake of fresh Air;—

11th this Day I sent a Letter Home which is the first I have had an oppertunity of sending since I Left Home.—

12th Nothing Extreordinery to Day.—

13th D[o]—

14 D[o]

15 D[o]

16 D[o]

17 we hear that the Enimy are Crossing the River[20] over into the Jerseys—

18 this four noon we are Assured that the Enimy have Lift Philadelphia & our advanced Parties have taken Possession. Genr[l] Lees Division is ordered to march Immediately for Corells ferry.[21] & at 3 O Clock we march.

Jersey. After his victory at Brandywine in 1777, he went home. As Dearborn notes, he returned in 1778 as a lieutenant-general and second in command to Clinton. Although not a member of the Carlisle commission, he arrived with the peace commissioners, who, of course, failed in their effort to negotiate a treaty. After marching with Clinton from Philadelphia to New York, Cornwallis again left for England, because of the illness of his wife. He returned to America in August, 1779, participated in the siege of Charleston and was left in command in the southern department. His march northward in 1781 resulted in his surrender at Yorktown. *Dict. Nat. Biog.*, IV, 1159–61.

19. The new arrangement of the American army (regulating size and organization of battalions, the number and rank of officers for each, etc.,) was resolved upon in the Continental Congress May 27, 1778. One reason for it was the dissatisfaction of American officers with foreign volunteers who had been promoted over their heads. *Journals of the Continental Congress*, XI, 538–43, 570.

20. The British crossed the Delaware River at Coopers Ferry in Philadelphia, on their way to Sandy Hook.

21. Coryell's Ferry ran from New Hope, Pa., to Lambertville, N. J. The encampment was made at Amwell, N. J., three miles from the ferry. W. S. Myers, ed., *Stryker's Battle of Monmouth* (Princeton, 1927), 60–9.

his Division Consists of three brigades viz: Poors, Hunt-ingtons²² & Varnoms.²³—

20ᵗʰ we Cross. Correllˢ ferry & Proceeded 3 miles & incamp.d

21ᵗ we Lay still. we hear the whole Army are on their way into the Jerseys. we hear the Enimy are on their way to New york, Govener Livingston²⁴ of Jersey has taken the field with 5000 millitia.

22ᵈ our Whole army Incamp.d about 3 miles from Cor-reels Ferry in Jersey.

23ᵈ the army march'd to Day towards the Enimy 10 miles, without Baggage, & Incamp'd at Hopewell.²⁵

24ᵗʰ a Detatchment of 1500 Pick'd men was taken to Day from the army to be Commanded by Brigadier Genr! Scot²⁶ who are to act as Light Infantry Dureing the stay of the Enimy In Jersey. Col? Cilley & I am in one Reg! of the Light Infantry— Genr! Scot march'd to Day to-wards the Enimy, who are at Allin Town²⁷ 14 miles from Prince Town, we march'd thro Prince Town & Pro-ceeded 3 miles towards allin Town & Incamp'd we have no Tents or baggage—²⁸

22. Jedediah Huntington (1743–1818) of Connecticut was made a brigadier-general in May, 1777. *Dict. Am. Biog.*, IX, 416–7.

23. James M. Varnum (1748–1789) of Rhode Island was made a brigadier-general in February, 1777. He was under Sullivan at Newport in 1778. He resigned in March, 1779, but was commissioned a major-general of Rhode Island militia. *Ibid.*, XIX, 227.

24. William Livingston (1723–1790), a lawyer and Whig, commanded the New Jersey militia in 1776 and the same year was elected first governor of his state, which office he held for 14 years. *Ibid.*, XI, 325–7.

25. Hopewell, Mercer co., N. J., 10 miles from the ferry and 14 miles north of Trenton.

26. Charles Scott (d. 1813) was colonel of the 5th Virginia regiment and a brig-adier-general. He was captured at Charleston in 1780 and was a prisoner on parole when the war ended. Heitman, *op. cit.*, 485.

27. Allentown, Monmouth, co., N. J., 10 miles southeast of Princeton. Washing-ton's main body was then about 19 miles from Howe's army.

28. On June 22, Washington issued orders from Coryell's Ferry regarding the bag-gage. Anticipating a rapid march and an early engagement with the enemy, he ordered the tents and heavy baggage separated from the army for a few days. Every able man

25th this morning we march.d within 5 miles of the Enimy—& Halted & Drew Provision. Sent a small Party of Horse to Reconoightir the Enimy. at 12 O Clock we ware Inform.d that the Enimy ware on their way to Monmouth Coart House.[29] Which is Towards Sandy Hoock. Our main army is Near Prince Town, we are now Prepared to Harress the Enimy. Genr! Scot 1500 men Genr! Maxwell[30] 1000 Col? Morgan 500—Genr! Dickerson[31] 1000—Millitia; & 200 Horse. the above Detatchmts are on the Flanks & Rear of the Enimy. Genr! Washington is in our Rear with 12000 men to support us— at 4 O Clock P: M we marchd to Allin Town & Incamp.d.— the Enimys Rear is 5 miles from us—

26th we march'd Early this Morning after the Enimy. the weather is Extreemly Hot, we are Obliged to march very Modirate. the Enimy Desert very fast. we are Join'd to Day by the Marquis De lefiette with a Detatchment of 1000 men. we advanced within three miles of the Enimy, & Incamp'd. the Enimy are about Monmouth Court House, on good Ground—

27th we march.d Early this morning within one mile of the Enimy & ware ordered by an Express from Genr! Washington to Counter March to where we Incamp'd Last night, & from thence to file off to English Town[32]

was to prepare for battle. Only the sick and wounded were to be left behind to guard the baggage. J. C. Fitzpatrick, ed., *The Writings of George Washington* . . . (Washington, 1934), XII, 105.

29. Monmouth Court House or Freehold, Monmouth co., N. J., is 17 miles northeast of Allentown and 22 miles southeast of Princeton. The town contained about 40 houses; the two most prominent buildings were the court house and the old English church. Myers, *op. cit.*, 113, *ff.*

30. William Maxwell (d. 1798) was colonel of the 2nd New Jersey regiment and in 1776 was promoted to the rank of brigadier-general. He resigned from the army in 1780. Heitman, *op. cit.*, 385.

31. Philemon Dickinson (1739–1809) was a major-general in the New Jersey militia. He worked with Gen. Maxwell in destroying bridges so as to delay Clinton's march while the main army came up. *Dict. Am. Biog.*, V, 302–3.

32. Englishtown, Monmouth co., N. J., is 5 miles northwest of Freehold.

(which Lay 7 miles on Our Left as we followed the Enimy) & their Join Genr! Lee Who was there with 2000
men. the weather Remains very Exceeding Hot. & water
is scarce we ariv.d at English Town about the middle of
the Day & Incamp'd. the Enimy Remain at Monmouth.
Genr! Washington with the Grand army Lays about 5
mile in our Rear. Deserters Come in in Large numbers.

28th haveing Intiligence this morning before sun Rise,
that the Enimy ware mooving, we ware Ordered, together with the Troops Commanded by the Marquis &
Genr! Lee (in the whole About 5000) to march towards
the Enimy & as we thought to Attact them. at Eleven
o Clock A. M. after marching about 6 or 7 miles we
ariv'd on the Plains Near monmouth Court House, Where
a Collumn of the Enimy appeard in sight. a brisk Cannonade Commens'd on both sides. the Collumn which
was advancing towards us Halted & soon Retired, but
from some moovements of theirs we ware Convince'd
they Intended to fight us, shifted our ground, form.d on
very good ground & waited to see if they Intended to
Come on. we soon Discovere'd a Large Collumn Turning
our Right. & an other Comeing up in our Front With
Cavelry in front of both Collumns Genr! Lee was on the
Right of our Line who Left the ground & made Tracks
Quick Step towards English Town. Genr! Scots Detatchment Remaind on the ground we form.d on until we
found we war very near surrounded—& ware Obliged to
Retire which we Did in good order altho we ware hard
Prest on our Left flank.— the Enimy haveing got a mile
in Rear of us before we began to Retire & ware bearing
Down on our Left as we went off & we Confin'd by a
Morass on our Right. after Retireing about 2 miles we
met his Excelency Genr! Washington who after seeing
what Disorder Genr! Lee.s Troops ware in appeer'd to be

at a Loss whether we should be able to make a stand or
not. however he order'd us to form on a Heighth, & Indevour to Check the Enimy, we form.d & about 12
Peices of Artillery being brought on to the hill with us:
the Enimy at the same time advancing very Rappedly
finding we had form.d, they form.d in our front on a
Ridge & brought up their Artillery within about 60 Rods
of our front. *When the brisket Cannonade Commenced on both
sides* that I Ever heard. Both Armies ware on Clear Ground.
& if any thing Can be Call.d Musical where their is so
much Danger, I think that was the finest musick, I Ever
heared. *however* the agreeableness of the musick was very
often Lessen'd by the balls Coming too near— Our men
being very much beat out with Fateague & heat which
was very Intence, we order.d them to sit Down & Rest
them Selves,— from the time we first met the Enimy until we had form.d as above mentioned several sevear
scurmishes hapened at Different Places & Times,— Soon
after the Cannonade became serious a Large Collum of
the Enimy began to Turn our Left. Some Part of our Artillery Play'd upon them very Briskly & they finding
their main Body ware not advancing, halted. the Cannonade Continued about 2½ Hours & then the Enimy
began to Retire from their Right. Genr! Washington being in front of our Reg.t when the Enimy began to Retire
on their Right he ordered Col.º Cilley & me with ab.t 300
men to go & attact the Enimies Right wing. which then
was Passing thro an orchard, but when they found we
ware about to attact them they formed & stood Redy to
Receive us, when we ariv'd within 200 yards of them
we form.d Batallion & advanc'd but having two Rail
fences to take Down as we advanced, (the Last of which
was within 60 yards of the Enimy) we Could advance but
slowly, the Enimy when we ware takeing Down the

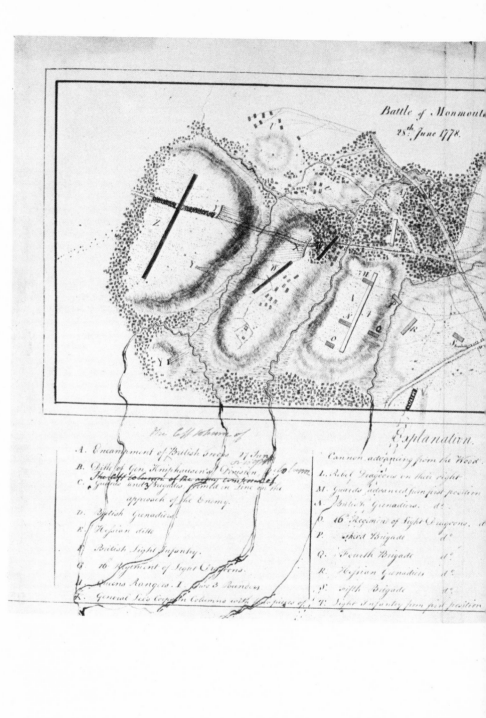

Battle of Monmouth
28th June 1778.

The Left Column of

Explanation.

A. Encampment of British Forces 27 June
B. Battle of Gen. Knÿphausen's Division
C. Guards and Brigades formed in Line on the
    approach of the Enemy.
D. British Grenadiers
E. Hessian ditto
F. British Light Infantry.
G. 16th Regiment of Light Dragoons.
H. Queens Rangers. 1 Two 3 Pounders
I. General Lees Corps in Column with pieces of

Cannon advancing from the Wood
L. Rebel Dragoons on their right
M. Guards advanced from first position
N. British Grenadiers.   d°
O. 16th Regiment of Light Dragoons. d°
P. Third Brigade   d°
Q. Fourth Brigade d°
R. Hessian Grenadiers. d°
S. Fifth Brigade d°
T. Light Infantry from first position

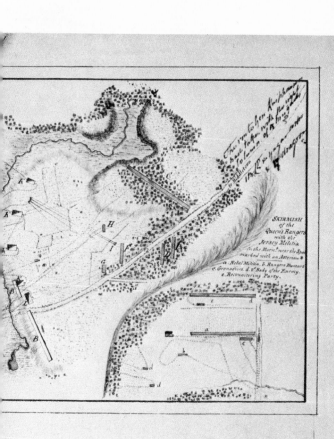

SKIRMISH
of the
Queen's Rangers
with the
Jersey Militia
in this Morass are the Spots
marked with an Attention
a. Rebel Militia. b. Rangers Bustard
c. Grenadiers. d. 1st Body of the Enemy.
e. Reconoitering Party.

V. Queens Rangers

V. First movement of the Light Infantry & Queens Rangers
to turn the enemy: & that of the fifth Brigade to
connect them with the Line.

W. Position to which General See retreated thro' the Woods
on the advance of the British Army, who drove him
& occupied it during the remainder of the Day. with the Light Corps
and sustaining Brigade had engaged
X. British Artillery. the morass when the whole fell back to
Y. Rebel Artillery. position in which the Hessian grenadiers
had remained I and from thence in Line
Z. Washington's Army. rest of the evening continued their
H. road to Freehold meeting march to join the left column begins
House. now #±25

M THE ORIGINAL MANUSCRIPT MAP IN THE **WILLIAM L. CLEMENTS LIBRARY**

Last fence, give us a very heavy fire which we Did not Return. after takeing Down the Last fence we march'd on with armes shoulderd Except 20 men who we sent on their Right to scurmish with them while we Pass.d the fences. the Enimy finding we ware Determined to Come to Close quarter, fil.d off from the Left & Run off upon our Right into a swamp & form'd in the Edge of it. we Wheel.d to the Right & advanc.d towards them. they began a heavy fire upon us. we ware Desending toward them in Open field, with Shoulder'd armes until we had got within 4 Rods of them when our men Dress'd very Coolly & we then gave them a very heavy fire from the whole Batallion. they had two Peices of artillery across a small Run which Play'd with grape very briskly upon us but when they found we ware Determin'd to Push upon them they Retreetd to their main body which was giving way & ware Persued by some Parties from our Line. we Persued until we got Possesion of the field of Battle, where we found 300 Dead & a Conciderable number of wound. among the Dead was Col? Mungton[33] & a number of other officers. the Enimy Retire'd across a Morass & form'd. Our men being beat out with heat & fateague it was thought not Prudent to Persue them. Great numbers of the Enemy Died with heat & some of ours. we Remain'd on the field of Battle & ware to attact the Enimy Early Next morning but they Prevented us by a Precipitate Retreet in the middle of the night. they Left 5 Officers wounded at Monmouth Court House the Enimies Whole Loss in the Battle of Monmouth was

327 kill'd

500 wounded

95 Prisoner

---

33. Lt. Col. the Honorable Henry Monckton of the 45th regiment, who was in command of the second battalion of British grenadiers. Myers, *op. cit.*, 296.

Our Loss—   63 kill'd
                  210 wounded
here Ends the famous Battle of Monmouth.[34]

29th we Lay Still to Recrute our men there being no Probibility of Coming up with the Enimy before they take Possession of the Heights Near Sandy Hoock[35] where their shipping Lay, it being but about 12 miles from Monmouth—

30th we Lay still to Day—

July 1[t] our whole Army March.d this morning (Except the Jersey Troops.) to Spots wood[36] 10 miles towards Brunswick. the weather Remains Extreemly Hot. vast numbers of our men fell Down with the Heat to Day & some Died.—

2[d] we March'd this Morning at 2 O Clock in the morning. Proceeded to Brunswick 10 miles & incamp.d. Genr! Lee is Arested to Day by Genr! Washington for Disobedience of orders in not attacting the Enimy & for making an unnessesary & shameful Retreet &c[37]   A General

34. When the British began moving from Philadelphia to New York, Washington marched his army north of them along a line which would eventually cross their route. As the enemy approached Freehold, Washington decided to attack before the long column could get to the coast. He sent Lee on ahead with orders to engage the enemy as soon as possible while the main army was brought up. On June 28 Lee approached the enemy, but instead of attacking, he tried to surround the British force, meanwhile issuing positive orders to Wayne and Lafayette *not* to attack. Washington rode up in time to stop a chaotic retreat as the British line wheeled and advanced on Lee's command. After reprimanding Lee, Washington himself took command, ordering Lee to the rear. As the main body of Washington's troops came up the British were driven back. During the night they retreated in haste to join their right wing at Middletown. For a comprehensive account of the battle, see Myers, *op. cit.*

35. Sandy Hook is a sandy peninsula 6 miles long extending northward on the New Jersey coast, 16 miles south of New York city. It separates Sandy Hook Bay from the Atlantic ocean.

36. After the battle of Monmouth, Washington made preparations to march northward, cross the Hudson and join Gates in the highlands of New York. The first day's march brought the army to Spotswood, Middlesex co., N. J., 10 miles northwest of Freehold. *Writings of Washington*, XII, 131 *ff.*

37. Washington, himself, described it as "an unnecessary, disorderly, and shameful retreat." The court-martial found Lee guilty on three counts and suspended him from the army for one year. *Ibid.*, XII, 133.

Coart Marcial is ordered to Set to Day for his tryal I
Obtaind Leave to go to Morris town[38] to Day to see after
my Baggage which Came from New hampshire together
with some slate stone & vunegar)—

3ᵈ I am at Morris Town. this Day.

4ᵗʰ was Celibrated as being the Anniversary of the Declaration of the amarican Indipendince By the whole army
being turnd out under armes. & the Artillery bing Inter-
spers'd thro the whole army Excipt thirteen Peices which
ware Placed on the Right of the army. the Celebration
began with a Descharge of the 13 Cannon on the Right of
the army Seconded by a Running fire first thro the front
Line of Cannon & musketry & then the second Line. suc-
seeded by three Cheers from the whole army after Pro-
claiming Perpetual & undisturb.d Independence to the
united States of America.[39]

5ᵗʰ the Left wing of our Army marches to Day towards
kings ferry— I go to to New Ark to Day—

6ᵗʰ the Right wing March'd to Day.

7ᵗʰ the Rear Line March'd to Day I Joined the Regᵗ at
Springfield[40] 6 mils from Elizebeth Town to Day.

8ᵗʰ we march'd 10 miles to Day to Crab Orchard[41] 5
miles from New Ark & Incamp'd.

9ᵗʰ we Lay Still to Day—

10ᵗʰ we march'd 10 miles to Slawterdam—[42]

---

38. About 30 miles north of Spotswood. While Dearborn was on this errand,
Washington moved the army to Brunswick. *Ibid.*, XII, 148.

39. This form of military celebration was known as a *feu de joie*, and the details of
its execution were outlined in Washington's General Orders of July 4. The army was
first paraded by the commander-in-chief. The *feu de joie* ended with a running fire
throughout the ranks, followed by three cheers.

40. Springfield, Union co., N. J., one mile from Milburn Station.

41. Crab Orchard was situated near the 18th century settlement called Second
River, up the Passaic River on the west side.

42. Slawterdam, Sloterdam or Slaterdam, stood on the east bank of the Passaic
River near the present site of Dundee Dam in Bergen County.

11th March'd 10 mils to Parammus[43] & Incamp'd.

12th we Lay still to Day. we hear that a french fleet is on our Coast.[44]

13th we Lay Still—

14th we March'd to kakaate—[45] we have the Ceartenty of the french fleets being at Sandy Hoock—

15th we March'd to kings ferry—

16th we Cross'd kings ferry—

17th we March'd to Peeks kill

18th we March'd 12 mils to Croten bridge[46]

19th we Lay still

20th we March'd 12 miles within 4 mils of White Plains[47] & Incamp.d.

21[t] we Lay still

22[d] as yesterday

24th we March'd to White Plains & Incamp'd.

25 Nothing new—

26 the york Regiments are taken from Genr[l] Poors Brigade & Col[o] Hasons[48] is Put in their stod—

27th Nothing new

28th Deserters Come in Conciderable numbers

43. Paramus, Bergen co., N. J., 2 miles from Rochelle Park.

44. Comte D'Estaing, with 18 ships and a land force of 4,000, had reached the mouth of Delaware Bay on July 8. From there he sailed up to Sandy Hook. John Fiske, *The American Revolution* (Boston & New York, 1891), II, 72.

45. Washington spelled it Kakiate. It is now New Hempstead, Queens co., N. Y.

46. The bridge spanned the Croton River near its mouth, on the road from Peekskill to Tarrytown.

47. Near the present site of White Plains, in White Plains township, N. Y. It was here that Washington fought the British on October 28, 1776.

48. Moses Hazen (1733–1803) was a French and Indian War captain of rangers. He settled in St. Johns, Quebec, and at the beginning of the Revolutionary War was suspected of Loyalist sympathies. However, he joined Montgomery's force in Canada and in 1776 was made colonel of the 2nd Canadian regiment. He helped plan a second invasion of Canada in 1778 which was abandoned. His regiment fought around New York, Philadelphia and Yorktown. Hazen was made a brigadier-general in 1781. *Dict. Am. Biog.*, 477–8.

29 we hear an Expedition against is form'd by Genr!
Sulivan & Count De Stange[49] against Rode Island[50] two
Brigades have march'd from here for that Place—
30th nothing new
31t we hear the french fleet have taken a Large number
of Prises & sent in to Different Ports—
August 1t Nothing new—
2d we hear the Enimy are block'd up in New port[51] &
that they had been Oblig'd to burn several frigates &
other vessels—
3d Nothing Extreordinary—
4th as yesterday
5th D°
6th D°
7th D°
8th D°
9th I got a fine dinner of Quohogs & Oisters to Day—
10th we are Dayly Expecting to hear that Newport has
falln into our hands with the garrison—
11th Nothing New—
12th as yesterday.

49. Charles Hector, Comte D'Estaing (1729-1794), served in the East Indies as a
brigadier-general before he entered the navy. In 1777 he was made a vice-admiral
and the next year commanded the French fleet sent to assist the colonies. In July,
1778, he arrived with his fleet off Sandy Hook, but being unable to get at the British
fleet anchored in New York harbor, he sailed off to attack Newport, Rhode Island.
A storm disrupted his plans and after making repairs, he sailed off to the West Indies.
Following his drawn battle with Admiral Byron in 1779, D'Estaing co-operated with
the Americans in an unsuccessful attempt to retake Savannah. He returned to France
in 1780. *Biographie Universelle* (Paris, 1855), XIII, 90-1.

50. The island of Rhode Island, including the city of Newport, near the mouth of
Narraganset Bay. The British had fortified Newport and environs in 1776. Major-
General Pigot was in command of the defences of the city, and a small fleet guarded
the harbor.

51. D'Estaing with his fleet, and the Continental troops under General Sullivan
were to make a joint attack on the British defences at Newport. The British fleet
refused to leave the harbor, so D'Estaing began to send ships in. The British then
began to scuttle their fleet, and would have lost all of it if Admiral Howe had not appeared off the coast. D'Estaing then abandoned his efforts in Newport harbor and put
out after the fleet under Howe. Winsor, *op. cit.*, VI, 593-4.

13th D?

14th d?

15th we hear Lord How^{52} has gone from N york to Pay Count De Astange a visit—

16th we hear that when Lord How Made his appearence off Rhode Island, the Count Waid anchor & stood after him. Lord How Put to see & the Count followed him & how they will make it nobody knows but Ministers. they have had very high Winds since they Put to sea for several Days.

17th at 9 O Clock this Morning 11 men ware to be Executed in Camp for Different Crimes. One of them was shot & the others Repreiv'd until fryday—

18th we have had a Long spell of fowl weather & high winds—

19th we hear a british frigate & Roegalley^{53} has got on shore in Jersey—

20th Nothing Extreordinery— I am Officer of the Day—

21^{t} we hear there has been a battle at Sea between the French & British fleets, & the British fleet is worsted & Return'd to N. York.

22^{d} Nothing New—

23^{d} I have a fine Dinner of Quohogs &c &c &c &c &c &c &c, to Day.

24th we hear to Day from Rhode Island that Count De Asstange has Returnd there; with a bum Cetch [bomb

---

52. Richard Howe, Earl Howe, (1726-1799), was vice-admiral and commander-in-chief on the North American station in 1776. He transported his brother's forces from New York to Philadelphia in 1777. His fleet moved up to Rhode Island in August, 1778, to engage D'Estaing, but a strong gale drove both fleets far apart and caused extensive damage. Howe returned to England the next month and declined further service. *Dict. Nat. Biog.*, X, 95-6.

53. Row-galleys were long single or half-decked boats with a low free-board. Usually they were propelled by oars, but they also carried spars and sails. Some of the larger galleys mounted two six pounders, fore and aft.

ketch] & Several Other Prises,—& that Genr! Sulivan
has taken several Redouts from the Enimy—54

25th Nothing new

26 D°

27th we hear Count Destange has gone to boston.

28th we hear Lord How has gone out to sea—

29th a Conciderable fleet is in the Sound supposed to
[be] bound to Rhode island—

30th I am Summoned as an Evidence upon a Genr!
Court Marcial for the Tryal of Maj^r Genr! St Clear—55

31^t nothing new—

Septem^r 1^t a skurmish hapen'd to Day near kings bridge
between a Party of our Indiens & a Party of the Enimys
foot & Hors, where Nine Indiens ware surrounded &
killd. a Party of Light Troops of ours Came to support
the Indiens & Drove the Enimy within their Lines after
killing a number & takeing several Prisoners—

2^d we hear Genr! Sulivan has had a battle on Rhode island   he was attact as he was Indevouring to Retreet off
of the Island. a Conciderable heavy Battle Insued. Sulivan Recovered the field & forc'd the Enimy within their
strong Holds with Cornsiderable Loss on both Sides—
the Next Day Genr! Sulivan made a safe Retreet from the
Island & brought his Baggage & Every other matter of[f]
with him—56

54. On the 19th, after three hours of heavy bombardment by Sullivan's artillery,
the British abandoned one redoubt. The following day they were forced to abandon
their entire outer line of defence. H. W. Preston, *The Battle of Rhode Island* (Providence,
1928), 30–1.

55. Arthur St. Clair (1736–1818) served in the British army from 1757 to 1762
and then settled in western Pennsylvania. A colonel in the Continental army in 1775,
he rose to the rank of major-general in 1777 and was placed in command of Ticonderoga, which post he abandoned as Burgoyne advanced on it. For this retreat he was
court-martialed, but completely exonerated. Yet he was never given an important
command thereafter. Following the war he was a member of the Continental Congress,
and later the first governor of the Northwest Territory. *Dict. Am. Biog.*, XVI, 293–95.

56. The first skirmish took place on August 29, near Butts Hill, at the middle of
the island, to which Sullivan had retired after the untimely departure of the French

3ᵈ we hear an Inglish Fleet has Lately ariv'd at New york —& that Count Destange is in Boston harbour. & that Genr! Sulivan has made a safe Retreet from Rhode island.

4ᵗʰ the Committee of Congress are now in Camp for the Purpose of New arraingeing the army nearly upon the brittish Plan—[57]

5ᵗʰ we hear Admirell Byren[58] has ariv'd with a Learge Fleet & has Block'd up Count De Astange in Boston harbour—

6ᵗʰ Nothing New—

7ᵗʰ we hear that an English fleet is Laying off New London—

8ᵗʰ the Enimy March'd a Learge body from New york into the Country about six miles & toock 5 of our Light Horse & 20 waggon Horses which ware feeding in a Meddow.

9ᵗʰ a small Party of our men in boats went across the sound Last night & burnt 3 vessels toock 10 men & killd 11 & toock a Large Quantity of Baggage. Genr! Poors, Pattersons & Learnards Brigades are Ordered to be Redy to March to Morrow morning at Nine o Clock.

10ᵗʰ we are Redy to march but Due not.

11ᵗʰ we march this morning at sun Rise towards Danbury 8 mils & incamp.

fleet from Newport. The British and Hessians under Gen. Pigot pursued Sullivan and made three determined attacks against the Continental lines, the last being supported by the cannon of two British ships of war which moved up the channel to enfilade the rebel lines. The battle lasted from seven in the morning to four in the afternoon, when the British forces were driven back to their entrenchments around Newport. Preston, *op. cit.*, 37–45.

57. The Committee of Arrangement consisted of Joseph Reed and Francis Dana. *Writings of Washington*, XII, 163.

58. Vice-Admiral John Byron (1723–1786) straggled into Sandy Hook Bay with the remnants of a poorly equipped fleet manned by a motley crew, after a stormy passage from England. It took him nearly two months to assemble his squadron and make repairs. He put to sea again in October, but D'Estaing had moved off to the West Indies. Byron followed him, and in 1779 two indecisive actions occurred off the West Indies. Byron returned to England the same year. *Dict. Nat. Biog.*, III, 613–5.

12th we March 8 miles & incamp.

13th we Lay Still to Day.

14th Our main army marchd to Day from White Plains towards fish kill—

15th Nothing New.

16th we march'd to Ridg field[59] 7 miles & Incamp'd.

17th we Lay still by Reason of a sevear storm.

18th we March'd to Danbury 10 miles & Incamp^d our main army is incamp'd at & Near fredricksburge[60] between this & fish kill—

19th Nothing Extreordinery to Day.

20th Genr^l McDoogels[61] Division arivd to Day & Incamp'd at Danbury, his Division Consisted of Nixons[62] & the N Carolina Brigades—

21^t We are ordered to hold our selves in Rediness to march at the shortest Notice.

22^d Nothing new.

23^d a heavy Storm to Day—

24th From all acounts, it appears, that the Enimy are about Leaving New York. Some Conjecture they are going to Boston, Others that they are going to Canada, Hallifax & the West Indies.[63]

25th Nothing new.

59. Washington's plan was to divide his army for the winter. One division, equal in size to Clinton's force, was left in the vicinity of White Plains, and in communication with the Hudson; the others were to be distributed at intervals towards the Connecticut River, in order to cover any movement of the enemy from Long Island Sound or a possible assault on Boston. Meanwhile all divisions would be within a sphere small enough to allow combined movements or the support of any one division in the event of a concerted enemy advance. *Writings of Washington*, XII, 426-7.

60. The ground selected for winter quarters was on the heights around Fredericksburgh, N. Y., between Fishkill and Danbury, Conn. *Ibid.*, XII, 460, *ff.*

61. Alexander McDougall (d. 1786), a colonel of the 1st New York regiment, was commissioned a major-general October 20, 1777. Heitman, *op. cit.*, 368.

62. John Nixon (1727-1815) of Massachusetts had been a brigadier-general since August, 1776. He served until September, 1780. *Dict. Am. Biog.*, XIII, 530.

63. The British had no intention of leaving New York City. The cause of this rumor was probably the redistribution of the army which the commander-in-chief ordered at this time, in order better to defend the city. *Clinton Papers*, Clements Library.

27 we have a Report that there has been an Ingagement between A French Fleet of 31 sail & a British fleet
of 33 sail, the Latter Commanded by Admiral Keppel,[64]
who it is said was killed in the action. & his fleet beat &
Oblige'd to Return into Port.

28th I Dined with Genrl Gates to Day. who shew me a
Letter he had Receivd from the Adjatant Genrl of the
french Troops at Boston giving an account of the above
mentioned Action—

29th Nothing Extreordinery.

30th as yesterday. we have very fine weather.

Octobr 1t Nothing Extreordinery to Day—

2d as yesterday.

3d Do

4th weather very fine for the Season.

5th we are in a state of suspence Respecting the Enimys
Leaving N. York.

6th this Day two men belonging to N. Hampshire (one
by the Name of Blare, belonging to Holderness, the other
Farnsworth of Hollis,) were taken up within the Lines
of our Army, with a Learge sum of Counterfit Money
which they brought from N. York. we hear that the
french have take[n] Domoneak & [have sai]l'd for Jamaka.[65]

7th A Special Coart marcial was ordered to sit to Day
for the Tryal of the two men above mentioned, of which
I was a member. they ware tryed for beings spys & haveing a Learge sum of Counterfit money with them Which
they brough[t] from N. York. they Confess'd they ware

64. Admiral Augustus Keppel, Viscount Keppel (1725–1786), was made commander
of the channel fleet in 1776 and of the grand fleet in 1778. With 30 ships he engaged a
French fleet of 32 sails under D'Orvilliers on July 27, off the French coast. Both fleets
were badly damaged and the action was indecisive, but the French were forced back
to port. Dict. Nat. Biog., XI, 39–40.

65. Dominica, one of the Leeward Islands, British West Indies, was captured by
the French from the neighboring island of Guadaloupe early in September. Writings of Washington, XIII, 120.

Guilty of bringing the Counterfit money & that they ware to send word to the Enimy: viz. Col?s Holland & Stark, & Esq! Cummins⁶⁶ & others what situation our army & Country is in, as Near as tha could; they ware both Condemn'd to suffer Death as Spys— our men had a Gill of Rum Extr? to Day on account of its being the anniverciry of the Glorious victory Obtaind over the british army at bemus⁸ Heights.—& the Officers in Generel had a Meeting at Evining had a social Drink & gave several toasts sutible for the Occasion.—& our men had a Grand sham fight.

8ᵗʰ Nothing Extreordinery to Day.

9ᵗʰ as yesterday.

10ᵗʰ we have a heavy & bold storm to Day.

11ᵗʰ We are ordered to be in the greatest Possible Rediness for marching. it is Said the Enimy are imbarcking as fast as Possible. *God grant it may be True.*

12ᵗʰ Nothing New

13ᵗʰ as yesterday

14ᵗʰ D?

15ᵗʰ D°

16ᵗʰ we are Prepareing for keeping up to Morrow.

17 this being the first Anniversary of the Glorious 17ᵗʰ of Octobʳ 1777. the field Officers of this Division Make an Entertainment for all the Officers of the Division, & Gentlemen of the Town.— we Eat Dinner on a small hill between two of the brigades.— after the officers of the three Brigades had assembled, on the hill by marching in Divisions 13 in Each, thirteen Cannon ware Dis-

66. The two officers were not in the regular army. Among the provincials attached to the British army were a Capt. Stephen Holland of the Prince of Wales American Volunteers and a Maj. William Stark of the New Hampshire Volunteers on half pay. Capt. Holland was directing espionage work in 1780, but whether Maj. Stark is the person to whom Dearborn refers, has not been determined. Mr. Cummins appears to have been a Tory civilian in New York City. *A List of the General and Staff Officers . . . under . . . Clinton* (New York, 1779), *passim*.

charg^d from Each Brigade at which time Gen^rl Gates arivd with a number of other Gen^rl Officers. there was then three Cheers from the whole Division. at Dinner we had about 350 Officers & other gentlemen. after Dinner there was 13 toasts Drank. & a Cannon Discharged for Each.— at Evining we Retire'd to the Town, & spent the Evining very agreably.

18th we are geting sober.—& Genr! Poors Brigad is ordered to march to Morrow.

19th we march at 10' O Clock towards Hartford. I Receiv'd News this Day by Express that my wife Lay Dangerously sick with a Nerveous Fever. In Consequence of which I got Leave of absince & set out for home this Evining.

24th I ariv'd at my House at 7 O Clock in the Evining. found my wife Senceless & almost Motionless, which was a very Shocking Sight to behold. at half after Eleven she Expired. much Lamented not only by her Relation but by all her Neighbours.—67 this was a very Trying Scene to me. I seem'd to be Quite alone in the world. Except my two Little Daughters who are two small to feel their Loss, or offer me any Comfort.—

25th the most Malloncolly Sunday I Ever Experiencd.

26th the Remains of My Deceas'd wife was this Day Interr.d, on which Occation there was a very Great Number of People assembled from several Neighbouring Towns who universally seemd Heartely to Mourn my Loss.—
27th _____

_____

67. Dearborn's wife was Mary Bartlett (1751-1778), to whom he was married in 1771. Their two daughters were Sophia, born in 1773, who married Dudley B. Hobart; and Pamela, born in 1775, who married Allen Gilman in 1798. Pamela died the following year, shortly after the birth of her child. *Maine Historical and Genealogical Recorder*, III, 3; Levi Bartlett, *Genealogical and Biographical Sketches of the Bartlett Family* . . . (Lawrence, 1876), 17.

Novem.ʳ 12ᵗʰ 1778

I sett out from home to Join the army.— went by Boston stayd 4 Days with Genr.ˡ Gates & went to Rhode Island. Tary'd 3 days with Genr.ˡ Sulivan, & the 26ᵗʰ ariv'd at Hartford. found Colᵒ Reid[68] & several of our Officers who set out with me the 28ᵗʰ for Danbury where Genr.ˡ Poors Brigade is Desten'd. after marching to Hartford & back to Danbury where I ariv'd the 30ᵗʰ—in a heavy storm of Rain Hail & Snow & to my Great mortifycation found we ware order'd to Hut once more. I find that the 2 men who ware try'd as spyes the 7ᵗʰ of octobr at Danbury, ware hang'd at Hartford Novem.ʳ 4ᵗʰ

Decem.ʳ 1ᵗ we are Loocking out ground to Hut on. Genr.ˡ Burguoyns army from Cambridg have Cross'd the North River on their way to virgenia, where they are to be station'd—[69]

2ᵈ we March'd 6 miles toward the Sound & Incampᵉᵈ Near where we are to build our Huts.—[70]

3ᵈ we are Laying out our Ground to Hut on.—

4ᵗʰ we began this Day to build Huts. we hear that Genr.ˡ Green[71] & Col. Beedle[72] ware taken a few Days

68. Col. George Reid (d. 1815) of the 2nd New Hampshire regiment. Heitman, *op. cit.*; 462.

69. Burgoyne's captured troops, the "convention army," were first interned around Cambridge, Mass., then removed to Rutland, Vt., for fear they might be rescued by the British from Newport, R. I. Congress next ordered them moved to the vicinity of Charlottesville, Va. Winsor, *op. cit.*, VI, 321.

70. Part of Washington's army was to winter at West Point and vicinity; another part was sent to Middlebrook, N. J. Dearborn's brigade was to be stationed at Danbury, Conn., which town had been burned the year before. *Writings of Washington*, XIII, 179.

71. Nathanael Greene (1741–1786) of Rhode Island was a brigadier-general at the siege of Boston and then commanded the defences of New York. He was commissioned a major-general in August, 1776. He served in the attack on Trenton, and in the engagements around Philadelphia. While at Valley Forge, he was appointed quartermaster general. He saw action at Monmouth and assisted Sullivan in the Rhode Island campaign. He was still engaged in procuring supplies at this time. *Dict. Am. Biog.*, VII, 569–72.

72. Dearborn probably meant Col. Clement Biddle (1740–1814) of Pennsylvania, who as commissary-general of forage was associated with Greene. Heitman, *op. cit.*, 102.

Since by a Party of Tories in Jersey where they ware Loocking out for Quarters for his Excellency.— we Likewise hear that Col° Alden[73] was not Long since killd & Inhumanely butcher'd by the Savages & Tories at Cherry valley,[74] & his L! Col° & Maj! made Prisoners.—

5th at twelve at Night we ware alarm'd by hearing that the Enimy are at Terry Town (below Peeks kill) in force. in Consequence of which a Detatchment of 1500 men from the three Brigades under Genr! Putmans[75] Command ware ordered to march. we marched two Hours before Day for bedford[76] which is 20 miles from our Camp. Where we ariv'd the afternoon of the same Day. Where we had a Maggazeine of Provision Collecting. when the Enimy found we ware Like to meet them they Immediately Retired on board their ships & Return'd to york. we Remained at bedford to night. we hear to Day that the Report of Genr! Green's being Taken is not True but Col? Ward[77] Commissary Genr! of Musters was taken at the Place where we heard Genr! Green was taken.

73. Col. Ichabod Alden commanded the 7th Massachusetts regiment. Lt. Col. William Stacey and Maj. Samuel Darby were taken prisoners. The former was detained for four years. *Ibid.*, 65, 185, 513.

74. On November 10, a party of Tories and Indians under Walter Butler and Joseph Brant, the Indian, had destroyed the village of Cherry Valley, N. Y., burning the houses and killing about 50 inhabitants. Fiske. *op. cit.*, II, 90.

75. Israel Putnam (1718–1790), a distinguished veteran of the French and Indian War, was appointed a major-general in June, 1775. He saw action at Bunker Hill, the siege of Boston, the battle of Long Island, and the engagements around Philadelphia. In May, 1777, he was given command of the highlands of the Hudson; here he was unable to obey orders. A paralytic stroke ended his military career in December, 1779. *Dict. Am. Biog.*, XV, 281–2.

76. Washington had received intelligence that 52 vessels including a bomb ketch were proceeding up the Hudson River. Messengers were despatched to all units of the army, ordering immediate preparations to march. Bedford, Westchester co., on the route from Danbury, Conn., is about 15 miles from Tarrytown, on the Hudson River. *Writings of Washington*, XIII, 365–6.

77. Col. Joseph Ward (d. 1812) had been aide-de-camp and secretary to Gen. Artemus Ward. He became commissary-general of musters early in 1777, and commissary-general of prisoners in 1780. Heitman, *op. cit.*, 568.

7th we Remain'd at bedford—

8th we march^{ed} to Ridgfield on our way to Camp.—

9th we Return'd to Camp— I understand Genr! Washington with the Grand army are Huting in Jersey at a Place Call'd Midle Brook between Morristown & Brunswick.— Genr! Putmans Command is Poors, Parsons-s & Huntingtons Brigades, Stationed about Danbury.

10th we have a very Sevear Storm of Snow & Rain to Day & we living in Tents.—

11th the weather very Cold, the Snow about 6 inches Deep.—

12th we are very busy at work upon our Huts, amongst the Snow.—

13 a very heavy storm of Rain,—& no bread for two Days.—

14th good weather—

15th we are Covering our Huts.—

16th we begin to git into our Huts.—

17th a heavy Rain—

18th fine weather—

19th we are in our Huts.—

20 Eight of our men appeard to be Poisened by Eating Chees. I have sent for the People who sold the Chees.—

21^{t} the Brigade is Mustered to Day

22 a sevear snow Storm.—

23^{d} Genr! Poor Col? Cilley & a number of other officers set out for home to Day. the weather is very Cold. the New arraingement of the army toock Place in our Hampshire Troops yesterday.— we have Try.d the People who sold the Cheese to our Soldiers which I suspected was Poisond but they ware thought to be Innosent—

24th we had a snow Last night & very Sevear Cold to Day.— our men are well Cloath'd & well Hutted.—

Christmas Day. the weather is so very Cold we take but very little notice of the Day—

26th we have a very Sevear Snow Storm

27th the weather seems more like Canada, then Connecticut.— the Honbl Sylas Dean[78] has made a voyolent attact upon the Lees—: (viz: Richard H. Lee in Congress, Arther Lee agent at the Court of Madrid, & William Lee our agent at the Courts of viane & Barlain.)—in the Fish Kill Paper. taxing them with unfaithfulness to the States.

28th there is a general uneaseyness among the soldiers of Genr! Putmans Division. on account of the Depresiation of our Currency the Consequences of which I fear will Prove unhappy

29th we have nothing new to Day.—

30th this is Thanksgiving Day throughout the Continent.—[79] our men have Half a Pint of Rum Each to keep it with.—

31t we hear the Enimy have releas'd all the Prisoners they had at Rhode Island by reason of their being scant of Provisions.—

January 1t 1779.—

Old time keeps on her Coars, we find another year has Commens'd. thro the Coarse of which it is highly Probable from the Present situation of affairs in the Different Quarters of the world Many Important Events will turn up.

2d Nothing new to Day.—

78. Silas Deane (1737–1789) had been sent to France as diplomatic agent for the colonies in 1776. Later he joined Benjamin Franklin and Arthur Lee, and together they negotiated the alliance with France. Deane was recalled in 1778 on insinuations made by Lee. He appeared in Congress on December 22 and 23 in defence of his conduct abroad. *Dict. Am. Biog.*, V, 173–7.

79. The Continental Congress established December 30, 1778, as a day of thanksgiving by a resolution passed on November 17. *Journals of the Continental Congress*, XII, 1139.

3ᵈ we have fine weather.—

4ᵗʰ we have a Detatchment of 200 men sent off to to Day who are to be Concidered as an advanced Post to this Division. they are Stationed Near the Sound.—

5ᵗʰ the face of the Earth is again Cover'd with Snow.— we have receiv'd a supply of Cloathing for the Hampshire officers from the board of war for that state.—

6ᵗʰ nothing Extraordinery to Day.—

7ᵗʰ I am Pr.s.dᵗ of a Brigade Coart Marcial, which sets for the Tryal of Several Theives to Day—

8ᵗʰ on Coart Martial.—

9ᵗʰ Nothing new—

10ᵗʰ we hear to Day that there has been a Duel fought between Genrᴵ Lee & Colᵒ Lawrence[80] one of Genrᴵ Woshingtons Aide de camps in which Genrᴵ Lee receiv'd a wound in the bellay by a Pistol shot.—

11ᵗʰ Nothing new—but flanking[81] &c.

12ᵗʰ as yesterday.—

13ᵗʰ we have a fine Snow to night

14 nothing Extreordinery.—

15 we hear a Duel has been fought between between Genrᴵ Arnold & a Cetisan of Phyladelphia. the latter, Receiv'd a wound—[82]

16 Nothing but flanking.—

17ᵗʰ as yesterday.—

18 Nothing new.—

19ᵗʰ flanking.—

---

80. Col. John Laurens (1754–1782), one of Washington's aides-de-camp, challenged Maj. Gen. Charles Lee to a duel over an abusive letter which Lee had written to Washington. The duel took place on December 23, 1778. Lee was wounded. *Dict. Am. Biog.*, XI, 35–6.

81. Flanking was a military maneuver in which a small party of men was detached from the advance column to cover the flanks of the main body against surprise.

82. This was a false rumor. From December 19, 1779, to January 26, 1780, Arnold was on trial by a military court in Morristown, N. J. Moreover, he still walked with difficulty and used a cane. I. N. Arnold, *The Life of Benedict Arnold* (Chicago, 1880), 249.

20th very Cold.—

21^t the old Story.—

22^d I went to the sound for Oysters—

23^d Returnd from Norwalk—[83]

24th Nothing new—

25th flanking

26 we hear the Enimy are coming to Pay us a visit.—fl.

27 we are making some preparations to meet the Enimy.—

28th Nothing new.—f!—

29th as yesterday f!—

30th fl.—

31^t Nothing new.

Febuary 1^t we have very fine weather

2^d Nothing N.— fl—

3 D^o

4th I am ordered to take Command of 400 men who are Detach'd from Gen^{rl} Putnams Division, & March to New London. to garrison that Town—[84] f!

5th I March'd for New London as far as fairfield.—

6th March'd to Milford.—

7th March'd to New Haven.—

8th March^d to Gilford—

9th March'd to Killingsworth.—

10th March'd to Lime.—

11th March'd to New London—

12th I am Reconoyrting the fortifycations in & about Town, & Procureing proper Quarters for the Troops.—

13th we live very happy here—

83. Norwalk, Fairfield co., Connecticut, 22 miles south of Danbury on Long Island Sound.

84. The defences of New London consisted of Fort Trumbull on a point extending from the west shore into the harbor of New London, and Fort Griswold on the east side of the harbor. The latter fort occupied the heights back of the town of Groton. Small redoubts and temporary intrenchments were built to cover the land approaches to the city.

14 Nothing new—

15 as yesterday.—

16th a fine Dance.—

17th Nothing new.—

18th a fine Dance & f!

19th Nothing important.—

20th I saw the British Tyrants Speech made at the Opening of his Parliment[85]—which appears more like a Dying spee[ch] then otherwise.—

21^{t} nothing new—

· 22^{d} we had an Elligant Ball. at which was a Learge numbar of very fine Ladies—& fl.

23^{d} I Dined with Genr! Parsons[86] at Esq. Mumfords at Groton. where I spent one of the most agreable after noons with x x x x x x I have had for some months.

24th nothing new—

25th as yesterday.—

26th we have remarkable warm weather—

27th we hear a Spanish Imbassador has ariv'd at congress with a learge sum of hard money—[87]

28th Sunday I go to meeting.—

March 1^{t} 1779.—

I was at a Dance on board the Confediracy frigate.— & f! a Prize brigantine with salt was sent in here to

85. The king's speech made at the opening of Parliament, November 26, 1778, reached this country early in February, 1779. It was printed in the *New Jersey Gazette* of February 10. The speech was brief and general, asking for renewed exertions to defeat Britain's enemies in North America and to restore to the Crown peace with honor.

86. Samuel H. Parsons (1737–1789) of Connecticut was commissioned a brigadier-general in August, 1776. During the year 1779 he was in virtual command of the Connecticut division, owing to the failing health of Gen. Putnam. Parsons was promoted to the rank of major-general in 1780. He was one of the directors of the Ohio Company, and was the first judge of the Northwest Territory. *Dict. Am. Biog.*, XIV, 270-1.

87. This was a false rumor. No Spanish ambassador was sent to this country, nor was any loan granted at this time. However, even Washington heard in February that a large loan had been obtained from Spain. *Writings of Washington*, XIV, 129.

Day— we are informd that a body of the Enimy from york made an attempt last week to Distroy Elesabath Town in the Jerseys but ware very Roughly handled by a body [of] our troops [that] happend to meet them & Obliged [them] to make tracks back Quick step but not without a conciderable loss.—[88] the same day a body of the Enimy march[ed] from Kings bridg to Hors neck[89] where we had a Guard of 100 men, the Enimy after Plundering the Inhabitants of their Houshold furniture & abuseing the women in a very shameful manner ware Oblig'd to make a Precepitate retreat finding they ware like to be cut of[f] by Genr! Putnams Division. our troops killd a number of them & made 52 Prisoners

2^d nothing new.—

3^d fine weather & f!

4th we had an Elligent Dinner two miles from Town at M! Rogers.s—to Day

5th nothing new.—

6 D°

7th D°

8th D°

9th — — — f! had an Eligent ball.

10 the Ship Defence of 18 guns ran on Shor near the mouth of this harbour & is Lost. Crew & Stores Save'd we are asured that Spain & the two Cissalees have acceeded to the Independency of america, & Rushia has refused assisting Great briton with men or stores—[90]

88. A detachment of British troops under Lt. Col. Stirling tried to surprise Elizabethtown in the early morning of February 25. The enemy set fire to a few buildings, but was driven off by Brig. Gen. Maxwell. The Americans suffered one killed; the British two. *New Jersey Gazette*, March 3, 1779.

89. Horseneck Point or Field Point, on the Connecticut coast, extends into Long Island Sound between Captain Harbor and Smith Cove, about 2 miles east of Port Chester, N.Y.

90. Spain did not enter into an alliance with France against Great Britain until April, 1779, but as she had made known her sympathies for the American cause, a committee in Congress had recommended the draughting of a treaty of alliance for

11th — — — — f!

12th I receive orders to march what troops are here (belonging to Genr! Poors Brigade) back to Reading,[91] toot sweet.—on some important matters—

13th Genr! Parsons Receiv'd orders to March the whole Detachment back to Camp.—

14 we have a severe Snow Storm to Day

15 we are prepareing to march.— f!

16 Capt Lloyds[92] Company from Col? Hazens Reg^t March'd to Day for camp   we had a fine Dance this Evining—

17 Nothing new.—

18 — — — — f!

19 the troops from Genr! Poors Brigade are ordered to march to morrow morning, for Camp. a snow storm to Day.—

20th the Hampshire troops march'd to day for Camp.—

21^t Sunday went to meeting & — — — f! receiv'd orders from Genr! Putnam to Join the Reg^t

22 nothing but—f.l.

23 I am to set out for Camp to Day— 14 of the Enimys transports ware stranded on Gardners Island[93] last night & one taken by one [of] our Privateers—

26th I ariv'd at Camp, found our Brigade under marching orders.

her signature. It was probably this action of Congress which prompted Dearborn's observations. The two Sicilies: the island and the province of Naples, under Ferdinand IV, had already opened their ports to American commerce, though not participating actively. Russia had twice refused aid to Great Britain, and by 1779 was advocating the protection of neutral shipping against Britain's fleet. *Journals of the Continental Congress,* XIII, 239, *ff;* George Bancroft, *History of the United States* (Boston, 1875) IX, X, *passim.*

91. Reading or Redding, Fairfield co., Connecticut, is on the Saugatuck River about 6 miles from Danbury.

92. Capt. Richard Lloyd of New Jersey, attached to the 2nd Canadian regiment. Heitman, *op. cit.,* 355.

93. Gardiner's Island lies off the eastern end of Long Island, separated from the mainland by Gardiner's Bay.

27 Col? Hazens Reg? has march'd for Springfield—. & one Hundred of the New Hampshire troops have march'd for Peeks kill.—

28th Nothing new— — f?

29th we hear the Enimy are Preparing to attact New London—

30th I take Command of the brigade—94

31^t fine weather.—

Aprill 1? I take Quarters at Col? Reads where Col? Hazen has Quarterd a very agreabl family.—

2^d weather Remarkable fine for the Season. fl.

3^d all the Officers of the Brigade turn'd out & Play'd a game at ball the first we have had this yeare.—

4 the brigade march'd to Reding meeting Hous to attend Publick worship.—

5th nothing new to Day.—

6th the brigade is marching by Divisions, viz 100 men in a day for Peekskill—

7th a Conciderable number of Masons had a feast to Day at Reading where a fine Collection of ladies attended—333.

8th the weather is very fine for the Season   it is said by the old men so forwar'd a Spring has not been known—

9th we had a very Desent Dance at my Quarters which we concider as the last we shall have this year—

10th the Peech trees are beginig to blow

11 the peech trees are in full blow—   the last of our Brigade march'd to Day—

12th nothing new to Day—

94. Poor's brigade at this time comprised the first three New Hampshire and the 2nd Canadian regiments. That the command should devolve temporarily upon a junior lieutenant-colonel was owing to an unusual chain of circumstances. Brig. Gen. Poor and Col. Cilley were on leave. Of the three colonels, Hale of the 2nd New Hampshire had been taken prisoner; Scammell of the 3rd New Hampshire had been promoted to adjutant-general; and Hazen of the 2nd Canadian had been sent north to build a military road to Canada. Among the lieutenant-colonels, Dearborn ranked below Reid and Antil, but the latter was a prisoner of war, and Reid was either on leave or detached on special duty.

13th I Rais'd a Seeige this morning of 2 months & march for Peeks kill. we had a very heavy thunder Storm last night—

14th arivd at Peeks kill found our brigade Quartered in Huts in the Highlands where we have no neighbors but Owls, Hedghogs, & Rattle snakes, & them in plenty.

15th a Small guard of ours was Surprisd this week in Gersey by a party of Tories from N. York & every man put to the bayonet on the Spot under the cover of a dark night.—^{95}

16th I have been recornoyrtering the mountain to day. & have moovd into a Hut my Self.

17th we ware oblige'd to walk 4 miles to day to find a place leavel enough to play ball.

18 we had a very severe frost Last night; I fear it will prove fatal to the fruit;

19th nothing new—

20th D^{o}.

21^{t} d^{o}.

22 d^{o}.

23^{d} we [have] certain Intiligence today of the capture of 8 of the Enimies vessels bound from N. york to Georgey: viz. one 20 gun ship one 16 gun Ship & 6 transports Containing 800 men 5000 Barrells of provisions 40000 Guineas—furniture for 2 Reg^{t} of Hors, a very learg Quantity of English good[s] & 24 British Officers— the above prises ware taken by the warren Frigate of 32 guns, the Ranger of 20 guns & the Queen of France of 20 guns.^{96}

95. The only raid reported at this time in the *New Jersey Gazette* was one on a post at Little Ferry in Bergen County. A British detachment under Capt. Van Allen seized a party of two officers and eleven men; two of the Americans escaped, and the rest were taken prisoners to New York. *New Jersey Gazette*, April 28, 1779.

96. The three American cruisers, with Capt. J. B. Hopkins as senior officer, left Boston on April 18 and captured a British privateer. From the crew they learned that nine British sail were leaving New York with supplies for the enemy in Georgia. The three American ships caught up with the transports off Cape Henry and captured

24th nothing new

25 we hear a body of the Enimy are Imbarking at york for the southward   Maj[r] Norris[97] & several of our officers ariv'd in camp to day from N. H.—

26th nothing new.—

27th D[o]

28th D[o]

29th D[o]

30th a Severe Snow Storm to day.

1[t] May— very pleasent—

2[d] we hear Col. Vanskoyk[98] has destroyed the OnOn-dogo tribe & Town of Indians   we hear a body of the Enimy are in the Jerseys.—

3[d] we Expect to march from this the 8th or 9th Ins[t]

4 nothing new.—

5th D[o]—

6th we are ordered to be hold our selves in redyness to march at the shortest notice—

7th Col[o] Cilleys Reg[t] is orderd to be redy to march to morrow.

8 Col[o] Cilleys Reg[t] is order'd to march to morrow morning—

9th Col[o] Cilley Reg[t] march'd to day & crossd the North River to New Windsor opposite Fishkill & orderd to march to East Town in Penselvania—

10 I am order'd to prepare to march

11 we are Drawing Cam[p] Equippage to day for the 2[d] & 3[d] Batt[lns]—

seven of them. Besides the cargo, twenty-four British army officers on board were captured. J. F. Cooper, *The History of the Navy of the United States of America* (London, 1839) I, 188–9.

97. Maj. James Norris (d. 1814) of the 3rd New Hampshire (Dearborn's) regiment. He had been wounded and taken prisoner at Hubbardton, July 7, 1777. Heitman, *op. cit.*, 415.

98. Col. Goose Van Schaick (d. 1787) of the 1st New York regiment received the thanks of Congress for his expedition against the Onondagas. *Ibid.*, 557.

12th we are prepareing to march—

13th as yesterday—

14th D^{o}

15 d^{o}

16th I am order'd to march to Morrow with the 2^{d} & 3^{d}
N. H. Battalions to Easton in Penselvania.—^{99}

17th we march to Fish kill—

18th Cross the North River & march'd 9 miles.—
Genr! Poor & Col^{o} Cilley arive'd to day from N. Hampshire.—

19th we March 14 miles to day.

20th we march'd 12 miles & ware Stop'd by a Storm.

21^{t} Stormy to day, we lay still— sold both my Horses
to day for 1800 dollers—

22^{d} Stormy to Day—

23 March'd to Sussex Court House—^{100}

24th March'd to Mount Hope, or Moravian village.

25th March'd within 4 miles of Easton—

26th Cross'd the Deliware to Easton & incamp'd
in Tents— found Genr! Sulivan & Genr! Maxwells
Brigade.—

27th Col^{o} Cilleys Reg^{t} is order'd to march to wiomen—^{101} where we all Expect to go soon—

28 Col^{o} Cilleys Reg^{t} March'd for wyomen to day—

29th I went to Bethleham—^{102}

30th Sunday I went to german Church— their manner
of worship appears very Sollom—

31 Nothing Extreordinery—

99. Easton, Northampton co., Pa., on the Delaware River at the mouth of the Lehigh, had been designated as the place where the western expedition was to be organized and outfitted. *Writings of Washington*, XIV, 492.

100. Sussex, Sussex co., N. J.

101. Wyoming, now Wilkes-Barre, Luzerne co., Pa., on the west bank of the Susquehanna, 18 miles west southwest of Scranton.

102. Bethlehem, Northampton co., Pa., on the left bank of the Lehigh River, 5 miles east of Allentown.

June 1ˢ I toock a touer round the country about 8 or ten mils from Camp to see what kind of inhabitents there was, & — — — — fˡ

2ᵈ — — — — — fˡ

3ᵈ I am on a genrˡ Court Martial for the tryal of some Tories who have been detected in Inticeing our Soldiers to desert to the Enimy—

4ᵗʰ as yesterday—

5ᵗʰ Dº— we hear that Genrˡ Lincoln has gain'd a very Conciderable victory over the Enimy near Charles Town in South Carolina. it is said he kill.d & toock 1400 of the Enemy—.[103] we are likewise assur'd that Colº Clark of Virgenia with a body of troops has taken a small fortress near Detroit. Garrison'd by Lˡ Govener Ham[104] & 101 men,[105] & the nex[t] day after takeing the fort, 20 Indian warrier returning from a scout came up to the fort not knowing it had been taken: the virgenians fire'd upon them & kill'd 18 out of the 20 the other two made their escape.

6ᵗʰ nothing new—

7ᵗʰ Dº

8ᵗʰ dº

103. This was a false rumor. Washington remained skeptical of the reports of a great American victory at Charleston, and waited in vain for confirmation of the story, which was printed in the newspapers. Gen. Prevost, in command of the British and Tories in Georgia, had marched on Charleston and demanded its surrender. The American defenders refused, and being without the equipment to carry on a siege, Prevost withdrew. Meanwhile Gen. Lincoln, hurrying to the support of the defenders, engaged the British at Stono Ferry, but not until June 20. Though the action was not decisive, the British withdrew to Savannah. David Ramsay, *History of the Revolution of South Carolina* . . . (Trenton, 1785), II, 24–31.

104. This name is crossed out, rewritten and otherwise obscured in the original text. Dearborn was obviously trying to spell Hamilton.

105. Col. George Rogers Clark (1752–1818) of Virginia had won over Vincennes (Indiana) to the American cause in July, 1778, without a battle, after he had subdued the Illinois settlements. He left a garrison of only two soldiers there. Lt. Gov. Henry Hamilton of Detroit easily captured Vincennes in December, 1778. Clark, who was at Kaskaskia, made a memorable winter march with his small force and recaptured the fort in February, 1779, sending Hamilton to Virginia as a prisoner of war. Winsor, *op. cit.*, VI, 722–8.

9 two men Inhabitents a sentenced to Suffer Death by a Court Martial for Inticeing Soldiers to desert to the Enimy & affording them their assistence to git to the Enimy.

10th Nothing new—

11th d.º

12th 3 penselvania Soldiers ware hanged to day for murder.—

13th nothing new.

14th we have the news from the southward confirmed, as follows viz. the Enimy made an attact upon the City of Charles Town in South Carolina & ware repuls'd, they made a second attact with fix'd Bayonets. Genr.ˡ Lincoln who was in the Rear of the Enimy came up & fell on the Enimy with great Sperit, put them to flight leaving 1483 dead & wounded, & 3000 of the tories laid down their arms— in Consequence of the above news, we fired a fude Joy ⌈feu de joie⌉— Lady Washington came to town to day, on her way from Head Quarters to Virginia—

15th Genr.ˡ Sulivan, the other Genr.ˡ & field officers waited on Misses Washington this morning to Bethleham 12 miles.—

16th All the Troops are order'd to march to Morrow morning for wyomen

Sullivan's Indian Expedition

THE *demoralizing effect of recurrent Indian raids on the settlers in western New York and the valley of the Susquehanna led to vigorous retaliatory measures in the summer of 1779. Acting under orders of Congress, Washington directed Brodhead to march , from Fort Pitt up the Allegheny River, while a larger expedition under Sullivan ascended the Susquehanna and Wyoming valleys. Their instructions were to destroy all Indian villages and crops belonging to the Six Nations, to engage the Indian and Tory marauders under Brant and Butler whenever possible, and to drive them so far west that future raids would be impossible. These operations consumed three months, during which the main army remained for the most part inactive near the Hudson above New York, waiting for Clinton to make the next move. In the South Lincoln, with the support of D'Estaing's fleet, laid siege to Savannah, but failed to rout the British from the city.*

EASTON June 17th 1779
Genr!s Maxwells & Poors Brigades with Col.s Procters¹ Reg.t of Artillary ware order'd to march this day for Wyoming under the Command of the Honb.e Maj.r Genr.l Sullivan, on an Expedition against the Savages between Wyoming & at Niagara—

---

1. Col. Thomas Proctor (d. 1806) of Pennsylvania had commanded the 4th Continental artillery since 1777. He resigned from the army in April, 1781. Heitman, *op. cit.*, 453.

18th The Army march'd at Sunrise, proceeded 12 miles to Hilliers Tavern,[2] & encamp'd our course to day about north.—

19th March'd at 4 oclock, A.M. proceeded 7 miles to Brinkers Mills,[3] where there is a Magazine of Provisions kept, here we halted & drew provisions. we pass'd this morning what is Call'd the Wind Gap of the blue mountains, a narrow pass that appears as if Nature desin'd it for a rode into the country, as it is the only place that this ridge of mountains can be pass'd for a very great distence. after drawing provisions we march'd 9 miles to Learns Tavern[4] & incamp'd our course to day about North.—

20th March'd at 9 oclock, pass'd the end of a mountain call'd Dogon point,[5] proceeded about 5 miles today & incamp[d6] the hous we left this morning is the last we shall see until we git to Wyoming.—

21[!] Enter'd what is Call'd the Great Swamp, proceeded 20 miles thro' a horrid rough gloomey country, the land cover'd with pine, Spruce lawrel bushes & hemlock. we eat breakfast at a streem call'd Tunkhannah, we pass'd an other call'd Tobehannah, & an other the Leahigh.[7] we likewise pass'd what is call'd the Shades of Death, a very gloomy thick part of the Swamp.—

2. The road to Wyoming had been surveyed by Lt. Benjamin Lodge, and opened "to allow the passage of waggons and carriages." The original manuscript maps of the Sullivan expedition are in the New York Historical Society. Facsimiles were printed to accompany Frederick Cook's *Journals of the Military Expedition of Major General John Sullivan* . . . (Albany, 1887). A comparison of the original survey with the U. S. Geological Survey indicates that the road ran along the route of the old Slate Belt Electric, through Belfast June, Belfast and into the town of Wind Gap. Hillier's Tavern stood in or near the present town of Wind Gap.

3. Brinker's Mills was in the vicinity of Scioto, Monroe co., Pa., about 20 miles north by west of Easton.

4. Learns Tavern stood at or near Tannersville, Monroe co., Pa.

5. Dogon's Point was probably Camelback Mountain.

6. The camp on the 20th was somewhere near Wiscasset, Pa.

7. Tunkhannock, Tobyhanna and Lehigh Creeks.

22[d] we March'd but 5 miles to a dessolate farm 7 miles from Wyoming.—[8]

23[d] we March'd to the fort at Wyoming[9] 7 miles, where we found several Reg[t]s incamp'd which are part of our army our course the 2 last days has been about N. West.—the whole Country from Easton to Wyoming is very poor & barren & I think such as will never be Inhabited. it abounds with dear & Rattle Snakes.—the land at Wyoming on both sides the river is very fine, & was very thickly Inhabited before they ware cut off by the savages, 20 miles up & down the river, after the Battle at this place last year in which more than 200 of the Inhabitents ware kill'd. the Savages burnt & destroy'd the whole country & drove off the cattle & horses, & strip'd the women & children of every comfort of life,—

we are now incamp'd on the bank of Susquehannah river, this river is at this place about 50 rods wide, & abounds with fish of various kinds, such as Shad, Bass, pike, Trout &c &c—

24[th] we are laying still. some skettering Indians are skulking about us.—

25[th] Nothing new.—

26[th] as yesterday.—

27[th] the 2[d] & 3[d] N. Hampshire Reg[t]s cross'd the river & moov'd 3 miles up to a place call'd Forty Fort[10] on Abrahams plains & incamp'd here in the remains of a stockhead fort. about 3 miles above this Fort the

8. Lt. Lodge labels this "Bullocks House."

9. Fort Wyoming was rebuilt in 1778 on the river bank about 10 rods below the junction of Northampton and River streets in Wilkes-Barre, Pa.

10. Forty Fort was built in 1770 on the high west bank of the Susquehanna, on the site of River and Fort streets in the borough of the same name, above Wilkes-Barre. It derived its name from the forty settlers who were sent out by the Susquehanna Company to take possession of the land in their behalf. *Report of the Commission to locate the site of the frontier forts of Pennsylania.* (Harrisburg, 1896), I, 438.

Battle[11] was fought between the 2 Butlers, viz. Col?
Butler of Wyoming & the more then savage butler
that commanded the Indians & Tories.—in which 250
men ware kill'd & skelp'd on our side & about 40 or
50 on the Enimies side. the next day after the battle
the Enimy contrary to their ingagements at the Capitulation of Forty Fort (in which was about 500
women & Children) burnt and destroy'd the whole settlement.

28th we are erecting some small works for the security
of our guards.—

29th as yesterday.—

30th nothing new

July 1[t] the two Tories[12] who ware condemn'd at
Easton war orderd to be executed to day. one of them was
hung. the other was pardon'd under the Gallows.—a
number of us discover'd a fine buck to day on an Island
which we surrounded & kill'd.—the army is waiting for
provisions that are coming up the River.—

2[d] I went with Gen! Poor & several other Gentlemen to day to vew the feild of action where the Battle
between the two Butlers was fought; we found a great
number of bones at & near the field of battle; among a
number of skul bones that we found none was without
the mark of the tommahok,—I saw one Grave where
73 of our men ware buried, & ware shewn a place wher
17 of our men after being taken ware made to set down in

11. Dearborn here refers to the Wyoming massacre. Maj. John Butler, commanding
about 1200 Tories and Indians, swept down on the valley, routing Lt. Col. Zebulon
Butler and about 360 militia who tried to check the raiders. Many of the settlers
were tortured and killed. The fort, containing women and children, surrendered
next day. Houses were burned, and more of the settlers perished in their flight. The
report of the massacre, somewhat exaggerated, spread rapidly throughout the colonies. Fiske, *op. cit.*, II, 88–9.

12. The two prisoners were Michael Rosebury and Lawrence Miller of Sussex
county, N. J. The former was hanged. Cook, *op. cit.*, 225.

a ring, 16 of whom they Immediately tommahawk'd, the other leap'd over the ring & made his escape.—

3ᵈ This is anniversary of the Battle of the two Butlers mentioned above.

4ᵗʰ this is the anniversary of the Declaration of American Independence, but as it is sunday we take no other notice of it then that of having a Sermon adapt to the Occation.—Colᵒ Cilleys & Courtlandts regᵗs cross'd the river & Joind us to day.—several dear & wild turkeys have been kill'd within a day or two with which this Country abounds.—

Monday July 5ᵗʰ Genˡ Poor made an Entertainment to day for all the Officers of his Brigade, to celibrate the Anniversary of the declaration of American Independence. 87 Gentlemen ware present at dinner, after which the 13 following Patriotick Toasts ware drank.—

1ˢᵗ 4th of July 76, the ever Memoriable Eara of American Indipendence.—

2ᵈ the United States.—

3ᵈ the Grand Counsel of America.—

4ᵗʰ Genˡ Washington & the Army.—

5ᵗʰ the King & Queen of France.—

6ᵗʰ Genˡ Lincoln & the Southern Army.—

7ᵗʰ Genˡ Sullivan & the Western Army.—

8ᵗʰ May the Counsellors of America be wise, and her Soldiers Invincible.—

9ᵗʰ A Successful & decisive Campaign.—

10ᵗʰ Civilization or death to all American Savages.—

11ᵗʰ the Immortal Memory of those heroes that have fallen in defence of American Liberty.—

12ᵗʰ May this New World be the last Asylum for freedom and the Arts.—

13ᵗʰ May the Husbandmans house be bless'd with peace, & his fields with plenty.—

the whole was conducted with such Joy & festivity as demonstrated an Independent Elevation of Spirit, on this Important & enteresting Occation.—

6th one Winslow a Soldier in the 3[d] N. Hampshire Reg[t] was drown'd this morning by going in to bathe—a very severe shower of thunder, hail, rain & wind came on at about 1 oclock P.M. many peices of the hail ware as large as hens Eggs but of a very erregular form.—

7[th] I eat part of a fryed Rattle Snake to day, which would have tasted very well had it not been snake.—

8[th] Nothing extreordinary.—

10[th] a detachment of 150 men was sent from the 2[d] & 3[d] N. Hampshire Reg[t]s under the command of Col[o]. Reid, towards Easton to repare the rodes & to help forward some waggons with provisions.

11[th] we receiv'd our New Commissions upon the new Arrangement to day, which we have been expecting for eighteen Months past.—I receiv'd several letters from N. Hampshire to day in one of which I am inform'd of being Married, but have not learnt to whome.—

12th nothing new.—

13 Col[o]. Butler, Misses Butler[13] & a number of other ladies honour'd us with a visit from town this afternoon, with whome we spent a very agreable afternoon.—

14th nothing new.—

15 we hear the Main body of the Enimy have retir'd from Kings ferry on the Hudsons river, but have left a post there.

16th I went with General[s] Sullivan, Maxwell, & Poor together with a number of other Gentlemen to vew the ground where the Battle of the Butlers was fought.

13. Zebulon Butler (1731-1795) led a band of Connecticut settlers into the Wyoming valley in 1769. After the massacre he fled with his family, but returned after the invaders had departed. He remained in Wyoming until the end of 1780, when he was stationed at West Point. "Misses Butler" refers to his second wife. *Dict. Am. Biog.*, III, 372.

17th we hear the Enimy are pursueing their savage plan of burning plundering & destroying defencless Towns, that they have burnt fairfield, Norwalk, & part of New Haven in Connecticut, & Bedford in N. York State.—[14] these things we may thank our good friends the tories for, what will not those hell hounds doo, there was a very striking instance of their more then savage barbarrity in the battle of the two Butlers. one Henry Pencel of wyomin who was fortunate enough to make his escape from the field of Battle onto an Island in the river, with one or two more without their arms; near night a small party of the Enimy came onto the Island, the foremust of which was John Pencel brother to s'd Henry, who upon discovering his brother call'd him a damn'd rebel, & threten'd to kill him. Henry fell on his knees & beg'd for his life, saying brother John I am in your hands I'll be your slave, I'll go with you, but pray spare my life, we have differ'd in sentiment & have met in the field of Battle, but as I am now fully in your power for god's sake don't kill me. but his unnaturel & more then savage brother, Cain like, deef to all his cries & Intreeties, damn'd him for a rebel, deliberately charg'd his gun & shot his brother, then tommahawk'd and skelp'd him. Immediately some savages cam up and ask'd him what he had done. he told them he had kill'd his brother henry, a dam'd Rebel, these savages curs'd his unnatural behaveyer & threten'd to serve him the same way. the above account I have from on[e] Mr Slocum a young fellow belonging to Wyoming who lay in the bushes so near pencel as to hear all that passed.—

18th nothing extreordinery—

14. Maj. Gen. William Tryon, Loyalist governor of New York, had led an expedition into Connecticut, which plundered and burned the towns mentioned between July 3 and 12. *Writings of Washington*, XV, 402, *passim*.

19th d?—

20th D?—

21? we are inform'd by a letter from one of Gen!
Washingtons Aides,[15] that Gen! Wain with a body of
light Infantry, on the night of the 15th Ins? surpris'd &
took a small Garrison near Kings ferry on Hudsons River,
call'd Stoney point.[16] the perticulers have not yet come
to hand, but it is said the number of men kill'd & taken
is about 600—& a quantity of Artillery & Stores &c.—

22d we have a confirmation of the news of yesterday,—

23d I went with several other Gentlemen 8 miles up
the River, to an old settlement call'd Lachawanee.[17] to
fish & hunt dear—where we stayed over night.—

24th came home with but few fish.—70 boats ariv'd
from Sunsbury[18] with provisions & stores to day—

25th 7 men belonging to what is call'd the German
Reg?[19] ware sentenced by a Gen! Court Martial to suffer
death for desertion.—

26 we are Inform'd that Gen! Parsons has had an Ingagement with a body of the Enimy near Wilton 7 miles
from Norwalk in Connecticut and finally repuls'd them.[20]

15. The aide was Major Caleb Gibbs (1748-1818) who commanded Washington's
Guards. Cook, *op. cit.*, 226; C. E. Godfrey, *The Commander-in-Chief's Guard* (Washington, 1904), 170-1.

16. Brig. Gen. Anthony Wayne with 1200 light infantry took the fort at Stony
Point in a brilliant assault with bayonets. The attack took place in the early morning
of July 16. Fiske, *op. cit.*, II, 112.

17. Lackawanna: Dearborn here refers to Pittston, Luzerne co., which is on the
Susquehanna River at the mouth of the Lackawanna, 9 miles northeast of Wilkes-Barre.

18. Sunbury, Northumberland co., Pa. is on the east bank of the Susquehanna,
one mile below the junction of its branches.

19. The German regiment was raised in Pennsylvania and Maryland in accordance
with a resolution of the Continental Congress. It was first commanded by Col. Nicho-
las Haussegger, later by Col. Henry L. P. Baron d'Arendt, who went on leave in
August, 1778, because of ill health. The commander of the regiment during Sullivan's
expedition was probably Lt. Col. Ludowick Weltner. Heitman, *op. cit.*, 27.

20. Washington had sent Brig. Gen. Samuel H. Parsons into Connecticut, where he
mustered some regulars and with the available militia routed the British who were
raiding Norwalk. So effective was the American resistance that the British did not

27th Gen! Poors Brigade moov'd down the river & Join'd the Main army at what is called the town.—²¹ the above mention'd deserters that ware orderd to be executed to day are pardoned by the Gen!—who has declar'd he never will pardon another man in like circumstances.

28 Col? Reid ariv'd with 80 waggons with provisions & Stores from Easton. the pack Horses are distributed in the several Brigades & Reg?s to day & mark'd.—

29th we are inform'd that a party of Savages with some british troops have taken a small fort²² on the west branch of the Susquehannah near Sunsbury, have plunder'd the Inhabitents of their cattle, horses & every other thing they could carry off.—& an other party has been down to a place call'd the Minnisinks²³ on the deliware river & have had an action with a party of our Millitia in which the Millitia ware rather worsted, & lost a number of men, but the Millitia being reinfors'd the enimy ware oblig'd to retreet—we likewise are inform'd that Gen! Clinton has moov'd up from New York & taken possession at Kings ferry again with his main body.

30th the Army under Gen! Sullivan is order'd to March to Morrow Morning, towards the Indian Settlement. a very severe campaign I expect we shall have.

Genr! Sullivans army at Wyoming consists of the Troops following viz:

renew their operations along the coast. G. H. Hollister, *The History of Connecticut* (Hartford, 1857), II, 378-9.

21. The town of Wyoming, or Wilkes-Barre.

22. The small fort was Freeland's Fort, which stood on Warrior Run, about 4 miles east of Watsontown, Northumberland co., Pa. The attack occurred about 9: A. M. on July 21, 1779. *Report of the Commission* . . . I, 381-3.

23. Minisink or Greenville, Orange co., N. Y., 5 miles east of Port Jervis on the Delaware River.

Maxwells Brigade consisting of Ogdons, Datens, Shreefs & Spencers Reg.[t]s.—[24]

Poors Brigade consisting of Cilleys, Reids, Scammells & Courtlands Reg.[t]s.—

Hands Brigade consisting of the German Reg.[t], Shots Corps, Spoldens Independent Company, & Hubley's Reg.[t] from penselvania.—[25]

Wyoming July 31.[t] 1779

this day the army Marches for Teogo,[26] in the following order:

Head Quarters Easton May 24th 1779

When the army shall be fully Assembled the following Arrangements are to take place:—

Light corps Commanded by Gen.[l] Hand	Armandts corps[27] Sholts D° 6 companies of Rangers W.[m] Butlers Reg.[t] Morgans Corps & all volunteers that may Join the army.	
Maxwell's Brigade to consist of	Ogdons, Daytons, Shreeves & spencers.	Regt.s & form the left of the front line—

---

24. Brig. Gen. William Maxwell's brigade consisted of the 1st New Jersey regiment under Col. Matthias Ogden, the 3rd New Jersey under Col. Elias Dayton, the 2nd New Jersey under Col. Israel Shreve, and Spencer's regiment under Col. Oliver Spencer.

25. Brig. Gen. Edward Hand's brigade consisted of the German regiment under Lt. Col. Ludowick Weltner, Capt. John Paul Schott's Independent Pennsylvania company from Ottendorf's corps, Capt. Simon Spalding's Wyoming Valley company, and Lt. Col. Adam Hubley's 11th Pennsylvania regiment.

26. Teoga is now Athens, Bradford co., Pa., on the west bank of the Susquehanna, 2 miles above the mouth of the Chemung River.

27. Charles Armand Tufin, Marquis de la Rouerie (1756–1793), came to America in 1777 and was commissioned a colonel. He raised a small cavalry corps of Frenchmen and was active in several battles. After the death of Count Pulaski in 1779, the remains of his corps were incorporated into Armand's command. Armand fought under Gates at the battle of Camden, and took part in the Yorktown siege. He was made a brigadier-general in 1783 and returned to France the following year. Townsend Ward, "Charles Armand Tufin . . . ", in Pa. Mag. of Hist. & Biog., II, 1–34. Lt. Col. William Butler (d. 1789) commanded the 4th Pennsylvania regiment. Heitman, op. cit., 138.

Poors Brigade   ⎫ Cilleys, Reids,
to consist of   ⎬ Scammells, & Courtlandts, Reg.s
                  ⎭ to form the right of the front line

Clintons Brigade[28] ⎫ late Livingstons Dubois.s Gainsworths,
to consist of   ⎬ & Oldens Reg.s to form 2^d line or Reserve.

The right of the first line to be coverd by 100 men draughted from Maxwells Brigade; The left to be coverd by 100 men draughted from Poors Brigade; Each flank of the 2^d line to be cover'd by 50 men draughted from Clintons Brigade: the Flanking division on the right to consist of Hartlies & Dattens Reg.s with a draught from the line of 100 men. the flanking division on the left to consist of the German Bat.^{ln} & 100 men draughted from the line.

The order of Battle & the Order of March are represented on the Annexed plan & are to be adherd to at all times when the situation of the Country will possibly admit, & where a deviation takes place, it must be carried no further than the necessity of that time requires.

The Order of March, The light corps will advance. by the right of Companies in files, & keep at least one mile in front.—Maxwells Brigade will advance by it right in files, sections, or platoons, as the country will admit.—Poors Brigade to advance by it left in the same manner.—Clintons Brigade will advance by the right of Reg.s by platoons, sections, or files as the Country will admit; all

28. Brig. Gen. James Clinton's brigade consisted of the 4th New York regiment, formerly commanded by Col. Henry B. Livingston, but now headed by Lt. Col. Frederick Weisenfels; the 5th New York under Col. Lewis Du Bois; the 3rd New York under Col. Peter Gansevoort; the 7th Massachusetts, formerly commanded by the late Col. Ichabod Alden but now under Lt. Col. John Brooks. Heitman, *op. cit.*, *passim.* Cook (*op. cit.*) states that the 2nd New York regiment under Col. Philip Van Cortlandt was attached to this brigade.

the covering parties & flanking divisions on the right will advance by the left, & those on the left, by the right;—the Artillery & pack horses will March in the Center. should the Army be attacked in front while

ORDER OF MARCH

Light Troops Commanded by General Hand

Flank Guard

Flanking Division

Poor's Brigade

Three Columns of Horses

Artillery Commanded by Colonel Proctor

Three Columns of Horses

Maxwell's Brigade

Flanking Division

Flank Guard

Clinton's Brigade

Reproduced from the diagram in Dearborn's original manuscript journal

on its march, the light Corps will Immediately form and repulse the Enimy. the flanking divisions will Indeavoor to gain the flank & rear of the Enimy, while the line is forming the pack horses will in all cases fall into the position represented in the annex'd plan. should the Enimy attack on either flank, the flanking division attacked will form a front & sustain the attack till reinforced, in which case a part of the light corps is to be Immediately detach'd to gain the Enimies flank & rear.

the covering parties of the 2^d line will moove to gain the other flank, should the Enimy attack our rear the 2^d line will face & form a front to the Enimy. the covering parties of the 1^t line will moove to sustain it while the flanking Divisions face about and Endeavour to gain their flanks rear. Shoould the light troops be

ORDER OF BATTLE

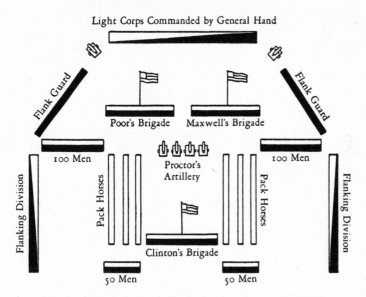

Light Corps Commanded by General Hand

Flank Guard

Flank Guard

Poor's Brigade   Maxwell's Brigade

Flanking Division   100 Men   Pack Horses   Proctor's Artillery   Pack Horses   100 Men   Flanking Division

Clinton's Brigade

50 Men   50 Men

Reproduced from the diagram in Dearborn's original manuscript journal

driven back, they will pass thro the Intervals of the main Army & form in the rear; should the Enimy in an Ingagement with the army when form'd, endeavour to turn either flank, the covering parties will moove up to lengthen the line, & so much as may be found necessary from the flanking division, will display outwards to prevent the attempt of the Enimy from succeeding; the light Corps will have their advance & flank guards at a good distance from the Main body—

the Flanking Divisions will furnish flank guards & the
2^d line a Rear Guard for the Main Army; when we find
the light Corps engag'd with the Enimy in front, the
front of the pack horses will halt and the rear close up,
while the collumns moove in a small distance Close &
display Columns, which will bring the horses in the position represented in the plan for order of Battle. should
the attack be made on either flank or Rear the horses
must be kept in the position they are in at the commencement of the attack, unless other orders are then given.—
    July 31^t 1779
                    After passing the forenoon at very severe
fatigue in loading the boats & pack horses, the army
moovd from Wyoming at 2 Oclock P. M with 120 boats
about 1200 pack horses & 700 beef cattle. we proceeded
to Lachawanea (10 miles) & Encamp'd. here has been a
very pleasant settlement, the land is very fertile & level.
the Inhabitants being drove off, & the place dessolated by
the Savages last year, it is now uninhabited. we have
had a remarkable rainey time for 10 days past & still
continues.—
August 1^t Sunday.—As the boats did not get up last night,
the army did not march till 4 oClock. P.M. proceeded 7
miles the way most horredly rough, we found great difficulty in giting forward the pack horses. it was late in
the evining before we ariv'd at our incamping ground.
our rear Guard did not arive till near day brake; we incamp'd on a fine piece of Intervale, which has been Inhabited, but shared the fate of Wyoming last year. this
place was Formaly Inhabited by savages & is called
Quilutimack.[29]—

29. Quailutimack, signifying "we came unawares upon them." The encampment
was made on the intervale two miles above Ransom, Lackawanna co., Pa., on the
west bank of the Susquehanna. Cook, *op. cit.*, 123.

2^d the army lay still to repair the pack sadles &c &c.— we took a number of fine fish with a sean to day—such as bass, pike, chubs &c &c—

3^d the army march'd at 7 oclock, proceeded 12 miles to some dessolated fields at the mouth of a creek call'd Tunkhannunk,[30] we had much better marching to day.

4th march'd at 6 oclock, proceeded 17 miles to a dessolated farm call'd Vanderlips, which is an excellent tract of land. we pass'd several dessolated farms to day, one of which was on a Streem 5 miles from where we incamp'd last night, call'd Meshoping;[31] the land we have march'd over to day is very Mountainous.—

5th march'd at 10 oclock, proceeded to Wyolusing[32] 10 miles. this has been an old Indian Town setuate on an Excellant tract of Intervale land, about 80 families of this town were Christianis'd by a Moravian parson & form'd into a reguler town, in the senter of which they had a Chappel. the land on this River being purchas'd by the Connecticut Company in the year 1770 or 71, the savages moov'd off further westward, & left this place in possession of a few Americans, who sence the commencement of this war have left it & Join'd the Enimy. this Town stood on a point of land round which the river makes a very learge bow or turn. above the town a learge streem emties into the river, called Wyolusing, the land here is cover'd with a very learge burthen of English Grass; on the Intervale near this place are much the leargest trees I ever saw, the growth is Black walnut & butterwood.

30. The encampment was made on the site of Tunkhannock, Wyoming co., Pa., at the mouth of Tunkhannock Creek, 32 miles north by west of Wilkes-Barre.

31. Meshoppen, Wyoming co., Pa., on the east bank of the Susquehanna River, 47 miles north by west of Wilkes-Barre.

32. Wyalusing, Bradford co., Pa., on the east bank of the Susquehanna at the mouth of Wyalusing Creek. Lt. Lodge's map indicates that the encampment was on the west side of the river.

6th we remain at Wyolusing to day to recruit our horses & cattle.—

7th the weather being rainey we lay still—

8th the Army march'd at 6 oclock. I had the flank Guard. passed several high mountains, & several dessolate farms proceeded to what is call'd the standing stone bottom,33 where there is a learge body of excellent land, that has been Improv'd;—Genl Sullivan is so unwell that he is not able to command the army and is oblig'd to proceed by water,—

9th march'd at 7 oclock, proceeded 3 miles to a dessolate farm, on the mouth of a streem call'd Wesawking,34 here we halted an hour, then proceeded 12 miles, to a learge body of clear Intervale cover'd with high Grass & incamp'd.—this place is within 4 miles of Tiogea & has been inhabited by both white People & Savages, & is Call'd Sheshekonunk;35 the land we march'd over to day is very fine indeed.—Genl Sullivan is not so unwell as he has been, & has resume'd the command of the army again.—the weather being very warm & our march very severe many of our men falter'd to day.—

10th the army lay still. the Genl & a number of the field Officers are reconnoitering the country, and Indeavouring to find a place wher the army can ford the river;—the General Course from Wyoming to Tiogea is near North.

11th the Army forded the river where the water was so deep and rapped that we found great difficulty in fording. after fording the river proceeded 3 miles & crossing the west branch of the river call'd the Tiogea branch

33. The encampment was made on the west bank of the river, opposite the present site of Standing Stone, Bradford co., Pa.

34. This stream is now called Wysox Creek. It empties into the Susquehanna from the north, 4 miles east of Towanda.

35. Sheshequin, Bradford co., Pa., 9 miles north of Towanda and 25 miles southeast of Elmira, N. Y. The old Indian town of Sheshequin was on the opposite side of the river on the present site of Ulster. Cook, *op. cit.*, 124.

ariv'd at Tiogea, setuate on the point where the west branch forms a Junction with the Sisquehannah; on both sides of the Tiogea branch are very learge bodies of clear Intervale, coverd with high grass, where there has been a learge Indian Settlement, & where Queen hester[36] (Queen of the Six Nations) resided until last fall, Col? Hartley[37] with a party of troops burn'd her palace: Gen! Sullivan has been fortunate enough to reach this place with his Army without any concider-able accident happening.

12th we are begining to erect works for the security of the troops & Stores to be left at this place.—the Gen! receiv'd intelligence this afternoon by a Small party that had been sent to make discoveries, that the Enimy appeer to be in great confusion & about mooving from Che-mong,[38] an Indian town 12 miles up the Tiogea branch, in consequence of which the whole army fit for duty march'd at 8 oclock P.M. in order to surprise the enimy at Che-mong;—on our march we pass'd several very difficult de-files, & as the night was very dark, & the path but little use'd, we found great difficulty in proceeding. Gen! Hand with his Brigade was to go round & fall in to the rode that leads from the town up the river, while Gen! Poor moov'd directly to the town & made the attackt if he found the enimy in possession of the town. at day brake

36. Queen Esther was the granddaughter of Madame Montour, a half-breed who married a Seneca chief. Esther's parents were French Margaret and Katarioniecha. With her husband, Eghohowin, a chief of the Delawares, Esther lived at Sheshequin until 1772. That year she and her people moved up the river to the mouth of the Chemung river. Queen Esther's village was burned by Col. Hartley in 1778 for her part in the Wyoming massacre. After Sullivan's expedition, no more is heard of her. Esther was a sister of Catherine of Catherine's Town. F. W. Hodge, *Handbook of American Indians* . . . (Washington, 1912), I, 938.

37. Col. Thomas Hartley (1748–1800) commanded the 11th Pennsylvania regiment. He had resigned in February, 1779. Heitman, *op. cit.*, 278.

38. Chemung stood on the left bank of the Chemung River, 3 miles above the present village of Chemung, in Chemung co., N. Y. Cook, *op. cit.*, 125.

we ariv'd at the Town but found it deserted, only two or
three scattering Indians ware seen running from the town.
the Town consisted of about 30 houses, situate on the
bank of the Tiogea. their houses ware built with split &
hew'd timber, cover'd with bark. there ware two learge
buildings which ware said to be publick houses. there
was very little left in the houses except baskets, buckets,
& skins. the houses had no chimneys, or flooers & ware
very dirty & smookey: about sun rise all the buildings
ware set on fire. on examination we found that a party
of the enimy incamp'd about 60 rods from the town last
night, & from all appeerences the enemy left the town
last evining, Gen! Hand with his brigade pursu'd the
enimy about 2 miles & was fired on by a party of Indians
from the top of a hill, who run off as soon as the fire was
return'd, Gen! Hand had 6 men kill'd & seven wounded,
three of the latter ware officers; the enimy ware pursued
by our troops but not overtaken.—we found a number of
very learge fields of corn, in the whole about 40 acres
about fit to roast, which we cut down & destroy'd,—
in doing which a party of our men ware fir'd on by a
party of tories & Indians across the river, [who] kill'd
one man & wounded 4; after compleeting the distruc-
tion of the corn, Town, &c. we return'd to Tiogea,
where we ariv'd at dark, very much fategue'd having
march'd not less then 30 miles, & the weather very
warm. Chemong lays about N. West from Tiogea.—

14th nothing new.—

15th 1000 chosen men under the command of Gen! Poor
are order'd to march to morrow morning up the river,
to meet Gen! Clinton, who is on his way to Join us with
his Brigade, & is in some danger of being attackt by the
Enimy before he can form a junction with our main army;
I am order'd on this Command.—

this afternoon a small party of Indians fir'd on some men who ware without our guards after horses & cattle kill'd & Scalp'd one man, & wounded another. a party was sent out in pursute of them but could not come up with them.

16th Gen! Poor march'd with his detachment at 10 oclock A.M. proceeded in two columns 13 miles up the Susquehanna over very rough ground. we incamp'd near the ruins of an old Indian Town call'd Macktowanunk.[39] the land near the river is generally good.—

17th we march'd early this morning. proceeded 12 miles to Owagea,[40] an Indian Town which was deserted last spring, after planting; about the town is a numbar of fruit trees, & many plants & hearbs that are common in our part of the country. here is a learge body of clear Intervale cover'd with Grass; our march to day has been very severe & fategueng, especially for the left Column (to which I belong,) as we had to pass several difficult steep hills & bad Morasses.—

18th we march'd early this morning, proceeded 14 miles to Choconnut,[41] the remains of a learge Indian Town, which has been likewise abandoned this summer. here we found plenty of cucumbers, squashes, turnips, &c—we found about 20 houses, which we burnt our days March has been more severe than yesterday, as we had besides hills & common swamps, one swamp of about 2 miles so cover'd with learge pines, standing & lying, which appear'd as tho several hurricanes had been very busey among them, since which a tremendious groath of bushes

39. Macktowanunck stood near the site of Barton, Tioga co., N. Y., which is on the north bank of the Susquehanna River at the junction of Butson Creek and Ellis Brook.

40. Owego, Tioga co., N. Y., is on the north bank of the Susquehanna River, about a mile above the mouth of Owego Creek.

41. This encampment was probably at Choconut Centre, Broome co., N. Y., about 3½ miles northwest of Binghamton.

about 20 feet high have sprung up, so very thick as to render passing thro' them Impracticable by any troops but such as nothing but death can stop.—at sunset we ware very agreably allarm'd by the report of a Cannon up the river which we suppos'd to be Gen! Clintons Evining Gun.

19th Our troops ware put in motion very early this morning after marching about one mile Gen! Poor receiv'd an express from Gen! Clinton informing him that the latter expected to be here by 10 oclock A.M. this day, in consequence of which we return'd to our old incampment, where Gen! Clinton Joined us at 10 oclock with 2000 men Including Officers, boatmen, &c—he has 208 bateaux with provisions, Ammunition &c. after mutial congratulations & Complyments, the whole proceeded down the river to Owagea & incamp'd. this evining the town of Owagea was made a bone fire of to grace our meeting; our general course from Tiogea to Choconnut is about N. East.—

20th we have a very heavy rain to day & no tents, but we are obliged to ride it out.—

21^t we march'd early, proceeded within 10 miles of Tiogea.—

22^d March'd at 6 oclock, & at 11 ariv'd in Camp, where we ware saluted with 13 Cannon & a tune on Col? Proctors band of Musick.—

23^d we are prepareing to march with all possible expedition.—about 5 oclock this afternoon a very shocking accident happened in our Brigade. a Soldier very accidentally discharge'd a musket charged with a ball & several buckshot, 3 of which unfortunately struck Cap! Kimbal[42] of Col? Cilleys Reg! who was standing at some

42. Capt. Benjamin Kimball of the 1st New Hampshire regiment. Heitman, *op. cit.*, 331.

distence in a tent with several other officers, in such a manner that he expired within 10 or 15 minutes, as universelly
lamented as he was esteem'd by all who knew him.—
one of the shot wounded a soldier in the leg who was setting at some distence from the tent Capt Kimbal was in.

24th the remains of the unfortunate Capt Kimbal was
Inter'd at 11 oclock A.M. with the honours of war, at-
tended by Genl Poor & almost all the Officers of the Brigade, with Col.^o Proctors Band of Musick;—the Army is
very busey in prepareing to march.

25th we find great difficulty in giting ready to moove
for want of a sufficiant number of horses, to Carry our provisions, Ammunitions, Stores &c.—however we are to
moove to morrow with out fail, with 27 days flower &
live beef,—our whole force that will march from here is
about 5000 men, Officers included, with nine peices of
Artillery.—3 of the Anyda Warriers ariv'd in camp this
afternoon who are going on with us, as guides.—two run-
ners ariv'd from Col.^o Broadhead[43] at Fort Pitt, Informing
that Col.^o Broadhead is on his way with about 800 men
agains[t] the western Indians.

26th our Army March'd at 12 oclock in the order laid
down in the plan of order of March & Battle. a garrison
of about 300 men is left at this place under the Command
of Col.^o Shreeve.—The army proceeded about 4 miles &
incamp'd.—Mr Lodge[44] a Gentleman who survay'd &
Measure'd the rode from Easton to this place, goes on
with [us] in order to take an actual survay of the country,
who measures the rode as we go on.

43. Daniel Brodhead (1736-1809) had raised a company of riflemen in 1775. He
was made a colonel of the 8th Pennsylvania regiment, and after Valley Forge was sent
to Fort Pitt. In April, 1779, he succeeded to the command of that post. With 600 men
he marched up the Allegheny and subdued the Indians in one month. He raided the
Delawares in 1781, but subsequently was removed from command at Fort Pitt. *Dict.
Am. Biog.*, III, 62-3.

44. Lt. Benjamin Lodge (d. 1801), detached from the 6th Pennsylvania regiment.

27th the Army March'd at 8 oclock. our march was very much Impeeded by the Artillery & Ammunition wagons, which we have to clear a rode thro the thick woods & difficult defiles.—the army was obliged to halt 7 hours at one defile to day for the artillery & baggage.— at 10 oclock P.M. we ariv'd [at] our incamping ground, a learg body of clear Intervale where we found about 70 or 80 acres of fine corn.—our march has not been more than 5 miles to day.—

28th as we had the corn to destroy before we could march, it was 2 oclock P.M. before we moov'd off the ground.—by reason of a high mountain that shuts down to the river so as [to] render passing with the artillery impractacable, we ware oblige'd to ford the river[45] twice before we got to chemong, with the artillery, pack horses, & one Brigade. the water was so high as render'd fording very difficult & dangerous. a conciderable quantity of flower, ammunition & baggage was lost in the river.— at 10 in the evening the rear of the army ariv'd at Chemong where we incamp'd, our march to day has not been more than 3 miles:—a small scout of ours return'd to day which informs that they discover'd a learg incampment about 6 miles from Chemong.—a small party of Indians fired on a party of our men to day that ware seting fire to some houses over the river, but did no dammage.

29th The army march'd at 9 oclock A.M. proceeded about 5 miles when our light troops discover'd a line of brestwork about 80 rods in their front, which upon reconoytering was found to extend about half a mile in length, on very advantageous ground with a learge brook in front. the river on their right, a high mountain on their

45. This mountain was probably Glory Hill, just northwest of Waverly, Tioga co., N. Y.

left & a learge settlement in their rear call'd New Town;[46] their work's ware very artfully mask'd with green bushes, so that I think the discovering them was as accidental as it was fortunate to us. Skurmishing on both sides commence'd after we discover'd their works, which continued until our Disposition was made, which was as followeth viz:—the Artillery to form in front of their works, cover'd by Gen! Hands Brigade, Gen! Poors Brigade & riflemen to turn the Enimies left, & fall in their rear, supported by Gen! Clintons Brigade: Gen! Maxwells Brigade to form a Corps dereserve; the left flanking division & light Infantry to pursue the enimy when they left their works.— at 3 oclock P.M. Gen! Poor began his rout by Collumns from the right of Reg's by files, we pass'd a very thick swamp, so cover'd with bushes for near a mile that the Collumns found great difficulty in keeping their order, but by Gen! Poors great prudence & good conduct, we proceeded in much better order than I expected we possibly could have done; after passing this swamp we inclin'd to the left, cross'd the creek that runs in front of the Enimies works:—on both sides this creek, was a learge number of new houses, but no land cleared. soon after we pass'd this creek we began to assend the mountain that cover'd the Enimies left.[47] Immediately after we began to Assend the Mountain, we ware saluted by a brisk fire from a body of Indians who ware posted on this mountain for the purpos of preventing any troops turning the left of their works. at the same Instant that they began their fire on us, they rais'd the Indian yell,

46. Newtown stood on the left bank of the Chemung River about 5 miles below Elmira, and one mile above the site of the battle.

47. The battle of Newtown was fought on Sunday, August 29, on the ground between the Chemung River and Baldwin Creek. Dearborn calls this creek "a learge brook." The mountain on the enemy's left was Sullivans Hill, later the site of a monument commemorating the event. The battle ground is six miles southeast of Elmira. Cook, *op. cit.*, 127.

or war whoop: the rifle men kept up a scattering fire while we form'd the line of Battle, which was done exceeding quick; we then advanced rappedly with fix'd bayonets without fireing a shot, altho they kept up a steady fire on us until we gain'd the summet of the Mountain, which is about half a mile, we then gave them a full volley which oblig'd them to take to their heels: Col? Reids Reg? which was on the left of the Brigade was more severely attackt then any other part of the Brigade, which prevented his advancing as far as the rest. after we had scowerd the top of the mountain, (in doing which L? Cass[48] of our Reg? tommohawk'd an indian with the Indians own tommahawk that was slightly wounded) I being next to Col? Reid on the left, finding he still was very severely ingag'd nearly on the same ground he was first attackt on, thought proper to reverce the front of the Reg? & moove to his assistence. I soon discover'd a body of Indians turning his right, which I turn'd about by a full fire from the reg? this was a very seasonable releaf to Col? Reid who at the very moment I fir'd on those that ware turning his right found himself so surrounded, that he was reduce'd to the nessessaty of retreeting, or making a desparate push with the bayonet, the latter of which he had began to put in execution the moment I gave him releaf; the Enimy now all left the field of action with precepetation, & in great confusion, pursued by our light Infantry about 3 miles, they lef[t] a number of their packs blankets &c on the ground.— half an hour before the action became serious with Gen! Poors Brigade the Artillery open'd upon their works which soon made their works too warm for them.—we

48. Jonathan Cass (d. 1830), who served as a private at Bunker Hill, was now 1st lieutenant of the 3rd New Hampshire regiment. At the end of the war he was a captain of the 2nd New Hampshire regiment. He remained in the U. S. army until 1801, when he retired a major. Heitman, *op. cit.*, 147.

found of the Enimy on the field of action 11 Indian warriers dead & one Squaw; toock one white man & one negro prisoners, from whome we learnt that Butler Commanded here, that Brant[49] had all the Indians that could be muster'd in the five Nations, that there was about 200 whites a few of which ware British regular troops. it seems their whole force was not far from 1000.—these prisoners inform us that their loss in kill'd & wounded was very great, the most of which they according to custom, carried off.—our loss in Gen! Poors Brigade, kill'd and wounded is

<table>
<tr><td></td><td>kill'd</td><td>wounded</td><td></td></tr>
<tr><td>Maj!̣ . . . .</td><td>0</td><td>1</td><td>Maj! Titcomb</td></tr>
<tr><td>Cap!̣ . . . .</td><td>0</td><td>1</td><td>Cap! Clays</td></tr>
<tr><td>L!̣ . . . .</td><td>0</td><td>1</td><td>died the same night</td></tr>
<tr><td>Non commis'd ⎫
& privates ⎭ . .</td><td colspan="2">3 . 29</td><td>L! McCawley[50]</td></tr>
</table>

our loss in kill'd & wounded in the whole Army except Gen! Poors Brigade was

kill'd 0   wounded . . . 4

at sunset the army Incamp'd on the ground lately occupied by the Enimy.—

30th the Army remain'd on the ground to day, destroy'd a vast quantity of corn & about 40 houses.—the Army by a request of Gen! Sullivans agree'd to live on

49. Thayendanegea, a Mohawk chief (1742–1807), received an education and was christened Joseph Brant. He served as secretary to the Superintendent of Indian Affairs in 1774, striving to keep the Iroquois on the side of the British. Aftᵣ. a visit to England he commanded the Indians on St. Leger's expedition in 1777, and directed the Cherry Valley massacre in 1778. At the end of the war Brant became the spokesman of the Indians who sought indemnities for their losses. Dict. Am. Biog., II, 604.

50. Lt. Col. Benjamin Titcomb (d. 1799) of the 1st New Hampshire regiment was first wounded at Hubbardton in 1777. He retired from the army January 1, 1781, after the New Hampshire line was rearranged. Capt. Elijah Clayes of the 2nd New Hampshire regiment died of his wounds on November 30. Lt. Nathaniel McCauley belonged to the 1st New Hampshire regiment. Heitman, op. cit., 545, 159, 364.

half a pound of beef & half a pound of flower p.r day for
the future as long as it may be found nessesary, our provisions being very short.—this night our sick & wounded
together with the Ammunition waggons & 4 of our heav-
iest peaces of Artillery are sent back to tiogea by water,
which will enable the Army to proceed with much
greater ease & rappidity.—our course from Chemong to
here is about N. West.—

31.t we march'd at 10 o'clock. the right Column
march'd on the hills some distence from the river, the left
collumn & Artillery march'd by the river. the land we
march'd over fine. found & destroy'd several fields of
corn & houses.—proceeded 4½ miles to where the Alli-
ganer & kaiyugea branches of the river unite. on the
point between these two streems was a very prety town
call'd Kannawalohalla,⁵¹ which from appeerances was
deserted this morning. some boats ware seen by our advanced parties going up the Allaganer branch. a number
of feather beds ware emtied in the houses. our soldiers
found several learge chests buried which ware fill'd with
a great variety of houshold furniture & many other articles; after halting here an hour we proceeded between
the two rivers on a fine plain about 5 miles & incamp'd.
a detachment was sent up the Allagana branch in pursute of the Enimy.

Septem.r 1.t the detachment that was sent up the river
in pursute of the Enimy return'd this morning. they
could not overtake the Enimy, but they found & destroy'd several learge fields of corn—

the Army march'd at 10 oclock, proceeded about 3
miles on a plain then came to what is call'd bair Swamp

51. Kannawalohalla stood on the present site of Elmira, at the junction of the
Chemung River and the mouth of Newtown Creek. The two branches to which
Dearborn refers may be the two divisions of the river as it passes on either side of
Big Island, below the city. Cook, *op. cit.*, 128.

which extends to French Katareens[52] 9 miles. the growth is pine, Spruce & hemlock exceeding thick, a small river runs thro it which we had to cross about 20 times. on both sides of this Swamp is a ridg of tremendeous hills, which the collumns ware oblige'd to march on, having a rode to open for artillery, we proceeded very slowly. at dark when we had got within about 3 miles of katareens town we found ourselves in a most horrid thick Mirery swamp which render'd our proceeding so difficult that it was 10 oclock in the Evining before we ariv'd at the town, where we found fires burning & every other appeerence of the Enimies having left the town this afternoon. this Town consists of above 30 houses there is a number [of] fruit trees in this town.—the streem[53] that we cross'd so often to day runs thro this Town & into the Seneca or kannadasegea Lake, the south end of which is but 3 miles from this town.

2^d the Army lay still to day to recrute; & to destroy the Town corn &c:—a very old Squaw was found in the bushes to day who was not able to go off with the rest, who informs us that Butler with the tories went from this place with all the boats the day before yesterday. the Indian warriers moov'd off their fammilies & Effects yesterday morning, & then return'd here & stay'd till Sunset. she says the Squaws & young Indians ware very loath to quit the town but ware for giving themselves up, but the warriors would not agree to it. several horses & cattle ware found at & about this place.—a party of light troops ware sent this morning to indeavour to overtake some of the Indians who left this place last evining, but return'd without being able to afect it.

52. Catherine's Town was an Indian village located on the high ground south of the present site of Havana, Schuyler co., N. Y., 19 miles north of Elmira. *Ibid.*, 129.
53. Catherine Creek.

3^d the Army march'd at 8 oclock. after proceeding about 3 miles over rough ground, came oposite the end of the Lake & then found good marching, the land very fine. proceeded 9 miles & incamp'd at 4 oclock P.M. near the side of the lake. This Lake is about 40 miles in length & from 2 to 5 in wedth & runs nearly North & South.

4th the army march'd at 10 oclock. proceeded 4 miles to a small village,[54] where we found several fine fields of corn. after destroying the village & corn, march'd on 8 miles further & incamp'd. the land we passed over to day is very fine.—

5th the Army march'd at 10 oclock. proceeded 5 miles to an old Indian town Call'd Candaia or apple Town[55]—where there is a very old orchard of 60 trees, & many other fruit trees.—the Town consists of 15 or 20 houses very beautifully situated near the Lake. in the Town are 3 Sepulchers which are very Indian fine, where I suppose some of their chief[s] are deposited. at this town we found a man by the name of Luke Sweatland,[56] who was taken by the savages at wyoming last summer, & was adopted into an Indian family in this town, where he has liv'd, or reather stay'd about 12 months he appeer'd quite overjoy'd at meeting some of his aquaintences from Wyoming who are in our army. he says the savages ware very much straiten'd for food from April until corn was fit to roast, that his being kept so starv'd prevented his attempting to desert, altho he had frequent oppertunities, by being sent 20 miles to the salt springs to make salt, which springs he says affords salt for all the Savages

54. This Indian village was called Condawhaw. It stood on the present site of North Hector in Schuyler co., N. Y., on the east shore of Seneca Lake. *Ibid.*, 129.

55. Kendaia, Seneca co., N. Y.

56. Luke Swetland (1729-1823) wrote a narrative of his captivity among the Seneca Indians which was published for the second time in 1875. No record of the first edition exists. Joseph Sabin, *A Dictionary of Books Relating to America* . . . (New York, 1934), XXIV, 380.

in this part of the country. he says the Indians ware very much allarm'd & dejected at being beat at New Town. they told him they had a great many wounded which they sent off by water—we destroy'd learge quantities of corn here. an express ariv'd this afternoon from Tiogea, by which I receiv'd a letter that inform'd me that Abnar Dearborn, a Nephew of mine about 16 years old, who was wounded in the Battle at New town, died of his wound the 2ᵈ Insᵗ—

6ᵗʰ the horses & cattle ware so scatter'd this morning that the army could not git redy to march until 3 oclock P.M. proceeded 3 miles & incamp'd. Oposite to where we incamp'd on the other side of the Lake we discover'd a settlement where we could se[e] some Indians driving horses.—

7ᵗʰ we toock up our march at 7 oclock proceeded 8 miles & came to the end of the Lake, where we expected the Enimy would give us an other battle, as they might have a very great advantage over us as we forded the outlet of the Lake. when we ariv'd in sight of the ford we halted, & several scouts ware sent out to reconoytir the adjacent woods, when we found the coast was clear, the army pass'd the ford, proceeded 3 miles by the end of the Lake and found a small settlement which we destroy'd & then proceeded 2 miles from the Lake & ariv'd at a learge town call'd Kannadasegea⁵⁷ which is consider'd as the Cappital of the senecas & is call'd the Seneca Castle.—it consists of about 40 houses very erregularly situated, in the senter of which is the ruins of a Stockade fort & block house. here is a conciderable number of apple & other fruit trees & a few acres of

57. Kanadaseaga (*the grand village*) stood on both sides of Kanadaseaga Creek, 1½ miles northwest of Geneva, N. Y. This was the capital of the Seneca nation. The ruins mentioned by Dearborn were all that remained of a stockaded fort built by Sir William Johnson in 1756. Cook, *op. cit.*, 130.

land clear cover'd with English grass. their cornfields which are very learge are at some considerable distence from the Town.—we found in this Town a white child about 3 years old which we suppose was a captive.—in the houses was left a number of Skins, some corn & many of their curiosities.—

8th the Army lay still to day. the riflemen ware sent to destroy a town about 8 miles from hence on the west side of the lake Call'd Gaghsconghgwa:—58we found a number of stacks of hay not far from this town which we set fire to.—a Scout of ours burnt a town to day about 10 miles N.-East from hence on the rode to the Kaiyugea settlement, call'd Skaigees or long falls.—59

9th by reason of a rain last night the Army could not March till 12 oclock.—all our sick & Invaleeds ware sent back this morning to Tiogea, under an escort of 50 men.— we proceeded about 3 miles thro old fields cover'd with grass, then enter'd a thick swamp call'd the 10 mile swamp. we proceeded 4 miles in this swamp with great difficulty, crossed a conciderable streem of water, & incamp'd.—

10th the Army march'd at 8 oclock. proceeded thro the swamp & pass'd a learge body of clear land cover'd with grass. after leaving the clear land march'd one mile & came to a Small Lake call'd konnondaguah. we forded the outlet of this lake, proceeded about half a mile & came to a very prety town call'd kannandaguah,60 consisting of about 30 houses, much better built then any I have seen before. near this town we discover'd very learge fields of corn, near which the Army incamp'd.—several

58. This town was situated on what is now Kershong Creek, 7 miles south of Geneva, N. Y.

59. Seneca Falls, Seneca co., N. Y., 10 miles east by north of Geneva, on the Seneca Outlet or River.

60. Canandaigua, Ontario co., N. Y., at the outlet of Lake Canandaigua.

parties ware order'd out this afternoon to destroy the corn &c.—

11th the Army Moov'd at 6 oclock. march'd 14 miles to an Indian town call'd Anyayea,[61] situate on a body of clear intervale near a small lake of the same name. this town consists of 10 or 11 houses. near it was several learge cornfields.—the land we march'd over to day is very good & a great part of it very thinly wooded & cover'd with grass.—it appeers as if it has been cultivated heretofore.

12th the weather being foul, the army did not march till 12 oclock. a small post is establish'd here, wher we leave our provisions & Ammunition except what will be nesessary to carry us to Chenesee (25 miles) & back again. one piece of artillery is left at this post. the Army march'd 11 miles this afternoon over a body of excellent land.

13 March'd at 7 oclock proceed[ed] 1½ miles to a town call'd Kanegsas or quicksea,[62] consisting of 18 houses situate on an excellent Intervale near a small lake. we found a learge quantity of corn, beens, Squashes, potatoes, water Mellons, cucumbers &c &c in & about this town:— the army halted here 4 hours, to destroy the Town & corn, & to build a bridge over a creek.—[63] at this town liv'd a very noted warrier call'd the Great Tree, who has made great pretentions of friendship to us & has been to Phyladelphia & to Genl Washingtons head Quarters since the war commenced, & has receiv'd a number of Presents,

61. Hanneyaye was situated at the foot of Honeoye Lake about a half mile east of its outlet, and south of Mill Creek, in Ontario co., N. Y. One of the houses was used as a fort, surrounded by kegs and bags of flour, under the command of Capt. Cummings of the 2nd New Jersey regiment. Cook, *op. cit.*, 130.

62. Adjutoa or Kanaghsaws stood between Lake Conesus and Hemlock Lake, 2 miles south of the town of Conesus, Livingston co., N. Y. *Ibid.*, 131.

63. The army, which was to march around the southern end of Lake Conesus, had to bridge one of the inlets of the lake.

from Genl Washington & from Congress, yet we suppose he is with butler against us.—

A party of Rifle men & some others 26 in the whole under the command of L! Boyd[64] of the Rifle corps was sent last night to a town 7 miles from here to make what discoveries he could & return at day brake—4 of his men went into the town found it abandoned but found 3 or 4 scattering indians about it, one of which they kill'd & Skelp'd & then returnd to L! Boyd after sunrise who lay at some distence from the town.—he then sent 4 men to report to Gen! Sullivan what he had discoverd, & moov'd on slowly with the remainder toward camp. after he had proceeded about half way to camp he halted some time expecting the Army along. he after halting some time sent 2 more men to Camp who discoverd some scattering Indians & returnd to L! Boyd again. he then march'd on his party towards camp, discover'd some scattering Indians, one of which one of his men kill'd he soon found himself nearly surrounded, & attackt by two or three hundred savages & tories he after fighting them some time attemp[t]ed to retreet, but found it impracticable 6 or 7 of his men did make their escape, the remainder finding themselves compleetly surrounded ware determin'd to sell themselves as deer as possible, & bravely fought until every man was killed but 2 which ware taken one of which was L! Boyd. some of the men that made their escape came to camp & inform'd the Gen! of the matter, upon which Gen! Hand with the light troops was order'd to march to the place of the action, but tow late. they left all their packs, hats, baggage &c wher the action began, which Gen! Hand found.—

64. Lt. Thomas Boyd of Thompson's Pennsylvania Rifles had been captured at Quebec in 1775 and was not exchanged until November, 1777. He was a first lieutenant of the 1st Pennsylvania regiment when he was killed at Genessee Castle. Heitman, *op. cit.*, 114.

after we had finish'd the bridge the army march'd on, proceeded 7 miles to the before mentioned Town & incamp'd—this town consists of 22 houses situate on a small river, that falls into the Chenesse river[65] about 2 miles below here, & is call'd Gaghchegwalahale.—[66]

14th the Gen! expected to have found the great Chennesee town within 1½ mile of here on this side the river, but upon reconoytering found that the town is 6 miles from here & on the other side of the river;[67] the army was imploy'd until 11 oclock in destroying corn which was found in great plenty. at 12 march'd, after fording the small river that the town stood on & passing thro a small grove, we enter'd upon what is called the great Chenesee flats, which is a vast body of clear Intervale extending 12 or 14 miles up & down the river & several miles back from the river, & cover'd with grass from 5 to 8 feet high & so thick that a man can git thro it but very slowly.—our army appeer'd to very great advantage mooving in the exact order of March laid down in the plan—but very often we that ware on hors back could see nothing but the mens guns above the grass.—after marching about 2 miles on this flat we came to the Chenesee river which we forded, passed over a body of flats on the other side & assended onto oak land, proceeded 3 miles & ariv'd at the town which we found deserted. here we found the bodies of L! Boyd & one other man Mangled in a most horred manner. from appeerences it seems they ware tyed to two trees near which they lay, & first

65. The Genessee River.

66. This town, also called Gathtsegwarohare, was 7 miles west of Kanaghsaws, on the east side of Canaseraga Creek, about 2 miles above its confluence with the Genessee River. The spot was later occupied by the "Hermitage," the ancestral home of the Carrols. Cook, *op. cit*, 132.

67. The Genessee Castle, stronghold of the Senecas, was located between Cuylerville and the west bank of the Genessee River, in Livingston co., N. Y. It had various names, including Chenandanah and Little Beard's Town. *Ibid.*, 133.

severely whip'd, then their tongues ware cut out, their finger nails pluck'd off, their eyes pluck'd out, then speer'd & cut in many places, & after they had vented their hellish spite & rage, cut off their heads and left them.—this was a most horrid specticle to behold—& from which we are taught the necessaty of fighting those more than divels to the last moment rather then fall into their hands alive.—

this is much the leargest Town we have met with. it consists of more then 100 houses, is situate on an excellent piece of land in a learge bow of the river.—it appeers the savages left this place in a great hurry & confusion, as they left leargequantities of corn husk'd & some in heeps not husk'd & many other signs of confusion.—

15th at 6 o'clock the whole Army ware turn'd out to destroy the corn in & about this town which we found in great abundence. we ware from 6 oclock to 2 P.M. in destroying the corn & houses. it is generally thought we have destroy'd 15000 bushels of corn at this place.—the meathod we toock to destroy it was to make learge fires with parts of houses & other wood & then pileing the corn on to the fire ading wood as we piled on the corn, which effectually destroyd the whole of it.—a woman with her child came to us to day who was taken at wyoming when that place was cut off. her husband & one child ware kill'd & skelp'd in her sight when she was taken. she informs us that butler & Brant with the tories & Indians left this place in a great hurry the 13 ins.^{t} & are gone to Niagara which is 80 miles from hence, where they expect we are going.—she says the Indians are very uneasey with Butler & their other leaders, & are in great distress.—we have now got to the end of our rout and are turning our face homeward. at 3 oclock we fac'd to the right about & march'd in high spirits, recross'd the Chenesee river & incamp'd on the Chenesee flats. this place lays about west from Tiogea.—

16th a number of fields of corn ware discover'd this morning at different places which employ'd the army until 10 oclock in destroying.—at 1 oclock P. M. we recross'd the streem at Gaghchegwalahale, & at 4 ariv'd at kanigsas or chockset & incamp'd—14 of L! Boyds party ware found this afternoon near to gether skelp'd. Honyose an onyda Indian of conciderable note that was with L! Boyds party was among the dead.—

17! the army march'd at sunrise & at 12 oclock ariv'd at Anyaye where we left our stores. found all safe.—

18th the Army march'd at 8 oclock proceeded to kannandaguah & incamp'd—4 Onyda Indians one of which is a Sachem, met us to day who say that 100 of the Onydas & Tuskorores set out with them to join us but meeting an Indian that left us sick at kannadasagea when we ware advancing, who told them we march'd on so rappedly that they could not overtake us so as to be of any service—they all return'd but these 4.—

19th the Army march'd to Kannadasegea, an Express ariv'd from Gen! Washington to day,[68] by which we are assured that Spain has declare'd War with England, & that the Grand Fleets of France & Spain have form'd a Junction at Sea.—

at several towns that our army has destroy'd we found dogs hung up on poles about 12 or 15 feet high, which we are told is done by way of sacrafice, that when they are unfortunat in war they sacrafice two dogs in the manner above mentioned, to appease their immaginery god. one of these dogs skins they suppose is converted into a Jacket & the other into a tobacko pouch for their god.—the

---

68. Washington's letter to Sullivan was dated at West Point, September 3. Spain declared war on Great Britain May 9, 1779. *Writings of Washington*, XVI, 222.

woman who came to us at Chenesee says the savages hung up dogs immediately after the Battle at New Town.—

20th 500 men are detach'd under the command of Col? Butler who is to march round the Kaiyugea Lake[69] & destroy the Kaiyugea Settlements on the East side of the Lake.—100 men under the Command of Col? Gansewort are order'd to go & destroy the Mohawk Castle on the Mohawk River & to proceed from thence to Albany.—the Army march'd this after noon, cross'd the outlet of the Seneca Lake & incamp'd.—

21[t] I was orderd with 200 men to proceed to the west side of the Kaiyugea Lake, from thence by the side of the lake to the south end, to burn & destroy what Settlements, corn &c. I might find. at 8 oclock I march'd proceeded an East course about 8 miles & found 2 or 3 wigwams in the wood[70] with some small paches of corn Squashes, water mellons & cucumbers & about 14 or 15 fine horses which we could not take. after destroying this little village, proceeded 4 miles to the lake where I found a very prety town of 10 houses[71] & a conciderable quantity of corn all which we burnt. we discover'd another small Town about a mile above this which we likewise destroyd. this place is call'd Skannayutenate.[72] after destroying this Town I march'd on one mile & came to a new town[73] consisting of 9 houses which we destroy'd & proceeded one mile & found one learg house

69. Cayuga Lake.

70. A settlement in the present town of Fayette, Seneca co., probably on Sucker Brook. Cook, *op. cit.*, 76.

71. This town was on the west bank of Cayuga Lake, in the northeast corner of Fayette, Seneca co., N. Y. *Ibid.*, 76.

72. Skannayutenate stood about 40 rods from the lake on the south side of Canoga Creek, a half mile northeast of Canoga, Seneca co., N. Y. *Ibid.*, 76.

73. Newtown, an Indian village, stood on the west bank of Cayuga Lake, a mile south of the present Canoga. *Ibid.*, 76.

which we set fire to & march'd on 2 miles further & incamp'd the land we March'd over to day is exceeding fine.—

22.ᵈ I march'd half an hour before sunrise proceeded about 5 miles & came to the ruins of a Town that a party of our men burnt when the army was advancing who mis'd their way & happen'd to fall in at this Town. about half a mile from this town I found a learge field of corn & 3 houses. we gathered the corn & burnt it in the houses.—this Town is call'd Swahyawanah.[74]—we march'd from this place about 5 miles & found a wigwam with 3 Squaws & one young Indian who was a cripple. I toock 2 of the Squaws who ware about 40 or 50 years old & march'd on about 3 miles & found one hut & a field of corn which I burnt & proceeded about 4 miles & incamp'd—

23ᵈ March'd at Sunrise proceeded without any path or track or any parson who was ever in this part of the country before, to guide us, & the land so horredly rough & bushey that it was hardly possible for us to advance.— however with great difficulty & fategue we proceeded about 8 or 9 miles to the end of a long cape[75] which I expected was the end of the lake, but found was not—from here we march'd off 2 or 3 miles from the Lake & then proceeded by a point of compas about 8 miles & came to the end of the lake & incamp'd. this lake is about 40 miles in length, & from 2 to 5 miles in wedth, & runs nearly N. and S. parralel with the Seneca Lake, & they are from 8 to 18 miles apart.

24ᵗʰ March'd at Sunrise. proceeded about 3 miles on the high land & came to an old path which led us to

74. Swahyawana stood in the northeast corner of the present town of Romulus, Seneca co., on the north bank of Sinclair Hollow Creek. *Ibid.*, 77.

75. Taghanic Point, formerly Goodwin's Point. *Ibid.*, 77.

two huts & some corn fields, which ware about one mile from where we first found the old path. after burning these two houses & corn I sent several small parties different ways to loock for a learge Town that I had been inform'd was not many miles from the end of the lake. the parties found 10 or 12 scattering houses & a number of learge corn fields on & near a streem that falls into the Lake: after burning & destroying several houses & corn fields, a small party that I had sent out discover'd the Town about 3 miles from the lake on the above mention'd Streem. this town & its surbubs consists of about 25 houses & is call'd Coreorgonet[76] & is the cappital of a Small nation or tribe called the . . . . my party was imploy'd from 9 oclock A.M. till sunset.—I expected to have met Col? Butler with his party at this town—

25th I march'd at sunrise for Katareens Town where I was order'd to join the main Army. I proceeded a due west point over a terible rough mountainous country about 18 miles & at 4 oclock P.M. ariv'd at Katareens, but the army was gone forward. I proceeded 6 miles in what is call'd the bair Swamp & incamp'd.—

26th March'd at Sunrise & at 12 oclock joined the army at Kannawalohala, which is 4 miles from where we fought the Enimy the 29 of August.—the army had a day of Rejoycing here yesterday in Consequence of the News from Spain.

27th some detachments ware sent up the Allegana river to destroy what houses & corn fields they might find.

28th the same parties that went yesterday ware sent again to day further up the river to destroy a tory Settlement that a small party discover'd yesterday & a learge

76. Coreorgonet stood on the west side of Cayuga inlet, about 3 miles from the end of the lake and 2 miles south of Ithaca. The tribe name left blank by Dearborn was, according to the Iroquois, Toderichroones. It was known to the English as Catawbas. *Ibid.*, 77.

detachment was sent off to compleet the destruction of the corn &c at & about Newtown. at 12 oclock Col.º Butler with his party ariv'd in Camp. on their route round the Lake they burnt & destroy'd several towns & a vast Quantity of corn.

29ᵗʰ the Army march'd to Chemong.—

30ᵗʰ ariv'd at Tiogea, where we were saluted with 13 Cannon which we answer'd with the same numbar. Col.º Shreeve who commanded the Garrison made an entertainment for the Gen! & Field Officers this afternoon. the afternoon was spent in festevity & mirth joy appeard in every countinence. we now have finish'd our campaign & gloriously too.—

Octob.ʳ 1.ˢ we are begining to prepare to march for Wyoming.

2ᵈ Gen! Sullivan made an entertainment for all the Gen! & Field officers to day, this evening we had an Indian war dance at Head Quarters. the Onyda Sachem was Master of cerimonies.—

3ᵈ the army is prepareing to March for Wyoming.

4 the Army march'd 15 miles down the River.—

5 the whole army Imbark'd on board boats, except what was nessassary to drive the pack horses & cattle. & the 7ᵗʰ ariv'd at Wyoming in high spirits. during the whole of this Severe Campaign, our loss in kill'd, died of wounds, & Sickness, did not exceed 60 men.—

8ᵗʰ Gen! Sullivan receiv'd an express this evining from Gen! Washington,[77] informing him that Count De Stang is on the coast near New York, with a fleet & Army, in consequence of which Gen! Sullivans Army is order'd to march the 10ᵗʰ ins.ᵗ for Head Quarters.

---

77. Washington's letter to Sullivan was dated at West Point, October 3. *Writings of Washington*, XVI, 398–9.

10th The Army March'd for Easton, & the 15th ariv'd there.—this army has marchd from Tiogea to Easton (150 miles, thro a mountanious rough Wilderness) in 8 days, with their artillery, & baggage:—an extreordinery march indeed.

16th 17th & 18 remain at Easton— we are inform'd that Count Destang has taken several ships of war, together with all the transports & troops the Enimy had at & near Georgea—he is expected dayly at New York.—

25th our army is to march the 27 Ins^t: towards Head Quarters.—

an express ariv'd this day from Head Quarters[78] which Informs that the Enimy have avacuated their posts at Kings ferry, & have retir'd to N. York.—

78. Washington's letter to Sullivan of October 25, written from West Point. *Ibid.*, XVII, 25–6.

The Yorktown Campaign

TOWARDS *the end of 1779 the British invaded the South and laid siege to Charleston, which surrendered in May, 1780. Clinton returned to New York, leaving Cornwallis in command of southern operations. Gates was unable to check the sweeping advance which followed, as Cornwallis overran the Carolinas. Late in 1780 Gates was replaced by Greene, who with Lafayette harassed Cornwallis and drew him northward and towards the coast, away from his supply base at Charleston. When Washington, at his camp on the Hudson, heard that the French fleet had sailed north from the West Indies, he conceived and in record time executed the stratagem which brought into play the combined arms of France and the United States, climaxed by the surrender of Cornwallis at Yorktown.*

OCTOB.ᵣ 28ᵗʰ 1779—
we this day receivd the particulars of a most horrid piece of cruelty commited by a party of British hors, which is as follows:—
a party of British hors under the ⌜com⌝mand of Col.º Simco,[1] made an excurtion into Jersey from Staten

---

1. John Graves Simcoe (1752–1806) came to America at the beginning of the war, and succeeded to the command of the Queen's Rangers in 1777. This raid into New Jersey resulted in his capture, but he was released by the end of the year. He was with Cornwallis at Yorktown in 1781. From 1791 to 1797 he was lieutenant-governor of Upper Canada. His *Journal* (Exeter, 1787) states that he landed at Sandy Point with about 100 rangers early on October 26, and proceeded in a circuit to Boundbrook,

Isl[and,] took a circuitous rout of about 30 miles, in which they burnt a forrage yard, & plunderd several defencless houses, on their return a small party of Millitia collected under the command of Cap.[s] van Voras & Wool,[2] tow Continental Officers who had been with Genr.[l] Sullivan on the western Expedition.— they form'd an ambuscade which they drew the Enimy into, killd several of them & made several prisoners, among the latter was Col.[o] Simco.— Cap.[s] Van Voras & Wool with several others on hors back pursu'd the Enimy some conciderable distance until they rallied & turnd upon their pursuers, who ware obliged to give way. Cap.[t] Van Voras being further advanced then any other, & his hors very much fatigued was overtaken by the Enimy & obliged to surrender himself prisoner; the party that took him conveyed him to the main party & after examining him, fell to hacking him with thier Swords in sight of Cap.[t] Wool & others of his party, after satisfying their more then Savage Spite they left him expiring on the ground. Cap.[t] Wool & some others immediately rode up to him & found him cut & hack'd in a most barbarous manner, his arms cut off, his head cut to pieces, & in fact appeerd to have been massacred by the most cruel Savages, this was done by the humane Britons, let every Briton blush at the idea.—

Novem.[r] 2.[d] Gen.[l] Sullivans army [page torn] at what is calld Smiths Clov[3] [torn] 18 miles from Kings ferry. w [torn] that the Enimy have left Rhodeisland—

Somerset Courthouse, Brunswick and South Amboy. At Somerset he destroyed some stores and forage and released some Loyalist prisoners. On his return he was attacked near Brunswick. *Dict. Nat. Biog.*, XVIII, 253.

2. Capt. Peter Van Voorhees of the 1st New Jersey regiment is listed as having been "taken prisoner and murdered by Tories near New Brunswick, N. J., 26th October, 1779." Capt. Isaiah Wool (d. 1794) of the 2nd Continental Artillery had been taken prisoner at Quebec and later exchanged. He resigned from the army in 1780. Heitman, *op. cit.*, 561, 606.

3. Smith's Clove was on the west side of the Hudson, in the highlands immediately behind West Point. *Writings of Washington*, VIII, 340.

7th we moovd 14 miles to a place calld Princton on the rode to Morristown—

9th His Excellency Gen! Washington paid us a visit—

12th Maj^r Clarkson[4] Adedecamp to Gen! Lincoln arivd from Georgey with the following intilligence:— on the 9thof octob^{rs} at day brake Count De Estang & Gen! Lincoln with about [torn] French & American Troops made an ap [torn] imies works at Savanah in Georgey [torn] was obstinate on both sides.— the American Standard was three times planted on the Enimies ramparts, but by the strength of the works & the brave resistence the Enimy made our troops ware repulsed, after loosing about 500 men among whom fell the brave Count Polasky.—[6] Count De Estang receivd two wounds but not dangerous.— Count De Estang was about imbarking for the West Indies when Maj^r Clarkson left him.— it is said a learge imbarcation has lately taken place at N. York, suposd destind for Georgey or carolina.—

Novr 16th I set out for home on furlough went the lower rode, the 7th of Decem^r arivd home. found all well. I spent a very agreable winter & spring.— in march I got married,[7] & after compleeting a settlement

4. Maj. Matthew Clarkson (d. 1825) had been aide-de-camp to Gen. Arnold, and later served in the same capacity with Gen. Lincoln from March, 1779, to July, 1782. He was taken prisoner with Lincoln at Charleston, S. C., on May 12, 1780. Heitman, *op. cit.*, 159.

5. For three weeks prior to the 9th, Gen. Lincoln with the support of Comte D'Estaing had besieged the British in Savannah. Fearing the approach of the autumnal gales, D'Estaing became impatient to move his fleet, and a sortie was planned. An informer revealed the plan of attack, and though a brave attempt was made to storm the fortifications, the Americans and their allies were repulsed with heavy losses.

6. Count Casimir Pulaski (*c*.1748-1779) fled Poland after participating in an unsuccessful rebellion in 1772. Franklin and Deane, who met him in Paris, sent him to America. He was placed in command of the Continental cavalry, but resigned in March, 1778. Congress then authorized him to raise an independent corps of cavalry. He was sent south to support Lincoln in the spring of 1779, was wounded October 9 at the siege of Savannah, and died two days later. *Dict. Am. Biog.*, XV, 259-60.

7. Dearborn married Dorcas Osgood Marble, daughter of Col. Osgood of Andover, Mass., and widow of Isaac Marble. Their son, Henry Alexander Scammell Dearborn, was named after Dearborn's colonel. *Ibid.*, V, 176.

of the accounts of the army with the State respicting the depreciation of our wages, set out for camp the 16th day of June, & the 23d arivd at West Point wher the Hamp. Troops lay—

West Point June 24th 1780
British fleet & Army that have been to the Southwar'd & after a long Seage taken the City of Charles Town in South Carolina & the troops there under the Command of Gen! Lincoln, have return'd to N York except a garrison which is left there,—& have landed in Jersey had an action with Gen! Maxwell & a body of Millitia, after which they retired to Elizabeth Town Point near their Shipping ware there reinforc'd & marchd towards Gen! Washingtons Camp,[8] & at the same time their Fleet moov'd up the river towards West Point.— the Enimys front was attack'd by the Rhodeisland Troops & a body of millitia at a place call[ed] Springfield[9] about 6 miles from Elizabeth's Town,   our troops behav'd with remarkable bravery, repulsd the Enimy several times, kill'd a very considerable number of them. the Enimy then set fire to the village & retired to their boats at Elizabeth Town Point & crossd over to Staten Island.

27th the Enimys fleet have moov'd down the river.

28th we are in dayly expectation of a French fleet & army on our coast to opperate with our army against N. York.

July 1t British Army are at Philips's Manner[10] about 20 miles up the River from N. York on the East side.

8. On his return to New York from the victorious siege of Charleston, S. C., Clinton sent an expedition into New Jersey to capture Washington's camp and stores at Rockaway. At Springfield the British were met by Gens. Greene and Dickinson, who with Maxwell's and Stark's brigades, Lee's cavalry and the available militia, turned them back. *Writings of Washington*, XIX, 64.

9. Springfield, Union co., N. J., on the Rahway River.

10. Phillipse Manor comprised a large part of Westchester, Dutchess and Putnam counties in New York. The Manor Hall is now surrounded by the city of Yonkers.

4th this being the Anniversary of the declaration of American Independence, the officers of the garrison assembled at Gen! M?Dougal's Quarters after drinking 13 toasts marchd in procession to Gen!s Poors & Pattersons Quarters &c and adjurned until Evining, at which time we met & took a social drink & retird.—

14th the weather is extreemly warm.

17th we are assur'd the French fleet with 6000 Troops have arivd at Rhodeisland,[11] the British soldiers desert in learge numbers.

we hear an English Fleet has ariv'd at N. York,[12] our recruits from New Hampshire are coming in.—

20th 21[t] we are very busey in driling our new leavies.

26th one man from Connecticut & one from New Hampshire ware Shot here to day for desertion.

we are told that Admirel Graves[13] with 15 or 16 men of war are laying not far from Rhode Island, & the French Fleet is block'd in.—   Gen! Clinton with 8 or 10000 Troops is imbark'd & mooving up the Sound towards Rhodeisland, it is supposd they intend making a cope de main on the French Troops.—

27th Gen! Washingtons Main Army is crossing Hudsons River at Kings ferry, & the troop are marching from West Point to join him. from appeerences we judge that he intends making an attack on New York while Grave & Clinton are absent.—

11. The French expeditionary force under Comte De Rochambeau arrived off Rhode Island on July 11. It numbered over 5500 men. *Dict. Am. Biog.* XVI, 61.

12. This was Admiral Graves' squadron, sent to reinforce Admiral Arbuthnot. *Dict. Nat. Biog.*, VIII, 439.

13. Thomas Graves, Baron Graves (1725?–1802) grew up in the navy. He commanded a ship in American waters under Admiral Byron in 1778, but was recalled and made an admiral. He sailed to America in 1780 with reinforcements for Admiral Arbuthnot. If Graves did appear off Rhode Island at this time, he took no action. In March, 1781, he unsuccessfully engaged the French fleet off Chesapeake Bay. Graves became commander in American waters in July, 1781, and was defeated by the French in September. Before he could refit and transport

August 1ˢᵗ we are inform'd the Enimy are Returning from Rhode Island,— we are likewise informd that a body of Savages & Tories have beseiged Fort Scheylar on Mohawk River, a body of Massachusets Millitia are orderd to march for the releif of Fort Schylar.—

2ᵈ the heavy Artillery & Stores are mooving from West Point down the River, a man was hanged here to day for a Spy & hors theaf.

4ᵗʰ Genˡ Poor is orderd to take command of a Brigade of Light Infantry. the N. Hampˢ Troops march from West Point to day to Kings firry where we find the main army crossing the river, Colˢ Hazens¹⁴ Regᵗ joined our Brigade to day. he commands our Brigade.—

6ᵗʰ we cross the River & march toward dobs ferry.—¹⁵

8ᵗʰ we incamp'd near dobs ferry at a place call'd Orange Town on the west side of Hudsons River about 24 miles above the City of N. York.— the Enimy have some arm'd vessels in the River in what is call'd Tarpon Bay,¹⁶ which is a few miles above us.—

9ᵗʰ we have a fine rain which was very much wanted.—

10ᵗʰ the whole Army pass'd a revew of Inspection before the Barren Stuben—¹⁷

reinforcements to Cornwallis at Yorktown, the latter was forced to surrender. *Ibid.*, VIII, 438–40.

14. Col. Moses Hazen of the 2nd Canadian regiment had been supervising the building of a military road to Canada. Recalled to the main army, he succeeded to the command of Poor's brigade. *Dict. Am. Biog.*, VIII, 478.

15. Dobbs Ferry, Westchester co., N. Y., on the east side of the Hudson, 20 miles north of New York City.

16. Tappan Bay or Tappan Sea is an expansion of the Hudson River about twelve miles long between Rockland and Westchester counties.

17. Friedrich Wilhelm Ludolf Gerhard Augustin, Baron von Steuben (1730–1794), a former staff officer and aide-de-camp to Frederick the Great, was sent to America by Franklin. He joined Washington at Valley Forge early in 1778 as a volunteer without pay, and was made inspector-general. He drilled the troops all winter and by the following summer he had built up a well disciplined army. He continued to drill the troops and wrote a manual of drill and field service for the United States army. He was sent south with Greene in 1780, and set up a base of supplies in Virginia for the southern army. Washington relied heavily on his advice in strategic and ad-

11th 12th 13th 14th 15th 16th the army is very buseyly imploy'd in instructing the new levies some of the Enimies armd vessels are daily passing & repassing up & down the River, indeavoring to prevent our small craft from coming down with provisions & Stores &c. there is more or less fireing from the Enimies vessels every day—

18th we are assured that a fleet of near 30 sail of Store Ships bound for Quebec have been dispers'd by a French Ship the greater part of which have been taken by the French & our privateers—& have arivd at Boston.— it is said a learge Imbarcatio[n] is taking place at New York. we have had 5 or 6 weeks of the most extreem heet that I ever experienc'd.— we are erecting works at dobs ferry in order to protect our boats in crossing.—

21^{t} the weather has very sudently changed from heat to cool.—

22^{d} altho we have a very learge proportion of new levies in our army, & the weather has been so remarkably warm, our troops are very healthy.—

23^{d} our army march'd at 7 oclock A.M. proceeded 10 miles down the river to a place calld the Tene Flie[18] & incamp'd oposite Kings Bridg. our left wing 1½ mile from the River. the Light Infantry 2 miles in front. the weather has been very warm, which render'd our march very fatigueing.—

Col? Hazen was arrested to day by Barren Stuben for halting his Brigade without leave.

25th the Light Infantry & three Brigades from the right wing march'd with 370 waggons down to Bergin point[19]

ministrative policy. He became a naturalized citizen and settled in New York. *Dict. Am. Biog.*, XVII, 601–4.

18. Tenafly, Bergen co., N. J., 16 miles north of Jersey City, and one mile west of the Hudson.

19. Bergen Point, Hudson co., N. J., on Newark Bay. It is now a part of Bayonne.

oposite the City of N. York, to collect forrage, & cattle. some cannonading hapen'd near Powlers hook,[20] but the Enimy did not chuse to make a serious attack. after collecting a learge quanti[ty] of forrage & 200 head of cattle, our troops returnd the 27$\underline{^{th}}$ our Army has been 4 days without meat, which has occasion'd many licentious practices, among the Soldiery. one man was detected in Robing an Inhabitents house to day & was hang'd on a tree without tryal by order of his Excellency Gen! Washington.—

28th we have a small supply of provision ariv'd.— the Country we now lay in is very pleasent & fertile, but a wors set of inhabitents never liv'd in any country.— we are assur'd that a very learge combin'd Fleet & army has gone against Jamaca.

the Country here suffers very much for want of rain.— two duels have been fought here within two days in which two gentlemen ware kil'd, & one wounded;—

Sept! 2^{d} the army is order'd to march to morrow morning.

3^{d} we have a very heavy rain.—

4th the Army march'd at 9 oclock A.M. cross'd Hacken Sack River & incamp'd about 8 miles to the westward of our late incampment;—[21]

5th our army has not been supplied with more then six days meat for eighteen days past.— Col? Hazen is honourably acquited by a court Martial

8th this evining ye Honb! Brigadeer Gen! Poor departed this life after labouring under a severe bilious fever 13

20. Powles Hook, also Paulus Hook is now gone. It was a point of land which projected into the mouth of Hudson River, directly opposite the southern tip of Manhattan Island.

21. General Orders for the day were issued from Kendekamack, known also as Steenrapie. Washington's headquarters were in Andrew Harper's house on the road to Morristown, about 4 miles south of Ramapo Pass. *Writings of Washington*, XIX, 499.

days, very universally lamented by the Gen!s & other
officers of the army.—²²

10ᵗʰ the remains of Gen! Poor was Interd at Hackin-
sack,²³ attended by his Excellency Gen! Washington, all
the Gen!s & most of the other officers of the army, together with a Reg! of Infantry, detachments of Cavelry,
Artillery, with a band of musick. the prosession was
truly Solemn & well conducted.
the death of so valuable an officer as the Gen! is a very
great loss to the army & to his Brigade in particular.

―――――――

―――――

by accounts from the Southward it appeers that Gen!
Gates has met with a defeat at a place calld camden,²⁴ in
Carolina has lost about 500 men & the baggage of his
army. it is said Barren De Calb²⁵ fell in the ⌈battle?⌉

12ᵗʰ a man was hang'd to day for plundering the
Inhabitents.—

13ᵗʰ the whole Army pass'd a revew to day before his
Excellency Gen! Washington. about 20 Indian cheefs accompanied the Gen! in the revew.—

14ᵗʰ from many reports it is expected that a Fleet from
the West Indias is near our coast, to coopperate with the
Fleet now at Rhode Island against N. York—

22. The *Dictionary of American Biography* mentions that the "circumstances of his
[Poor's] death are shrouded in uncertainty," and reports the rumor of a fatal duel;
but there is no reason to doubt Dearborn's statement regarding the death of Gen. Poor.

23. Hackensack, Bergen co., N. J., 12 miles north of New York City.

24. Camden, Camden co., S. C. The battle took place August 15, on low land
between two swamps, 5 miles outside the city. Cornwallis commanded the British
force. Despite the gallantry of Kalb and other officers, Gates and his troops, largely
composed of militia, were routed with heavy losses.

25. Johann Kalb (1721–1780), a German who had served in the French army and
adopted a title, came to America with Lafayette in 1777. He was given the rank of
major-general and spent the winter at Valley Forge. In April, 1780, he was sent to
relieve Charleston, S. C. There he joined the unfortunate expedition under Gates.
During the battle of Camden, Kalb was mortally wounded, and died August 19 at
Camden. *Dict. Am. Biog.*, X, 253–4.

17ᵗʰ we are informd that Admiral Rodney²⁶ with 13 Ships of the line has arivd at N. York, from the West Indias.—

His Excellency Gen! Washington has set out to day to meet the Count Deroshambo, (Commander of the French army at Rhodeisland) in Connecticut to hold a conference.²⁷

18ᵗʰ at evining the Army was orderd to be in rediness to march Instantly.—

19ᵗʰ the weather being rainy the army did not march.

20 the army marchd to our old Incampment at Orrange Town,²⁸ & incamp'd.

22ᵈ at day brake this morning 2 cannon & one Hoytres began to play briskly a [on?] a ship of war that lay in the river, the wind & tide being unfavorable for the ship she was not able to git out of reach for more then an hour—

the French Minister Plenipotentiary²⁹ arivd in Camp to day on his way to Rhodeisland. Col? Pickering³⁰ ariv'd

26. George Brydges Rodney, Baron Rodney (1719–1792), after a long naval service, was in retirement in France from 1775 to 1778. He returned to England and was commissioned an admiral, but was not given a command until the end of 1779, when he was sent to the Leeward Islands station. He had two indecisive actions with the French, then sailed for New York. Admiral Arbuthnot quarrelled with him, and he returned to the West Indies. In 1781 he seized the island of St. Eustatius, but the French retook it. Rodney resigned his command to Hood and sailed for England on August 1, 1781. *Dict. Nat. Biog.*, XVII, 81–7.

27. Jean Baptiste Donatien de Vimeur, Comte de Rochambeau (1725–1807), entered the French army in 1742 and served on the continent in the wars against England. He was made commander of the expeditionary force sent to America in 1780, and reached Rhode Island in July. Washington conferred with him at Hartford on September 22, and agreed that until France could gain superiority in American waters, nothing extensive should be attempted. Rochambeau's army wintered in Rhode Island. *Dict. Am. Biog.*, XVI, 60–3.

28. Orange, Essex co., N. J., 13 miles west of New York City.

29. César Anne de la Luzerne (1741–1791). He succeeded Conrad Gérard de Rayneval, France's first minister, in September, 1779. J. B. Perkins, *France in the American Revolution* (Boston, 1911), 294.

30. Timothy Pickering (1745–1829) of Massachusetts had been adjutant-general of the Continental Army and a member of the Board of War before succeeding Greene

Sept.r 25.th

Treason of the blackest dy, is this day fortunately discover'd. Maj.r John Andre Adjutant Gen.l of the British Army taken within our lines in disguise acting as a spy. upon which Maj.r Gen.l Arnold immediately deserted from his Command of West Point, on board a British sloop of war that lay in the River below Kings Ferry. being convinced his hellish plot would soon be brought to light, & his only safety was in flight. the plan was as follows

he had agreed to put the Enemy in possession of the important Post call'd West Point together with the stores & Garrison this night, & a body of the Enemy were imbarked at New York for the purpose, & had not a superintending providence almost miraculously interpos'd in our behalf by throwing Maj.r Andre into our possession after he thought himself quite secure, & out of our reach, the Enemy would undoubtedly soon been in possession of our most important Post, which would

Dearborn's entry for September 25, 1781, concerning the discovery of Arnold's treason

also in camp, who supersedes Maj. Gen. Green as Quarter Master General.—

Sept. 25th

Treason of the blackest dy, is this day fortunately discoverd.[31] Maj. John Andre[32] Adjutant Gen. of the British Army taken within our lines in disguise acting as a spy, upon which Maj. Gen. Arnold immediately deserted from his Command of West Point on board a British sloop of war that lay in the River be[l]ow Kings Ferry, being convinced his hellish plot would soon be brought to light & his only safety was in flight. the plan was as follow[s:] he had agreed to put the Enemy in possession of the Important Post call'd West Point together with the stores & garrison this night, & a body of the Enemy ware imbark'd at New York for the purpose, & had not a superintending providence almost miraculously interpos'd in our behalf by throing Maj. Andre into our possession after he thought himself quite secure, & out of our reach, the Enemy would undoubtedly soon been in possession of our most important Post, which would have been a capital loss to America;— as soon as this plan was discoverd two Brigads ware detach'd & sent to West Point.

as quartermaster-general. Under Presidents Washington and Adams, he served as postmaster general, secretary of war, and secretary of state. *Dict. Am. Biog.*, XIV, 565–8.

31. This sentence was copied from the official announcement of Arnold's defection published in General Orders dated at Orangetown, September 26, 1780. *Writings of Washington*, XX, 95.

32. Maj. John André (1751–1780) was aide-de-camp to Sir Henry Clinton and had just been made adjutant-general of the British army in America. He directed much of the secret service, particularly the treason correspondence with Benedict Arnold. Before turning West Point over to the British, Arnold demanded a personal interview with some British officer. André met him up the Hudson River on September 21. Unable to return to New York by boat, André started overland in disguise, with plans in his boot. He was seized on September 23 by American soldiers, to whom he revealed his identity. A board of officers examined him and advised Washington that he was a spy rather than a prisoner of war. Accordingly he was hanged on October 2, after vain efforts on the part of Clinton to have him exchanged. *Dict. Nat. Biog.*, I, 397–8.

26th one Joshua Smith[33] was taken up on suspicion of being an accomplice of Arnolds—

29th a Board of Gen! Officers set to day for the Tryal of Maj^r Andre—

30th a Gen! Court Martial sits to day for the Tryal of Smith—

Octob^r 1st Maj^r Andre was orderd to be hanged at 5 oclock P.M. but in consequence of a Flag from the Enemy the execution was put off

2^d at 12 oclock this day Maj^r Andre was executed. he discoverd great firmness & candor on the occasion; he was one of the most promising yong Gentlemen in the British Army, had been an Aid-decamp to Genl. Clinton & was lately appointed Adjutant Gen! to the British army in America.—

3^d we hear an other Arrangement of the Army is in contemplation.—

7th the Army march'd, when the following disposition was made.

Gen! Washington with the main Army near Princton in Jersey—

Gen! Green with the New Jersey, New York, New Hampshire troops & Starks Brigade[34] at West Point.

9th we took post at West Point.

10th the Massachusets & New Hampshire Millitia at this Post ware dismis'd.—

the 1st & 2^d New Hampshire Reg^{ts} posted on Constitution

---

33. Joshua Hett Smith (d. 1818), a lawyer, member of the New York state convention of 1775, and a brother of the chief justice, was implicated in Arnold's treason because his house was the meeting place of Arnold and André, and because he guided André part way on his return to New York. However, Smith was acquitted by a military court. He was later imprisoned by civil authorities, but escaped to New York City. He went to England after the war. F. S. Drake, *Dictionary of American Biography* (Boston, 1876), 843.

34. Earlier in the year Stark's brigade had consisted of four regiments under Sherburne, Angell, Webb and Jackson.

Isle,[35] the 3ᵈ & Hazens Regᵗ on the Table at Nelsons Point oposite West Point.—

17ᵗʰ the Honbᵉ Majʳ Genˡ Heath[36] takes command at West Point to day. Genˡ Green is orderd to take Command of the Southern Army. Genˡ Gates is under an arrest, for his conduct at the Battle of the 16ᵗʰ of August near Camdon.—

18ᵗʰ we begin to talk of Hutting.—

19ᵗʰ & 20ᵗʰ we are loocking out ground to Hut on.—

21ᵗ Genˡ Heath being informd of a large party of the Enemy coming out by way of Kings Bridg for the purpose of forrageing & plundering about crum pond,[37] our Brigad was orderd to march to oppose them.

we marchd this afternoon & at 10 oclock in the evining arivd near croten bridg twenty miles from our camp, where we expected to meet the Enemy at day brake, but ware disappointed. we remaind there until the morning of the 23ᵈ & returnd to Camp.—

24ᵗʰ we marchd to Soldiers fortune[38] about 3 miles to the Eastward of our camp to build huts for winter.—

we are informed that the combind fleet of France & Spain have fallen in with & taken more then fifty English marchantmen bound from England to the East & West Indies.—

27ᵗʰ we are begining to build huts

29ᵗʰ we are this day inform'd in Genˡ orders of a very fortunate event that has taken place at the Southward.

35. Constitution Island is on the east side of the Hudson, opposite West Point. It is separated from the mainland by a marsh. Nelson's Point is now Garrison, N. Y.

36. William Heath (1737–1814) of Massachusetts was made a major-general in 1776, but was employed for staff work. He was stationed in Boston in 1777–78 in command of the Eastern District. In 1779 he was transferred to the Hudson, and commanded West Point after Arnold fled. *Dict. Am. Biog.*, VIII, 490.

37. Crompond, N. Y.

38. An outpost in the highlands opposite West Point.

Col? Williams[39] of Carolina having receiv'd intelligence of a body of British Troops & tories consisting of about 1400—hundred commanded by Col? Fargarson[40] being on their way to Charlotte in North Carolina—rallied the country & mounted 1000 [1600?] on hors back in order to be able to meet the Enemy at a pass calld Kings mountain he there fell in with the Enemy & a severe action ensewed in which Col? Williams' party was finally successful, the British commander kill'd with 130 of his men, & 800 made prisoners of war together with 1500 stand of arms.— but unfortunately for us the Brave & enterpriseing Col? Williams receiv'd a mortal wound the latter part of the action.—[41]

Nove.[r] 8th I was orderd on a Gen.[l] Court Martial to act for the tryal of Col? Hazen at West Point.[42]

19th all the troops at this Post fit for duty are orderd to be prepar'd for a march with 4 days provision cook'd by the morning of the 21.[t]—

39. Col. James Williams of the South Carolina militia was killed in the battle of King's Mountain on October 7, 1780. Heitman, *op. cit.*, 595.

40. Lt. Col. Patrick Ferguson (1744–1780) joined the British army before he was fifteen. In 1776 he invented the first breech-loading rifle used in the army and formed a corps of riflemen equipped with this type of arm. Ferguson was severely wounded in the battle of Brandywine. In 1779 he dislodged the Americans from Stony Point and was then sent south. After the siege of Charleston, Ferguson trained the Loyalist militia of South Carolina. He was killed at King's Mountain on October 7. *Dict. Nat. Biog.*, VI, 1212–4.

41. Hearing that militia was advancing towards Augusta, Cornwallis despatched Ferguson to cut it off. But when Ferguson learned that a thousand "mountain men" were assembled at Watauga, bent on his destruction, he abandoned his pursuit of the militia and began a retreat towards Charlotte. He was intercepted, however, and forced to make a stand. On the night of October 6 he camped on the southern end of King's Mountain. Meanwhile the mountaineers, after a forced night march, reached the base of the mountain with reinforcements from the Carolinas. They surrounded Ferguson's position and began the attack the following day. After three charges and countercharges, during which Ferguson and many of his men were killed, the remainder of the British force, under De Peyster, surrendered to the Americans. Winsor, *op. cit.*, VI, 479, *passim.*

42. Col. Moses Hazen was involved in a dispute with Maj. James Reid over the date of the latter's commission, but there is no indication in Washington's papers that a court-martial was ordered. *Writings of Washington*, XX, 306.

21ˢᵗ six Batallions under the command of Brigadeer Genˡ Stark march'd towards the Enemies lines as a covering party to several hundred teams that ware collected & sent down as a forrageing party near the Enemies lines.—[43] we proceeded within about 10 miles of Kings Bridg on the several roads leading thereto, & remaind until the teams ware loaded, we toock every meathod to provoke the Enemy to come out & attack us but to no purpose.— after remaining out six nights without any covering but the heavens, (three nights & three days exposed to heavy rains & hard marching,) returnd to camp. the main Army under the Command of his Excellency Genˡ Washington is mooving to winter Quarters.

Decemʳ 1ˢᵗ this day receiv'd the account from Majʳ Talmag[44] of Colᵒ Sheldons Regᵗ of Horse,[45] who with 60 dismounted dragoons crossd the Sound in whale boats, & surpris'd Fort Saint George on Long Island,[46] brought of[f] 1 Lᵗ Colᵒ 1 Capᵗ 1 Lᵗ & 60 men, dismantled the fort, burnt a Schooner ladend with wood in a harbour & return'd without the loss of a man.—

6ᵗʰ his Excellency Genˡ Washington arivd at New Windsor[47] 8 mile above west Point & toock Quarter for the winter

the Pencelvania & Jersey Troop are stationd in Jersey for

43. The British lines included Fort Washington and the chain of fortifications in the vicinity of Laurel Hill, including Fort George.

44. Benjamin Tallmadge (1754–1835) joined a Connecticut regiment in 1776 and became a major in 1777. He participated in the battles around New York and Philadelphia and in the battle of Monmouth. He distinguished himself by destroying Fort St. George in 1780. From 1778 on he directed much of Washington's secret service. *Dict. Am. Biog.*, XVIII, 284-5.

45. Col. Elisha Sheldon of Connecticut commanded the 2nd Continental Dragoons. Heitman, *op. cit.*, 493.

46. The raid took place on the night of November 23. Tallmadge dated his report to Washington November 25. Fort St. George was on Smith's Point, Long Island.

47. New Windsor, Orange co., N. Y., on the west bank of the Hudson, between Newburgh and West Point.

the winter—[48] the whole of New England troop at & about West Point, the New York troop at and about Albany—

10 the New Hampshire Troop moovd into Huts, the best ever built in America—call'd New Hampshire village.—[49] we are informd that the most severe Hurricane hapen'd in the west Indias about the middle of Octob^r last that was ever experiencd there. almost totally distroy'd many of the Islands, together with all the shiping there.—

16. the New Hampshire line is arrangeed agreable to the New arrangement. Col? Cilley, Lt Col? Titcomb & Capt N. Hutchins retire.[50]

20th I am about seting out on command to New Hampshire

28th ariv'd in New Hampshire & had the pleasure of finding my fammaly well.

May 10th 1781 after finishing the business I had to do with the State,[51] set out for Camp where I ariv'd the 17th found our troops at New Hampshire village.—

the 14th Ins^t Col? Green & Maj^r Flagg[52] of the Rhode-Island Reg^t being on the line ware surprised & most in-

48. The Pennsylvania line was quartered about four miles from Morristown, and the Jersey line was in and around Pompton. *Writings of Washington*, XX, 418.

49. The New Hampshire village was just above Peekskill Creek, Putnam co., N. Y., in the vicinity of Cat Hill.

50. The retirement of these officers resulted in the transfer to the 1st New Hampshire regiment of Alexander Scammell as colonel and Dearborn as lieutenant-colonel. Heitman, *op. cit.*, 41, 190, 483.

51. By act of Congress on Nov. 4, 1780, the states were called upon to furnish specific quantities of provisions for the army. Washington wrote to Gov. Weare of New Hampshire on this head on December 10. Following the mutiny of the Pennsylvania Line in January, 1781, Washington again addressed the governors on the pressing need of cash to pay the soldiers. *New Hampshire Historical Collections*, II, 172–4. When Dearborn returned to camp in May, 1781, he brought with him cash for the New Hampshire troops. *Provincial and State Papers . . . of New Hampshire*, X, 543–4. His business in New Hampshire doubtless concerned the matters of food and money.

52. Col. Christopher Greene, who had been on the Quebec expedition with Dearborn, and Maj. Ebenezer Flagg of the 1st Rhode Island regiment. Heitman, *op. cit.*, 229, 260.

humainly butcher'd, together with 12 of their party, by a body of the Enemy consisting mostly of refugees.— 30 of our party ware made prisoners.

18th we are inform'd that Gen! Philips[53] with about 3000 troops has taken possession of Williamsburg in Virgenia. his Excellency Gen! Washington has gone to Hartford in Connecticut suppos'd to hold a conference with Gen! De Roch Shambault.[54]

26th we hear Gen! Green has taken Possession of Camdon in South Carolina where Lord Corn Wallis has had a garrison for several months.—[55]

June 7th Lord Cornwallis & a body of troops under the command of Gen! Arnold have form'd a Junction in Virgenia.—

June 12th we are assured that Gen! Green has taken several of the Enemies Posts in South Carolina, & has a prospect of confining the Enemy in that State to Charles Town.—

21st 22d & 23d Our Army took the Field near Peeks Kill.— we are in expectation of being Join'd by the French Troops from Rhode Island in a few days—

July 1st I was appointed D[eputy]. Q[uarter]. M[aster]. G[eneral]. & Joind the department.[56]

53. Maj. Gen. William Phillips (1731?-1781) commanded the artillery under Burgoyne in 1777, and was held a prisoner of war until he was exchanged for Gen.Lincoln early in 1781. He died of a fever at Petersburg, Va., on May 13. *Dict. Nat. Biog.*, XV, 1106-7.

54. The conference was held at Wethersfield on May 22. The French were represented by Rochambeau, Chastellux and Jacques Melchior. Comte Barras St. Laurent, Chef d'escadre of the French navy, was unable to attend because of the sudden appearance of the British fleet off Newport, Rhode Island. *Writings of Washington*, XXII, 100, *passim*.

55. This rumor probably refers to Greene's siege of the village of Ninety-Six, near the Saluda River. Camden was evacuated by the British under Rawdon on May 10, 1781, it being untenable.

56. The appointment was made at the request of Col. Timothy Pickering, quartermaster-general. Dearborn succeeded Maj. Richard Platt, resigned. H. P. Johnston, *The Yorktown Campaign . . .* (New York, 1881), 112.

July 2^d our whole Army march'd at 3 oclock A M. without baggage, towards New York.[57]

3^d at Sun rise we arriv'd near Kings Bridg, where a scurmish happend between a detachment of our troops consisting of about 800 men & a body of the Enimy, in which we had three commission'd officers & 55 non commission'd & privates kill'd & wounded. 1 officer & 5 privates only of the former— the loss of the Enemy was about equel to ours according to the best accounts we can procure.— the intentions on our side was to have drawn the Enimy out so far from their works as to enabled us to cut of[f] their retreat,—but they ware to[o] caucious.— after Gen! Washington had had sufficiently reconoiter'd their work &c. we moovd back about two miles & lay until next morning.— it appeerd from many circumstances that the Enimy ware very much allarm'd at our sudent appeerence before their works.—

The Duke Delason[58] with his legend ⌐legion¬ of French Troops joind us near kings Bridg this morning—

4th we march'd towards White Plains & incamp'd about 3 miles to the southward of them,—& sent for our baggage.—

5 the French Army under the command of the Count De Rochambo arriv'd near White Plains, & the 6th they joind us & incamp'd on our left, a body of as fine Troops as the world can bost of (I beleave) a few hours after their joining us our army was paraded & revew'd by the Count De Rochambo.—

57. An elaborate plan for attacking New York City had been discussed at Wethersfield.

58. Armand-Louis Gontaut Biron, Duc de Lauzun (1747–1793), arrived in America with a cavalry corps in 1780, as part of the French force under Rochambeau. He spent the winter at Lebanon, Conn., and was later active in the Yorktown campaign. Rochambeau sent him back to France with the news of Cornwallis' surrender. E. M. Stone, *Our French Allies* (Providence, 1884), 308, *passim*.

18th several of the Enemies ships (that went up the rive[r] some days agoe in order to interrupt our transportation of Stores & provisions by water) find their situation reather uncumfortable return'd, & at dobs ferry our battery (of 2 eighteens, two twelves & 2 hoytrers[59]) gave them a very handsom salute, one of their largest ships was set on fire by a shell from our hoytrers, after being shot through in near twenty places, which put the crew into such confusion that about 20 jumpd overboad some of which reach'd the shore.

21[t] at 9 oclock in the evining the whole of our army, together with the French march'd (except a sufficient numbar to guard the Camp) & at day brake ware paraded before the Enemies work at Kings bridg,— a party of our horse, with some Millitia from Connectut, went on to Frogs neck,[60] (a nest of tories) & the Duke Delozen with his Legion & Col? Scammell, with a corps of Light Infantry, went onto Morissenia[61] (the place of randisvoos for Delensees Infamus Corps of horse theives, & murderers)[62] a considerable numbar of horses, Cattle, & sheep, together with about twenty of the above mentioned corps ware taken & brought off, & the remeinder dispers'd, except what ware killd.

after remaining two days in front of their works, & making use of every meathod in our power to induce them to give us Battle, & having had a sufficient opper-

59. Howitzers.

60. Throg's Neck or Throg's Point, Westchester co., N. Y., extending into Long Island Sound. It is the present site of Fort Schuyler.

61. Morrisiana, at the junction of the Bronx and East rivers. The action occurred on July 3. Washington had planned a joint action with De Lauzun, but it failed. *Writings of Washington*, XXII, 330, *passim*.

62. Col. James De Lancey (1746–1804) commanded a troop of Loyalist horsemen, nicknamed ''Cowboys'' because of their cattle raids in Westchester county. Washington sent out an expedition on July 21 to reconnoiter the enemy's posts at Kingsbridge and to cut off De Lancey's raiders, but few of the horsemen were captured. J. C. Fitzpatrick, ed., *Diaries of George Washington* (Boston, 1925), II, 241–3.

tunity for reconnoitering every part of their works & the country adjacent, we returnd to Camp without the loss of one man.—

by a letter from the Marquess De Lafiatte we are informd of an action that hapened near Williamsburgh in Virgenia between Gen! Wain with about 800 men & Lord Cornwallis.s main army, in which we lost about 100 killd & wounded, & one piece of artillery. the Enemies loss was conciderable,[63] the Enemies numerous posts in South Carolina & Georgey, established at such an amazing expence of men & money, are at last by that excellent officer Maj! Gen! Green intirely reduced, except *barely* Charles Town, & Savanah; in which two places the remains of their shatterd & worn out army are confined; after all the boastings of the British Ministry of their glorious conquests of the Carolinies & Georgey.

the British Army in Virgenia under the Command of the Celibrated Lord Corn Wallis, who was to compleet the conquest of all the States to the Southward of the Hudson River this Campaign is now confined to the Town of Portsmouth wher[e] he can be covered by ships of War.—[64] Pensacola the cappital of West Florida is captured by the Spainyards & the whole Provinc put under Spanish government.[65] Tobago, a british west India Island is taken by the French, & by various accounts, it appears that the British affairs in the Est Indies ware a very bad aspect.—

63. Generals Wayne and Lafayette engaged Cornwallis at Jamestown Ford, Va., near Green Spring Farm. On July 6, with a small reconnoitering party, they forced the British army back across the James River. Jared Sparks, ed., *Correspondence of the American Revolution* . . . (Boston, 1853), III, 347–50.

64. Portsmouth, a seaport of Norfolk co., Va., stands on the left bank of the Elizabeth River. By blockading the mouth of this river or the entrance to Hampton Roads, the British source of supplies could be cut off. At the same time, an attacking French fleet could sail up the river within range of the city and bombard the British position.

65. Gov. Galvez of New Orleans, with a land and sea force, captured Pensacola on May 9, 1781. Winsor, *op. cit.*, VI, 739.

our old Friend the old Continental money is at last dead.
very great pains has been taken by many ranks & orders
of People for many years past, to take the life of our said
friend, which has been performd after a strugle of more
then six years.—[66]

Augus.^{t} 10th
we remain near Dobs Ferry, nothing extraordinery
hapened.—

18th there is preparations for mooving, but when or
where is uncertain.

21^{t} the French Army, with a detachment of the American Army consisting of about 2500 together with our
Park of Artillery march'd towards Kings Ferry, with
Gen! Washington at thier head,— from the 22^{d} to the
27 the Army & baggage was crossing the Hudson at
Kings Ferry— as soon as the Army was over the River
the line of march was taken up,— the distination of
this Army being an intire secret, it occasioned a great variety of conjectures, but an attack on Staten Island was
more generally expected, by the Country & Army.[67] our
Troops after marching 9 miles in one Column, & then
proceeded in two columns until we arrivd at Prince
Town, from thênce to Trenton in one column— at Trenton vessels ware collected to receive our Artillery, heavy
baggage, & some part of our troops, which proceeded
down the Delliware to Christiania creek, then up said

66. In 1780 Congress began to retire the depreciated paper issued earlier in the war
by means of a tax on the states payable in the old bills. Silver was exchanged at the rate
of 1 to 40. A new paper issue was offered of less than one twentieth of the face value
of the old. Although the new bills were redeemable in specie after five years, actually
they were not exchanged until 1790. D. R. Dewey, *Financial History of the United
States* (New York, 1903), 36–40.

67. The march to the Chesapeake was begun on the 19th. The destination of the
army was kept secret, and the enemy under Clinton logically expected an attempt on
New York by way of Staten Island. By the time Washington's combined forces began
to head directly towards Princeton and Trenton, on the 30th, it was too late for
Clinton to intercept the move against Cornwallis.

creek to Christiania bridg, from whence the Artillery &
Stores ware transferd by land to the Head of Elk, about
12 miles, & there reship'd.—[68] our Troops that march'd
by land pass'd Philadelphia the 2ᵈ of Sepᵗ. by this time
it is generally supposed that Lord Corn Wallis & his
Troops in Virginia is our object.— the 29ᵗʰ ulᵗ a Fleet
of British Men of War arriv'd at New York consisting of
12 ships of the line & some Frigates, under the command
of Admiral Whood,—[69] A large French Fleet is hourly
expected on our coast. on the 6ᵗʰ the American Troops
arriv'd at the Head of Elk, & began to imbark our Artillery & Stores. the 7ᵗʰ the French Troops arriv'd & began
to imbark their Artillery & Stores.— we have certain
intilligence of the Arrival of A French Fleet in the Ches-
opeak bay consisting of 28 Ships of the line & some Frigates, & that they have landed 3000 men.—[70] the French
Fleet captured on their passage a Frigate on board of
which was Lord Rawden[71] on his way from Charles Town
to England; the 9ᵗʰ and 10 the French Granidiers, light
Infantry & artillery, together with the American Artillery, light Infantry, & one Battalion of Jersey Troops imbark'd on board vessels & the 11ᵗʰ proceeded down the

68. Washington ordered the route of march from Philadelphia to the head of Elk
River by way of Darby, Chester, Wilmington on Christiana Creek, and Christiana
Bridge. Elk River rises in Chester co., Pa., flows south to Elkton, Maryland, and enters
Chesapeake Bay in Cecil county. *Writings of Washington*, XXIII, 23, 68, *ff.*

69. Admiral Samuel Hood, Viscount Hood (1724–1816), was inactive in the war
until 1780, when he was sent to the West Indies. The next summer he took his ships
to New York to reinforce Admiral Graves. Together they were defeated by a superior
French fleet off Chesapeake Bay, and failed to help Cornwallis. Hood then returned
to the West Indies. *Dict. Nat. Biog.*, IX, 1157–63.

70. The French fleet arrived off Chesapeake on August 31. Fiske. *op. cit.*, II, 278.

71. Francis Rawdon-Hastings, 2nd Earl of Moira and 1st Marquis of Hastings
(1754–1826), came to America in 1773 and took part in most of the Revolutionary
campaigns. In 1778 he was appointed adjutant-general with the rank of lieutenant-
colonel. He fought in the siege of Charleston in 1780, and defeated Greene at Hobkirk's
Hill in 1781. He left America because of ill health. On his way to England his ship
was captured, and he was taken to Brest, but was exchanged in a short time. *Dict.
Nat. Biog.*, IX, 117–22.

Bay as far as Annapolis, where we remain'd until the 15th & then put down the bay.

12 the other Battalion of Jersey Troops, Hazins Reg^t & the Rhode Island troops imbark'd in flat Bottom boats (which we transported from Hudsons River,) & proceeded down the Bay. the main body of the French Troops, & the two New York Reg^ts march'd on to Baltimore & from thence to Annapolis, & there imbark'd on board vessels (sent up from the French Fleet,) & proceeded to James River.— the first division of our Troops arriv'd in James River the 20th & the remainder the 24th we proceeded up the River about 40 miles & landed.—(I was attack'd with a Billious fever the day before we left Annapolis which continud very severe until after I landed.—)

we found the Enemy at York Town strongly fortified & about 5000 strong exclusive of a large body of negros which they had stolen from the Inhabitents. York Town is situate on York River, twelve miles from Williamsburg where we found the Marquiss De Lafiate with the Troops under his command. our Troops landed about five miles from Williamsburg, march'd & found the Army near that Town.— the French Fleet consisting of 36 sail of the line with a numbar of frigates, lay in the mouth of the bay & in the mouths of the rivers.[72] the   th a British Fleet under Admiral Graves appeer'd of[f] the Bay consisting of 21 ships of the line & a numbar of Frigates.[73]

---

72. Comte De Grasse stationed his fleet so as to blockade all possible approaches to York and Gloucester by sea. These included (1) the passage between the "Middle Ground" and Cape Henry (2) the passage from Lynhaven Bay into the James River (3) Burwell's Ferry across the James River from the Williamsburg Road to Suffolk (4) the passage between "The Spit" and the shoals of the "Middle Ground" which cut off the mouth of Chesapeake Bay as well as the mouth of York River. The York peninsula was blockaded by the combined land forces under Washington.

73. The British fleet under Admiral Graves appeared off Chesapeake Bay on September 5, and was routed by the French fleet the same day. Fiske, *op. cit.*, II, 279.

the French slip'd their cables & 24 ships put to sea came up with the British & had a parcial action the British made off. the French took two frigates & return'd to their Station.—

27th L.t Col.º Connaway[74] of the british was taken near york Town.—

28th the whole Army march'd from Williamsburg to york Town, & incamp'd near the Town;— we have authentic accounts from the Southward of an action between Gen.l Green & the Enemy in that Quarter, in which the Enemy lost 300 kill'd 400 taken prisoners & ware totally defeated; our loss was 250 kill'd & wounded, among which was a numbar of officers of distinction.—[75] we are inform'd the Enemy have lately burn'd New London & New Haven in Connecticut. it is said the Infamous Arnold headed the party that perform'd those brilliant exploits.—[76]

Octobr 1 our army is carrying on their opperations against York. have Obliged the Enemy to abandon their out works.—[77] Col.º Scammell (being Officer of the day)

74. The prisoner's name is given as Lt. Col. John Connolly in *The Pennsylvania Gazette* for Oct. 10, 1781, which adds that he was "paroled in Hanover in Virginia." As there is no such name in the British Army List, he must be Dr. John Connolly, who held this rank in the provincial forces of Sir Henry Clinton. Connolly was Lord Dunmore's agent at Fort Pitt, and helped to foment "Dunmore's War" in 1774. He was captured the following year and kept a prisoner until early in 1781. R. G. Thwaites and L. P. Kellogg, eds., *Documentary History of Dunmore's War 1774* (Madison, 1905), 42.

75. This was the battle of Eutaw Springs, S. C., fought September 8 between Greene's southern army and a British detachment under Lt. Col. Stuart. Winsor; *op. cit.*, VI, 493-4, *passim*.

76. When Clinton learned that Washington had marched south, he ordered a raid into Connecticut in the hope of diverting part of the allied armies. Arnold invaded and burned New London, his boyhood town. Forts Griswold and Trumbull were taken, and some shipping was destroyed. New Haven was not attacked. This was Arnold's last military exploit. Fiske, *op. cit.*, II, 281-2. Arnold's letter to Clinton, in *N. Y. Gazette & Weekly Mercury*, Sept. 24, 1781.

77. From the day of its arrival, Washington's army had worked steadily on the construction of redoubts and approaches to the enemy lines. On September 29, the British outposts were abandoned, as well as the advanced redoubts, and Cornwallis withdrew to the security of his main line of defense. The abandoned works were immediately taken over by Washington's troops.

was reconnoitering the Enemies works this morning when a small party of their Hors sallied out, & took him prisoner, & after having him in possession, one of the horsmen came up in his rear, put his pistol near his back & shot him. the ball enter'd between his hip bone & his ribs & lodg'd in him. he was carried into Town, & the next day came out on Parole. his wound appeers rather dangerous.

6th New Hampshire has met with one more cappital loss. the unfortunate Col? Scammell this day expired, in consiquence of his wound receiv'd the 1st ins^t universally lamented by all who knew him. the loss of so great & good an officer must be very severely felt in the Army at large; but in the New Hampshire line, in perticular.—

9th I have so far recover'd my health as to be able to go into Camp & do my duty this day.

our batteries Open'd this day on the Enemies works, & our approaches are going forward briskly.

10th and 11th we burn't a 50 gun Ship of the Enemies & two smaller ones with our shells.—[78] this night we broke ground within about 250 yards of the Enemies works, where batteries will be erected immediately.—

12th a very heavy fire is kept up on both sides to day. but our men continue at work in the advanced works.— we have not had as much as one man p^r day kill'd on an average since we began our approaches. (very fortunate indeed.)

15th last evining two of the Enemies redoubts ware taken by assault between seven & eight oclock;— one by the American light Infantry, the other by the French; without firing a gun, the bayonet alone was used— about 100 prisoners ware taken in both, & about forty kill'd,

78. The Charon, anchored off shore at Yorktown, was burned by a hot shot from the French land battery. Two transports anchored close to her were also burned. Johnston, *op. cit.*, 140.

A PLAN
OF THE ENTRANCE OF CHESAPEAK BAY,
with JAMES and YORK RIVERS;
wherein are shewn the Respective Positions (*in the beginning of October*)
1.° OF THE BRITISH ARMY Commanded By LORD CORNWALLIS,
AT GLOUCESTER *and* YORK *in* Virginia;
2.° of the American *and* French Forces *under* General Washington,
3.° *and* of the French Fleet *under* Count de Grasse.

By an Officer

Scale of Miles

LONDON.
Publish'd by Wm Faden Charing Cross, Nov.r 26.th 1781.

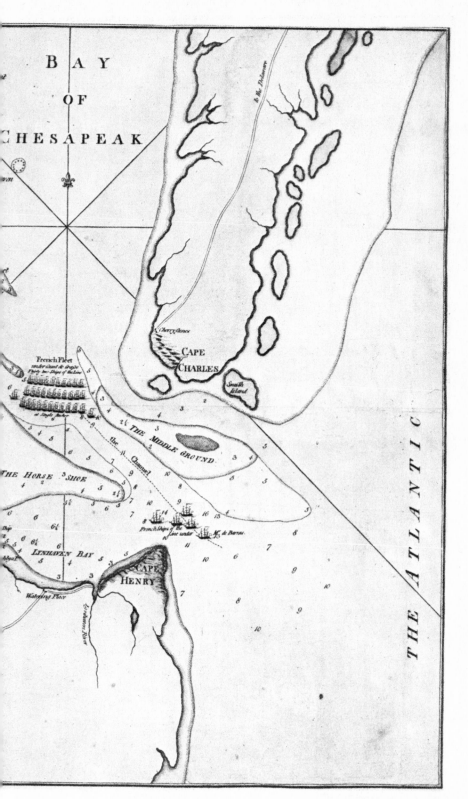

BAY

OF

CHESAPEAK

to the Delaware

Cherrystone

CAPE
CHARLES

South Island

French Fleet
*under Count de Grasse
Thirty two Ships of the Line*

at Single Anchor

THE MIDDLE GROUND

the ll Channel

THE HORSE SHOE

French Ships *of Line under M.r de Barras*

LINHAVEN BAY

CAPE
HENRY

Watering Place

Linhaven River

THE ATLANTIC

our loss about 70 kill'd & wounded;[79] immediately after those works ware carried (every thing being previously prepared) a third parallel was began which included the two redoubts taken, & by morning the trenches ware nearly compleet, together with a cover'd way from our first parallel to the last. our men continued at work this whole day in compleeting the trenches, & in prepareing for erecting several batteries.— the Enemy kept up a brisk fire of small royals & such cannon as they had (which wair mostly nines & twelve pounders,) but did very little dammage, altho our works are within 200 yards of their main lines.

16th the Enemy made a faint sortie last night, but ware soon repulsed, a small party pass'd our right & spiked up six cannon in a battery in our first parallel, where there hapen'd to be but a few men, but ware immediately drove off by the french who ware nearest the battery with the loss of eight kill'd & six taken prisoners;[80]

sixteen deserters came out this morning who say the Troops are very much fatigued, with excesive hard duty. & that they are very sickly.—[81]

17th four years this day since Gen! Burgoyne & his Army surrendered to the American Armies at Sarratoga— we had a numbar of very warm Batteries opend this morning in our advanced Parallel, which made the Enemies situation so very disagreable.— that about the

79. The two redoubts were on the extreme left of the British fortifications, near the river. No. 9 redoubt was taken by a detachment under Col. William Deuxponts. No. 10 redoubt was assaulted by a force under the command of Lt. Col. Alexander Hamilton, and was captured in ten minutes. *Ibid.*, 141-7.

80. The object of this sortie by the British was to cripple some unfinished batteries being erected very close to their lines. The detachment was led by Lt. Col. Abercromby. He was opposed by Comte de Noailles, who had command of the supports that night. *Ibid.*, 148-9.

81. Illness, more than enemy fire, reduced the number of Cornwallis' effectives and influenced his decision to capitulate, according to a letter from Cornwallis to Clinton dated Oct. 20, 1781. *Clinton Papers*, Clements Library.

middle of the day his Lordship was induced to send out a flag, with some proposels for a Capitulation.—soon after, a Cessation of Hostilities took place, & the evening was taken up in negotiation between two Officers of our Army, & two of the Enemies, on the Terms of capitulation. 19th

the Treaty between Gen! Washington & his Lordship ended this fournoon by a Capitulation being agree'd on & rattified by both parties, & this afternoon the Troops march'd out & laid down their Armes, both at York & Gloster,[82] amounting in the whole (including those in the Hospital,) to 7,054 including Officers. one hundred Ships & vessels of different kinds ware at York when the Seige commenced the whole of which ware distroyd & taken, about 1000 seamen ware made prisoners.— our troops took possession of the Enemies principle works previous to their marching out, their Troops ware very sickly. 2000 ware in the Hospitals of Sick & wound'd at York & Gloucester was taken 74 pieces of Brass ordnance, between two & three hundred pieces of Iron, 8000 stands of armes & very conciderable quantities of ammunition, Quarter Masters Stores, clothing; & provisions.—

The Prisoners ware sent to the back parts of Virginia & Maryland, except a large proportion of the Officers which went on Parole to New York.—

28th after collecting the different kinds of Stores, leaveling our works, & making the necessary arrangments, we are now prepareing to leave this Place. The French troops which came from the West Indeas have imbark'd & joined the Fleet.— the Army under the Gen! Count Roshambau is to winter in Virginia.—

82. Now Gloucester Point, on the left bank of the York River, directly opposite Yorktown.

A large British Fleet appeered off the mouth of the Bay this afternoon,[83] the French are prepareing to go out to see them.—

all the Troops belonging to the Eastward of Pennsilvania are to return to the North River, & the others to join Gen! Green in Carolina.—

I am severely handled by the ague & fever.—

we find our selves embarresed for want of teams to transport our baggage, as very nearly the whole of our oxen are dead & sick (of which a large proportion of our teams ware composed) with a distemper not known yet, to the Northward of this State. it is not uncommon for cattle to die within two days after the first appeerence of the disorder. it is call'd (by some) the bloody murren. The urine of the cattle appears bloody immediately after they are taken, & continues so until they die, if cattle are brought only fifty miles from the northward to the sea coast, in the months of August or September they are generally more or less affected by this distemper. it is said here, that the hides of cattle that die with it cannot be made into leather.— no remedy or relief has yet been found out for it.—

Novemr 6th from the 28 ult we have been busily ingaged in collecting vessels, & Imbarking Troop, Artelliry, Stores &c. our sick & invaleads ware first imbark'd & sent off for the head of Elk. this day nearly all the Troops will Sail for the same place.—

our waggons go by land, the greatest part of which go to the Southward with the Troops & Stores that are to Join Gen! Green.—[84]

Articles of Capitulation, Settled, Between His Excellency Gen! Washington, Commander in chief of the com-

83. This was Admiral Graves' fleet of 35 sail, bringing Clinton's delayed reinforcements to Cornwallis.

84. The war did not end with the defeat of Cornwallis. The British were still active in the Carolinas and in Georgia, where Gen. Greene carried on against them.

bined Forces of America & France, His Excellency the
Count De Roshambeau L.ᵗ Gen.ˡ of the Armies of the King
of France, great cross of the Roial and Military order of
Saint Lewis, Commanding the Auxillery Troops of his
Most Christian Majesty in America, and His Excellency
the Count De Grass,[85] L.ᵗ Gen.ˡ of the Naval Armies of
His Most Christian Majesty, com.ʳ of the order of Saint
Lewis, Commander in Chief of the Naval Army of
France in the Chesapeek, on the one part, & the Right
Honorable Earl of Corn Wallis, L.ᵗ Gen.ˡ of His Britan-
nick Majesties forces, Commanding the Garrisons of
York & Gloucester, & Thomas Simmons[86] Esq.ʳ Com-
manding His Brittanick Majesties Naval forces in York
river in Virginia on the other part.—

Article 1ˢᵗ—

The Garrisons of York & Gloucester, including the Officers & Seamen of his Britannick Majesties Ships as well
as the Marines, to Surrender themselves Prisoners of
War, to the combined Forces of America & France, the
land Forces to remain Prisoners to the United States, the
Navy to His Most Christian Majesty.—

Article 2ᵈ—

The Artiliry, Armes, accoutrements, Military chest, &
Public Stores of every denomination, unimpaired to the

85. François Joseph Paul Grasse, Comte de Grasse-Tilly (1723-1788), commanded
a squadron in the West Indies in 1779 and 1780, and again in 1781. On September 5
he defeated Admiral Graves off Chesapeake Bay and began a blockade which later
prevented Cornwallis from receiving reinforcements and supplies. De Grasse was
captured by Admiral Rodney in 1782. *Biographie Universelle*, XVII, 374-5.

86. Capt. Thomas Symonds (d. 1793) obtained post rank in 1771 and commanded
Admiral Montagu's flagship on the American station until 1774. Later he served
under various admirals along the American coast. In December, 1780, he transported
Arnold's force to Virginia and remained in the Chesapeake all winter. There he was
trapped with the land forces of Cornwallis by De Grasse's fleet. His ship was burned
and sunk by a hot shot from a French land battery. B. F. Stevens, *Clinton-Cornwallis
Controversy* (London, 1888), II, 459.

Heads of departments appointed to receive them,— Granted.—

Article 3.ᵈ—

at 12 oclock this day the two redoubts on the left Flank of York, to be delivered, the one to American Infantry, the other to a detachment of French Granadiers. the Garrison of York will march out to a place to be appointed in Front of the Post at 2 oclock precisely with Shouldered Armes, colours cased, & drums beating a British or German march.[87] they then are to ground their Armes, & return to their Encampment, where they will remain until they are dispach'd to the place of their destination, two works on the Gloucester side will be delivered, at one oclock, to a detachment of French & American Troops appointed to possess them; the Garrison will march out at 3 oclock in the afternoon; The Cavalry with their swords drawn, Trumpets sounding, & the Infantry in the manner prescrib'd for the Garrison of York, they are likewise to return to their incampment, to remain until they can be finally march'd off. Granted

Article 4ᵗʰ—

Officers to retain their side Armes, both officers & soldiers to keep their private property of every kind, & no part of their baggag or papers to be at any time subject to a search, or inspection, the Baggage & papers of officers & Souldiers taken during the seige to be likewise preserved for them, it is understood that any property obviously belonging to the Inhabitents of these States in the possession of the Garrison shall be subject to be reclaim'd.— Granted—

87. The tune selected was "The World Turned Upside Down." Johnston, *op. cit.*, 155.

Article 5th—

the Soldiers to be kept in Virginia, Maryland, & Pennsilvania, & as much by Reg[ts] as possible, & supplied with the same rations of provisions as are allowed to soldiers in the service of America. A field officer A field officer from each Nation, Viz British, Anspack, & Hessian,[88] and other Officers in proportion of one to fifty men to be allowed to reside near their respective Reg[ts] to visit them frequently & be witness of their Treatment, & their Officers may receive & deliver clothing & other necessaries for them, for which purpose pasports are to be granted when applied for.— Granted

Article 6th—

The Gen! Staff, and other officers not imploy'd as mentioned in the above article, & who chuse it, to be permited to go on parole to Europe, to New York, or to any American maretime Port, at present in possession of the British forces, at their own option, & proper vessel to be granted by the Count De Grasse to carry them under flag of truce to New York within twenty days from this date if possible, & they to reside in a district to be agreed upon hereafter until they embark, the Officers of the civil department of the Army & navy to be included in this article, pasports to go by land to be granted to those for whom vessals cannot be furnished. Granted—

Article 7th—

Officers to be allowed to keep soldiers for servants according to the common practice of the service, servants,

88. Among the German provinces represented by the British mercenaries were Hesse-Cassel, Hesse-Hanau, Brunswick, Waldeck, Anhalt-Zerbst and Anspach-Bayreuth. E. J. Lowell, *The Hessians . . . in the Revolutionary War* (New York, 1884), 2–3.

not soldiers not to be considered as prisoners, & be allowed to attend their masters.—

Granted—

Article 8th—

The Bonetto sloop of war to be equiped & navagated by its present Cap[t] & crew, & left intirely at the disposal of Lord Cornwallis, from the hour the capitulation is signed, to receive an Aid Decamp[89] to carry dispaches to Sir Henry Clinton, & such soldiers as he may think proper to send to New York, to sail without examination when his dispaches are ready his Lordship ingaging on his word the ship shal be delivered to the order of Count De Grasse, if she escapes the dangers of the seas, that she shall not carry off any Public stores, any part of hur crew that may be deficient on hur return, & the soldiers passengers to be accounted for on hur returning,

Granted—

Article 9th—

The Traders to preserve their property & to be allowed three months to dispose of, or remoove them, & these Traders are not to be considered as prisoners of war.— The Traders will be allowed to dispose of their goods; the Allied Army having the right of preemtion; the Traders to be concidered as prisoners of war on parole

Article 10th—

natives or inhabitents of different parts of this country

89. The bearer was Lt. Col. Robert Abercromby (1740–1827), of the 37th regiment. He fought in America during the French and Indian War and throughout the Revolution. He later distinguished himself in India and rose to the rank of general. *Dict. Nat. Biog.*, I, 47–8.

at present in York & Gloucester are not to be punished
on account of having join'd the British Army

{ this Article cannot be assented to,}
{ being altogether of civil resort.   }

Article 11th—

{proper Hospitals to be furnished for the sick and
{wounded. they are to be attended by their own Surgeons on Parole, they are to be furnished with medicine
& Stores from the American Hospital.} — {The Hospital Stores now in York & Gloucester shall be delivered for the use of the British sick & wounded; pass-
ports will be given for procureing them, & other supplies
from New York as occation may require proper Hospitals will be furnished for the reception of the sick &
wounded of the two Garrisons}

Article 12th—

Waggons to be furnished to carry the baggage of the
Officers attending the Soldiers, & two Surgeons when
traveling on account of the sick, attending the Hospitals, at Public expence. Answer they will be furnished if
possible.—

Article 13th—

the shiping & boats in the two garrisons with all their
Stores, guns, tackling, & riging shall be delivered up in
their present state to an officer of the Navy appointed to
take possession of them, previously unloading the private property, part of which had been on board for security during the seige.—Granted—

Article 14th—

no article of Capitulation to be infringed on, on pretence

of reprisal. if there be any doubtful expressions in it they are to be interpreted according to the meaning and common acceptation of the word.

Granted—

Finished at York in Virginia
this 19th day of Octob.^{r} 1781—
and in the 6th year of our
Independence^{90}

Novr 13th I arrived at the Head of Elk but few of our vessels have yet arriv'd. the winds have been remarkably unfavorable; we have snow & cold weather.—

24 having nearly compleeted the transporting of the Artillery & stores from the head of Elk, to Christiania, where they are ship'd & convay'd to Philadelphia, I set out with the first division of troops towards Hudsons River, our troops had a very fatiguing march, the weather very unfavorable, frequent storms of both rain & snow.—I arriv'd at Hudsons River the 3^d of Decr the Troops arriv'd the 7th.— Genl Heaths Army had got into winter Quarters when we arrived.—

the N. York & Jersey Troops together with the Park of Artillery winter in Jersey, the Rhode Island troops in Philadelphia, where Genl Washington will remain some part of the winter.—

the New Hampshire Troops winter above Albany, on the Hudson & Mohock rivers,—

Decem.^{r} 10th we have a deep snow.— have taken Quarters at New Windsor.—^{91}

90. Dearborn's copy of the text of the capitulation follows the official version, with only a few changes in words and punctuation. The original was signed by Cornwallis, Symonds, Washington, Rochambeau, Barras and Grasse.

91. The upper half of this page of the original manuscript is missing. It probably contained an entry dated between December 7 and December 10.

Peace Negotiations

THE *surrender of Cornwallis was followed by the resignation of the British ministry, and the king was forced to accept a cabinet pledged to negotiate an immediate peace and willing to recognize the independence of the United States. Carleton replaced Clinton as commander-in-chief, and while skirmishes continued for a time in the South, the British finally withdrew their forces late in 1782. A preliminary treaty of peace was formulated in November, but the final articles were not signed until September 3, 1783. Carleton then evacuated the last of the British army from New York City.*

JUNE 20th 1782
after compleeting the Public business[1] I was ordered to perform by the Commander in Chief, &c.—I set out for Camp.

29th I arriv'd at Head Quarters at Newburgh on the Hudson River.[2]

1. On January 31, 1782, Washington wrote a circular letter to the several states, urging them to recruit such men as would bring their draft quotas, fixed by a Resolution of Congress, up to their limits, thereby insuring a respectable fighting force in the field. Dearborn was ordered to deliver this message, addressed to the state of New Hampshire, and wait for an official statement regarding the exact number of men which could be counted on from that state. *Writings of Washington*, XXIII, 476–80.

2. Washington's headquarters were at Newburgh, 8 miles north of West Point, in a stone mansion now owned by the state. Here the army was disbanded June 23, 1783.

July 9.ᵗʰ I [s]et out from Newburgh to Join my Reg.ᵗ at Saratogea.

17.ᵗʰ I Joind my Reg.ᵗ—

in the month of April last Sir Henry Clinton Commander in Chief at New York, was recall'd and Sir Guy Carleton arriv'd to take command of the British Army in America,—who brought over some pretended terms for a peace or truce, which ware with propriety totally rejected by Congress.

A total change in the British Ministry having taken place[3] has flattered us to believe that we shall soon have a peace, but I fear it will only serve to enable Briton to act with more vigor against us.—

a very severe and bloody navel ingagement hapened on the 12.ᵗʰ of April in the West Indias, between Admiral Rodney & Cound De Grass, in which the french ware unfortunate, not being able to bring but part of their fleet to action. after a very obstinate ingagement the Action terminated in favor of the English, the French having lost 6 ships of the line one of which was the Ville De Parris in which was Count De grass.[4]

July 19.ᵗʰ we hear that a conciderable body of the Enemy have appeerd on the Mohawk River, have kill'd some men, taken some, & drove off a learge numbar of cattle.[5]

July 27.ᵗʰ I began to erect some fortifications at this Garrison for its better securety.—

3. Lord North resigned as prime minister in March, 1782. He was succeeded by Charles Watson-Wentworth, 2nd Marquis of Rockingham (1730-1782), a Whig who had opposed the war. Lord Shelburne was made home secretary and Charles James Fox foreign secretary. *Shelburne Papers*, Clements Library.

4. The battle took place off the island of Dominica. Five thousand casualties resulted and De Grasse was taken prisoner. Fiske, *op. cit.*, II, 288.

5. Washington reported this incident in a letter to Congress dated July 9, 1782. Just before he paid a visit to the defences at Saratoga on June 29, a party of British, Loyalist Refugees and Indians came down the Mohawk, captured a guard of Continental troops stationed at a mill, and destroyed the mill. *Writings of Washington*, XXIV, 405, ff.

30th altho we keep constant scouting parties at a conciderable distence, on different parts of the Lakes George
and Champlain, no parties of the Enimy have yet been
discovered.— more plentiful harvests ware never known
in this Country than there is at present.—

August 2d we receiv'd accounts of the States of Holland's having declared the thirteen united States of America independent.[6]
it is reported that a new set of Commissioners have arrived at New York from Briton with new and fresh par-
dons for us Rebels:—[7] we hear that the French Army is
on their march from Virginia to the Northward, it is
hoped that the Campaign will not terminate in the manner we feared it would not long since.—

8th we are inform'd that a French Fleet has arriv'd in
the Chesapeek Bay consisting of 13 sail of line of Battle
Ships,—and likewise that the States of Holland have ac-
knowledged the independency of these States, through
the authority of their High Mightin[e]sses, and have ut-
terly refused to make a seperate peace with Briton.—
All these things are for us.—

a small scout of mine toock a new whale boat in Lake
George belonging to the Enemy, which had been se-
creted by a small party that had come over the lake for
the purpose of plundering the inhabitents and carrying
some poor defenceless man to Canada.

20th we are inform'd that the French Fleet that arriv'd
in the Chesapeek Bay a few week[s] agoe has arrivd in
Boston Harbour.—

6. The Netherlands did not sign a treaty of amity and commerce with the United
States until October 8, 1782; but in April John Adams had been officially recognized
as minister from the United States. S. F. Bemis, *The Diplomacy of the American Revolution* (New York, 1935), 169.

7. There was no truth in this rumor. The United States now had ministers abroad
with whom peace negotiations would be opened.

a general Peace is much talk'd of,

22.ᵈ went to Stillwater to an Ordination in the woods, &c &c

Sept.ʳ 1.ˢᵗ we are informd from authority that the Enemy have left Savannah in Georgey—[8]

Sept.ʳ 2 we hear that our main Army have taken the field—[9]

15 the French Army have arriv'd from the Southward & incamp'd near our main army.

20 Peace & the Enemies Leaving New York is all the talk.

25 we are informd from prety good authority that an action has happened in the East Indies between the French & British fleets in which the French ware victorious. the British Admiral by the name of Hughes, with several other ships fell into the hands of the French.—[10]

28.ᵗʰ the Enemy in all parts of this Continent appeer to have no intentions of prosicuting the war any further. no fighting has happened for a long time.

an other revolution has taken place in the British Ministry, on account of the death of the Marquess of Rockingham, first Lord of the Treasury, to which vacancy Lord Shelborn[11] was appointed by yᵉ King which occasiond the resignation of Charles Fox & some others. it is feard that this revolution in the British Ministry will have

8. The British evacuated Savannah on July 11, 1782.

9. The main army, except the garrison at West Point, which was left intact under the command of Maj. Gen. Knox, was moved from West Point on August 31, 1782, to a camp at Verplank's Point. *Writings of Washington*, XXV, 100, *ff*.

10. Admiral Sir Edward Hughes (1720?–1794) commanded the fleet in the East Indies from 1773 to 1777 and again from 1778 to 1783. He fought five indecisive battles with the French fleet under De Suffren in 1782–83. *Dict. Nat. Biog.*, XXVIII, 172.

11. Sir William Petty, 2nd Earl of Shelburne and 1st Marquis of Lansdowne (1737–1805), succeeded Rockingham as prime minister in July, 1782. He had pledged himself not to grant independence to the United States, but his commissioners were forced to alter this policy. Charles James Fox (1749–1806) resigned as foreign secretary and formed a coalition with Lord North. *Shelburne Papers*, Clements Library.

a tendency to prolong the war, as those Ministers that ware for Peace are no longer in Office.—

we have had various accounts of a Treaty for Peace, said to be on foot between Briton, France, Spain, Holland & America and that a congress of Agents from the different Powers has been seting at Paris several months, from which we expect much. a speedy & honorable Peace is the general cry of America, & I believe great Briton is far from being averce to Peace—

Octob.ᵣ 5.ᵗʰ having heard much said of several springs of an uncommon kind that are situate about twelve miles west from this garrison, I was induced to pay them a visit this day in company with several other Gentlemen.[12] I was much disappointed in finding the quality or taste of the water as well as the very extreordinery situation of it infinitely more curious then I expected, the water is clear, the taste is hard to describe; to me it appeered at first tasting to partake much of alkoline qualities, but on drinking freely it appeerd to be between good porter & cyder in taste and was not ungreatful to my taste, many are excessive fond of it. a frequent use of those waters have, as common report sais,) proov'd a cure for many different disorders, such as the rumetism, gout falting sickness, ague & fever, many cutanious disorders, scorbutic and venereal complaints, and for all kind of external ulcers. indeed those waters have proovd so effectual in curing many old & stubborn complaint[s] of vairous kinds, that people from many parts of the country flock to the spring, for almost all kind of disorders, there is three or four of the spring within a space of eighty rods, one of them is quite a curiosity, the water is containd in a stone that has without doubt, been formd from the water itself. of a conick figure resembling

12. Saratoga Springs, Saratoga co., N. Y.

a sugar Loaf in shape: it is abou.t eighteen feet in circumference at the ground, about five feet in highth, and about
two feet over at the top, at which place it has a cavaty
in the senter about ten inches over, which remains nearly
of the same bigness to the bottom of the stone, which
cavaty contains the water, which boils not much unlike
a pot over the fire constantly. & at the full of the moon
boils over the top. but at other times the surface of the
water is from six to twelve inches below the top of the
cavaty.— it appeers very evident from many circumstances that this stone has been formd by the over flowing of the water as those waters petrefy wherever they
run, and forms large bodies of soft stone, around it[s]
courses.— one other of those springs is contained in a
large body of stone of the above discription, not less. then
forty feet in circumference but not more then 4 feet above
the surface of the ground. The water is contain'd in a cavaty of about three feet one way & six the other, & so deep
that the bottom has not been found by any that I have
heard of: from this there is a conciderable discharge constantly: another of those springs is larger & calculated for
bathing.— there is such a constant fermentation in the
water of those springs that it cannot be confind in any
close vessel, & if it is but a few hours in an open one
it looses all its medicenal quallities, & becomes quite
insiped:—

Octob.r 17.th this being the Anniversary of the Capture
of Gen.l Borguoyn & his Army, we had an entertainment at which was all the Officers of the Garrison, &
some other Gentlemen. we spent the day & Evening
in festivity & mirth. the Soldiers had a gill of spirits
over their allowence servd out to them, to enable them
to keep the day with the spirit, as well as with the
understanding

a small scout from this Garrison toock up one Fifield from New Hampshire, in the State of Vermont, with Enlisting orders from the Enemy in Canada. he is sent to Albany in Irons for tryal.

24.th we are inform'd that our main Army is about going into winter Quarters, at and about West Point, & that the French Troops are going to winter Quarters in the State of Connecticut;—

Octob.^r 25.th we ware honoured by a visit of Count Viomenel[13] a Maj.^r Genl in Count Roshambaus Army. after reconnoitering the different works that ware occupied by Genl Burgoyns Army & ours, spent the Afternoon in shooting small game in the woods.—

Novr 3.^d 1782 we hear from Head Quarters that a general Peace is very nearly agreed on by the several contending Powers:—[14]

by a Flag of mine that has returnd from Canada, I am inform'd that the whole of our Prisoners in that Quarter are sent to New York, to be exchang'd, except about 300 women & children which are sent over the Lake to this place, on their way to their respective homes, on parole.

Novr 6.th I receiv'd orders to march to Join the Main Army. the 7.th I march'd the same day I was relieved by the Rhode Island Reg.^t—[15] the 9.th imbarcked the Reg.^t at Albany & on the 12.th arrived at Newburgh & Join'd the

13. Antoine Charles du Houx, Baron de Vioménil (1728–1792), was second in command of the French army in America, under Comte de Rochambeau. *Biographie Universelle*, XLIII, 583.

14. The provisional treaty of peace was signed in Paris, November 30, 1782. The House of Commons refused to accept it because the terms were too generous. As a result, Shelburne resigned in April, 1783, and the new cabinet composed of the Fox-North coalition promised to obtain better terms. The definitive treaty was thereby delayed another year, but when it was signed it read virtually the same as the provisional articles. *Shelburne Papers*, Clements Library.

15. Washington ordered the relief of the New Hampshire troops in his letter to Lord Stirling dated October 30, 1782. They were to be relieved by the Rhode Island troops under Col. Olney. *Writings of Washington*, XXV, 307.

Main Army, about 3 or four miles back of Newburgh & New Windsor where they ware huting for winter,— the 2^d New Hampshire Reg^t march'd from the Mohawk River & Joind the Main Army likewise.—

Novr 14th we began to build huts—

20th we hear that Gibralter has surrenderd to the Spaniards, & that a very large French & Spanish Armiment is proceeding against Jamaca.—[16]

25th we are inform'd that a large imbarcation is taking place at New York, supposed for the West Indies. [17] it is said that Sir Guy Carleton is to command it—

Decem^r 13th 1782

I set out for home on furlow and the 20th arrived & found all well.—

March 1^t 1783 by a reformation in the new Hamp^r line in which the two Reg^{t}s ware reduced to one Reg^t & one Batallion, I being the Junier Col^o was deranged;[18] & thus ends my millatery life, after almost eight years servus. I Joined the army 1^t of June, & received my discharge the 18th of June 1783 so that my serveces exceeded 8 years by about 1 month.

16. This rumor was false. Gibraltar was besieged by Spain from August, 1779, to February, 1783, when news of the preliminary treaty of peace was received. J. D. Bethune, *A History of the Late Siege of Gibralter* (Edinburgh, 1786), *passim*.

17. Washington learned that many transports had been sent down to New York from Halifax and Quebec, and that four regiments had received embarkation orders. But no troops sailed from New York in November, and the city was not evacuated until November 26, 1783. *Writings of Washington*, XXV, 435.

18. Lt. Col. George Reid was senior to Dearborn and consequently was retained as commander of the New Hampshire troops until November 3, 1783. Heitman, *op. cit.*, 462.

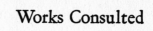

Works Consulted

Works Consulted

BOOKS

ADAMS, HENRY, *History of the United States of America* (New York, 1889–91), 9 volumes.

ARNOLD, ISAAC N., *The Life of Benedict Arnold; His Patriotism and His Treason* (Chicago, 1880).

BABCOCK, KENDRIC C., *The Rise of American Nationality 1811–1819* (New York and London, 1906).

BANCROFT, GEORGE, *History of the United States from the Discovery of the American Continent* (Boston, 1859–75), 10 volumes.

BARTLETT, LEVI, *Genealogical and Biographical Sketches of the Bartlett Family in England and America* (Lawrence, 1876).

BASSETT, JOHN SPENCER, editor, *Correspondence of Andrew Jackson* (Washington, 1926–33), 7 volumes.

BEMIS, SAMUEL FLAGG, *The Diplomacy of the American Revolution* (New York, 1935).

BETHUNE, JOHN DRINKWATER, *A History of the Late Siege of Gibralter* (Edinburgh, 1786).

Biographie Universelle (Michaud) ancienne et moderne . . . (Paris, 1854– 65), 45 volumes.

BRITTON, N. L., and ADDISON BROWN, *An Illustrated Flora of the Northern United States, Canada . . .* (New York, 1896–98), 3 volumes.

BURPEE, L. J., and A. G. DOUGHTY, editors, *Index and Dictionary of Canadian History* (Toronto, 1911).

COFFIN, CHARLES, compiler, *History of the Battle of Breed's Hill* . . . (Saco, 1831).

The Lives and Services of Major General John Thomas . . . Major General Henry Dearborn (New York, 1845).

COOK, FREDERICK, editor, *Journals of the Military Expedition of Major General John Sullivan against the Six Nations of Indians in 1779 with Records of Centennial Celebrations* (Auburn, 1887).

COOPER, JAMES FENIMORE, *The History of the Navy of the United States of America* (London, 1839), 2 volumes.

CURREY, J. SEYMOUR, *The Story of Old Fort Dearborn* (Chicago, 1912).

The Cyclopedia of American Biographies (Boston, 1897–1903), 7 volumes.

DEARBORN, HENRY, *An Account of the Battle of Bunker Hill. Written for the Port Folio, at the Request of the Editor* (Philadelphia, 1818).

DEARBORN, HENRY A. S., *Defence of Gen. Henry Dearborn Against the Attack of Gen. William Hull* (Boston, 1824).

DEWEY, DAVIS RICH, *Financial History of the United States* (New York, 1903).

Dictionary of American Biography (New York, 1928–37), 21 volumes.

Dictionary of National Biography (London, 1908–09), 22 volumes.

Documents Relative to the Colonial History of the State of New-York (Albany, 1853–87), 15 volumes.

DRAKE, F. S., *Dictionary of American Biography* (Boston, 1876).

DUNNACK, HENRY E., *Maine Forts* (Augusta, 1924).

EMMONS, RICHARD, *The Battle of Bunker Hill, or, The Temple of Liberty; an Historic Poem in Four Cantos* (Boston, 1872).

FARROW, EDWARD S., *Farrow's Military Encyclopedia* . . . (New York, 1895), 4 volumes.

FELLOWS, JOHN, *The Veil Removed; or, Reflections on David Humphreys' Essay on the Life of Israel Putnam* (New York, 1843).

FISKE, JOHN *The American Revolution* (Boston and New York, 1891), 2 volumes.

FITZPATRICK, JOHN C., editor, *The Diaries of George Washington, 1748–1799* (Boston and New York, 1925), 4 volumes.
The Writings of George Washington from the Original Manuscript Sources, 1745–1799 (Washington, 1931—), 26 volumes to date.

FRENCH, ALLEN, *The First Year of the American Revolution* (Boston and New York, 1934).

FROTHINGHAM, RICHARD, *The Battle Field of Bunker Hill: With a Relation of the Action by William Prescott* . . . (Boston, 1876).

GODFREY, CARLOS E., *The Commander-in-Chief's Guard* (Washington, 1904).

GOODWIN, DANIEL, *The Dearborns; a Discourse Commemorative of the Eightieth Anniversary of the Occupation of Fort Dearborn* . . . (Chicago, 1884).

HEITMAN, FRANCIS B., *Historical Register of Officers of the Continental Army During the War of the Revolution April, 1775, to December, 1783* (Washington, 1914).

HILDRETH, RICHARD, *The History of the United States of America* (New York, 1880), 6 volumes.

HODGE, FREDERICK WEBB, editor, *Handbook of American Indians North of Mexico* (Washington, 1912), Smithsonian Institution Bureau of Ethnology, Bulletin 30, 2 volumes.

HULL, WILLIAM, *Defence of Brigadier General W. Hull. Delivered before the General Court Martial, of which Major General Dearborn was President* . . . (Boston, 1814). *Memoirs of the Campaign of the North Western Army of the United States, A. D. 1812* . . . (Boston, 1824). *Report of the Trial of Brig. General William Hull;* . . . *Taken by Lieut. Col. Forbes* . . . (New York, 1814).

JACOBS, JAMES RIPLEY, *Tarnished Warrior, Major-General James Wilkinson* (New York, 1938).

JAMES, MARQUIS, *The Life of Andrew Jackson* (New York, 1938).

JOHNSTON, HENRY P., *The Yorktown Campaign and the Surrender of Cornwallis 1781* (New York, 1881).

Journals of the Continental Congress 1774–1789 (Washington, 1904–37), 34 volumes.

KINGSFORD, WILLIAM, *The History of Canada* (Toronto, 1887–98), 10 volumes.

LOWELL, EDWARD J., *The Hessians and the Other German Auxiliaries of Great Britain in the Revolutionary War* (New York, 1884).

M'AFEE, ROBERT B., *History of the Late War in the Western Country* . . . (Lexington, 1816).

McKAY, GEORGE L., compiler, *American Book Auction Catalogues 1713–1934, a Union List* (New York, 1937).

McMASTER, JOHN B., *A History of the People of the United States* . . . (New York, 1883–1913), 8 volumes.

MYERS, WILLIAM STARR, editor, *The Battle of Monmouth by the late William S. Stryker* (Princeton, 1927).

NICKERSON, HOFFMAN, *The Turning Point of the Revolution or Burgoyne in America* (Boston and New York, 1928).

PAINE, RALPH D., *The Fight for a Free Sea; a Chronicle of the War of 1812* (New Haven, 1920).

PARKER, FRANCIS J., *Could General Putnam Command at Bunker Hill?* (Boston, 1877).

PERKINS, JAMES BRECK, *France in the American Revolution* (London, 1911).

PRESTON, HOWARD W., *The Battle of Rhode Island, August 29th, 1778* (Providence, 1928).

PUTNAM, DANIEL, *Account of the Battle of Bunker's-Hill; by H. Dearborn, Major-General of the United States' Army. With a Letter to Major General Dearborn* . . . (Boston, 1818).

QUAIFE, Milo M., *Chicago and the Old Northwest* (Chicago, 1913).

RAMSAY, DAVID, *The History of the Revolution of South-Carolina, from a British Province to an Independent State* (Trenton, 1785), 2 volumes.

Report of the Commission to Locate the Site of the Frontier Forts of Pennsylvania (Harrisburg, 1896), 2 volumes.

ROBERTS, KENNETH, editor, *March to Quebec* (New York, 1938).

SABIN, JOSEPH, *Bibliotheca Americana. A Dictionary of Books Relating to America, from its Discovery to the Present Time* (New York, 1868–1936), 29 volumes.

SMITH, JUSTIN H., *Arnold's March from Cambridge to Quebec; a Critical Study, Together with a Reprint of Arnold's Journal* (New York, 1903).

Our Struggle for the Fourteenth Colony: Canada, and the American Revolution (New York, 1907), 2 volumes.

SPARKS, JARED, editor, *Correspondence of the American Revolution; Being Letters of Eminent Men to George Washington* . . . (Boston, 1853), 4 volumes.

STEVENS, BENJAMIN FRANKLIN, editor, *The Campaign in Virginia 1781. An Exact Reprint of Six Rare Pamphlets on the Clinton-Cornwallis Controversy* . . . (London, 1888), 2 volumes.

STONE, EDWIN M., *Our French Allies* . . . (Providence, 1884).
SWETT, SAMUEL, *History of Bunker Hill Battle* (Boston, 1827).
THWAITES, REUBEN GOLD, and LOUISE PHELPS KELLOGG, editors, *Documentary History of Dunmore's War 1774* (Madison, 1905).
WALDO, S. PUTNAM, *The Tour of James Monroe, President of the United States, in the Year 1817;* . . . (Hartford, 1818).
WENTWORTH, JOHN, *Early Chicago. Fort Dearborn; An Address at the Unveiling of the Memorial Tablet to Mark the Site of the Block-house* . . . (Chicago, 1881).
WILKINSON, JAMES, *Memoirs of My Own Times* (Philadelphia, 1816).
WILLIAMSON, WILLIAM D., *The History of the State of Maine* . . . (Hallowell, 1832), 2 volumes.
WINSOR, JUSTIN, editor, *Narrative and Critical History of America* . . . (Boston and New York, 1884–89), 8 volumes.

MANUSCRIPTS

British Headquarters Papers of Sir Henry Clinton, including 350 maps, in the William L. Clements Library of the University of Michigan.
Papers of Lord Shelburne, 1st Marquis of Lansdowne, in the William L. Clements Library of the University of Michigan.
DEARBORN, HENRY A. S., *The Life of Major General Henry Dearborn* (Brinley Place, 1822), 7 volumes, in the Maine Historical Society, Portland, Maine.
Secretary of War Military Letter Book, volumes I–II, War Department Archives, in The National Archives, Washington, D. C.

PERIODICALS

Bulletin of the Fort Ticonderoga Museum, volume I, number 5 (1929).

Maine Historical and Genealogical Recorder, volume III (1886).

Massachusetts Election! American Nomination. Major-General Henry Dearborn for Governor. Hon. William King for Lieut. Governor. (Boston, Office of the Yankee, n.d.).

New Jersey Gazette, volume II (1779).

The New-York Gazette: and the Weekly Mercury (1781).

Pennsylvania Gazette, and Weekly Advertiser (1781).

Pennsylvania Magazine of History and Biography, volume II, number 1 (1878).

Royal Society of Canada, *Proceedings and Transactions*, series 2, volume 9 (1903).

Index

Index

254 INDEX

Newark, N.J., 130
Newark Bay, 201
Newburgh, N.Y., 102, 112, 209; Washington's headquarters at, 229, 230; 235, 236
Newburyport, Mass., 38, 90
Newcastle, Me., 94
Newport, R.I., blockade of, 132; 140
Newspapers, in Fishkill, N.Y., 143; *New Jersey Gazette*, 146, 147, 150; *Pennsylvania Gazette*, 218; *New York Gazette & Weekly Mercury*, 218
Newtown, battle of, 177, 178, 179, 183, 190, 192
Niagara, 155, 188
Nichols, Francis, captured at Quebec, 76
Niger, H.M. frigate, 85
Ninety-Six, S.C., 211
Nixon, John, 136
Nixon's regiment, 45
Noailles, Comte de, 220
Norridgewock, Me., 43
Norridgewock Falls, 44
Norris, James, 151
North Carolina brigade, 136
North Hampston, N.H., 4
North Hector, N.Y., 182
North, Lord, 230, 232
North River, *see* Hudson River
North Yarmouth, Me., 95
Northern Department, 112
Northwest Territory, 146
Norwalk, Conn., 145; reported burned, 161; raid on, repulsed, 162
Nottingham, N.H., 4, 35, 96
Nova Scotia, 86
Nunnery, at Quebec, 58

Ogden, Matthias, 164
Olney, Christopher, 235
Oneida, Indians, 107, 121; guides for Sullivan, 175, 189, 193
Onondaga Indians, 151
Orange, N.J., *see* Orange Town
Orange Town, 200, 204; General orders issued from, 205
Oriskany, 101
Osgood, Col., 197
Oswald, Eleazer, captured at Quebec, 76
Oswego, N.Y., 101
Ottendorf's Corps, 164
Owego, N.Y., 173, 174

Palace Gate, Quebec, 69
Paramus, N.J., 131
Parker, Francis J., 8
Parker's Flats, 39
Paroles, of American officers at Quebec, 84, 98
Parsons, Samuel, sketch of, 146; 148, 162
Passaic River, 130
Patterson, John, sketch of, 111, 113, 199
Patterson's brigade, 135
Paulus Hook, *see* Powles Hook
"Paxton Boys," 41
Peace, negotiations, 229; commissioners of, 231; treaty of, 235
Peekskill, N.Y., 113, 131, 141, 149, 150, 211
Peekskill Creek, 210
Pencel, Henry, 161
Pencel, John, 161
Pennsylvania troops, 209; mutiny of, 210
Penobscot Bay, 93
Pensacola, Fla., 214
Percy, Sir Hugh, sketch of, 87
Petersburg, Va., 211
Petit Passage, 88
Philadelphia, Pa., 36, 98, 113; Howe retires to, 117, 118; 121; evacuation of, 122, 123; Arnold in command at, 144; 185; Washington marches through, 216; 228
Phillips, William, 211
Phillipse Manor, 198
Pickering, Timothy, sketch of, 204; 211
Pigot, Gen., 132, 135
Pioneers, 50; attack at Quebec, 72
Piscataqua River, 32, 96
Pittsburgh, Pa., 20
Pittston, Me., 14, 15, 39
Pittston, Pa., *see* Lackawanna
Plains of Abraham, 56, 57, 62
Platt, Richard, 211
Pleasant Bay, 92
Point Levis, 35, 56, 60, 80
Pointe aux Trembles en Bas, Quebec, 58, 59, 60, 83
Pompton, N.J., 210
Poor, Enoch, sketch of, 101; at Saratoga, 111, 152, 159, 160, 171, 172, 174, 175, 177, 199, 200; death of, 202; burial of, 203
Poor's Brigade, 111; marches towards Fish Kill, 112; 124, 131, 135, 139, 140; winter camp of, 142; 148, 149, 155; at Wyoming, 163; regiments in, 164, 165; 177, 178; losses in, 179; 200